Interview with John Lennon, New York, 1975

QUESTION: What were the Beatles really trying to do? And why all the hostility when you broke up?

JOHN: When it gets down to the nitty-gritty, it's the song, you know. And, if anything, the Beatles were figureheads. I could speak [about them] more succinctly later on when I thought about it. I call it a divorce, right? But when I thought about it, obviously, I could change my mind.

QUESTION: What did the Beatles actually contribute to their generation?

JOHN: I have a picture of it now. There was a ship sailing to the new world. I saw this group on the ship, maybe the Stones were up there too, but I just said, "Land ho!" So we were all part of it. We were in the crow's nest. We contributed whatever we could. I can't designate what we did or didn't do, how each individual was impressed by the Beatles physically, or whatever. And we were all on this ship together, our generation. What we did was wake up the avant-garde in music and film. I mean, not just the Beatles, but rock 'n' roll itself, you know. And this so-called avant-garde was asleep, and we were going around in circles.

THE LOST BEATLES INTERVIEWS

Geoffrey Giuliano is the acclaimed author of a number of internationally bestselling music biographies, including *The Beatles: A Celebration*, *John Lennon: My Brother* (co-author), *Dark Horse: The Private Life of George Harrison*, and *Blackbird: The Life and Times of Paul McCartney*. **Brenda Giuliano**, co-author, has acted as chief researcher, photo editor, and copy consultant on all of Geoffrey Giuliano's previous works. **Timothy Leary**, the controversial philosopher of the Woodstock Nation, currently resides in Beverly Hills 90210.

GEOFFREY GIULIANO
and BRENDA GIULIANO

THE LOST BEATLES

INTERVIEWS

Afterword by Dr. Timothy Leary

A PLUME BOOK

PLUME

Published by the Penguin Group
Penguin Books USA Inc., 375 Hudson Street,
New York, New York 10014, U.S.A.
Penguin Books Ltd, 27 Wrights Lane,
London W8 5TZ, England
Penguin Books Australia Ltd, Ringwood,
Victoria, Australia
Penguin Books Canada Ltd, 10 Alcorn Avenue,
Toronto, Ontario, Canada M4V 3B2
Penguin Books (N.Z.) Ltd, 182-190 Wairau Road,
Auckland 10, New Zealand

Penguin Books Ltd, Registered Offices:
Harmondsworth, Middlesex, England

Published by Plume, an imprint of Dutton Signet,
a division of Penguin Books USA Inc.
Previously published in a Dutton edition.

First Plume Printing, January, 1996
10 9 8 7 6 5 4 3 2

Ⓟ REGISTERED TRADEMARK—MARCA REGISTRADA

The Library of Congress has catalogued the Dutton edition as follows:

The lost Beatles interviews / Geoffrey Giuliano.
p. cm.
Transcripts of interviews with the Beatles and their associates,
conducted 1963–1993 by Giuliano and others.
ISBN 0-525-93818-4 (hc.)
ISBN 0-452-27025-1 (pbk.)
1. Beatles.   2. Rock musicians—England—Interviews.
I. Giuliano, Geoffrey.   II. Beatles.
ML421.B4A5   1994
782.42166'092'2—dc20

[B]   94-29575
CIP
MN

Printed in the United States of America
Original hardcover design by Steven N. Stathakis

BOOKS ARE AVAILABLE AT QUANTITY DISCOUNTS WHEN USED TO PRO-
MOTE PRODUCTS OR SERVICES. FOR INFORMATION PLEASE WRITE TO
PREMIUM MARKETING DIVISION, PENGUIN BOOKS USA INC., 375 HUD-
SON STREET, NEW YORK, NY 10014.

CONTENTS

THE LOST BEATLES INTERVIEWS

THE LOST BEATLES INTERVIEWS

ACT THREE: THE INNER CIRCLE / Friends and Family

---

*Interview conducted by journalist other than Geoffrey Giuliano. See acknowledgments for specific credits.

FOREWORD: OLD TIMES NEW

Charlie Lennon

Foremost amongst the tribulations of being uncle to one so famous as John Lennon is knowing how to accurately assess the impact of someone who, at the same time, is an international hero and also simply "Our John." To be sure, John possessed an almost magical talent, but I prefer to remember him as the lanky, good-natured young boy who used to tease me about my rapidly receding hairline (hair being a very major part of the Lennon family fortune, as you know) and goad me for not making it down to his place in Surrey often enough. Whenever I did find the time to visit him, however, it was as if time stood still. Inside the privacy of his plush Tudor mansion it was all slaps on the back, silly evenings spent playing Scrabble, and lovely long dinners together tucking into some very memorable Liverpool fryups.

Although John and his dad, Fred, went through some relatively rough patches together, I resisted ever getting myself in the middle and, hence, was able to stay friends with both sides. That these two loved each other devoutly was never in question. Things just got off to a rather bumpy start between them early on and left a lot of scars. It's sad, of course, but it's not really too unheard of in families today, is it?

Charlie Lennon is John's uncle and resides proudly in the Liverpool suburb of Sefton Park, the Beatles' hometown stomping grounds.

FOREWORD

As far as the longstanding public perception of my elder brother and, indeed, the entire Lennon clan are concerned, I must tell you, however many books, magazines, or newspapers you've read over the years, the true story of John Lennon, the Beatles, and his proud and accomplished family has yet to see the light of day. Of all the punters out there in the trenches, I must say that Geoffrey Giuliano so far outdistances them all in his sterling commitment to accuracy, insight, and detail as to leave all the other latterday Beatle pundits scratching around in the dust. To say that Geoffrey is the world's foremost authority on the Beatles is to subtly understate; for my money (and I've read them all) Mr. Giuliano *is* Beatle literature.

Inside this book you will find something very precious and rare, the world's foremost popular composers and performers discussing their life and work in their own words. Now, for the first time, you can hear John waxing philosophical about his views on world peace, drugs, and his masterful music. Eavesdrop as Geoffrey chats privately with George Harrison about his spiritual views and the ever rolling juggernaut that was the Beatles. Paul too speaks candidly about the tragic murder of John, the flawed charm of Brian Epstein, and the challenge of forever playing the role of the congenial Beatle.

In addition to the Beatles themselves, the author introduces us to the complex secret inner circle of the group. He provides us with never before published interviews with Auntie Mimi, Pete Best, John's sister Julia Baird, Jo Jo Laine, and many more. Even I learned a thing or two about the Beatles I didn't know, and this after sitting down with John many times as he opened his heart about the unnatural highs and lows of being part of the most lauded group of all time. Unlike any other work ever on the Fab Four, *The Lost Beatles Interviews* finally gives those closest to the phenomenon a platform from which to speak. It's been a long time coming, but at last the Beatles' incredible story has finally been told accurately by the principals directly involved. That means quite a lot to me personally, as I'm sure it does to everyone who ever loved them.

New Year's 1993
Liverpool, England

INTRODUCTION
THE LURE OF BEATLESPEAK

Reinventing their persona with the release of almost every new album, the Beatles constantly challenged themselves and thus their listeners to perpetually reevaluate not only their music but their complete personalities as well. Positioned dead center as the group's searing spiritual heart, George Harrison became the conscience of a generation, pushing the perimeters of our own life experience to include the concepts of innate spirituality and the possibility of unquestioning, uncompromising, unalloyed love.

"The more aware I've become the more I realize that all we are doing is acting out an incarnation," Harrison intoned to *Look* magazine way back in 1968. "It's just a little bit of time which is both relevant and very irrelevant too. Every moment is surcharged with the possibility of either forgetfulness or surrender to the Divine. All life is worship of God in a way and all we're doing is trying to pass it on to more people. My idea of God is that you're not doing it for yourself particularly but for everyone else. For whoever wants it."

To assimilate such ideas as an impressionable preteen back then was the foggy outline of everything I hoped for and the obtuse beginning of my own internal search. I suspect it was the same for many of you as well.

John Lennon, however, was a different proposition altogether. Pre-

Yoko John was still the archetypal working-class, intellectual, upscale acidhead. His own inner radar ever on look out for deeper, more meaningful levels of experience to help shape his already generously overloaded sensory framework. Once Yoko settled in for the duration, however, things quickly changed and Lennon became forever tangled in her wacky, often self-indulgent, artsy head space.

What isn't generally known is that towards the end John had pretty much rejected Yoko's influence over his work in favor of the straight-ahead pop/rock idiom that reached out and grabbed him as a kid back in Liverpool.

Paul McCartney's story, meanwhile, is considerably less complex. He caught the show-biz bug early on from his charismatic, piano-playing dad and the old Hollywood movies that sparked into the cluttered front parlor of the McCartneys' humble two-up-two-down. Aside from a brief psychedelic/avant-garde detour in the middle sixties the wide-eyed entertainer has pretty much stuck to that credo proliferating a long string of pretty, toe-tapping, largely inconsequential ditties tailor-made for the undemanding international top ten. Staunchly denying the deep river that runs through him, McCartney could have been a hell of a musician but settled on triple-platinum rock stardom instead. Pity.

All of which brings us to Ringo. Intrinsically much more than the lucky drummer who won the pools when he first sat down to keep time for the savage young Beatles, he remains one of the most well-loved bit players in the checkered history of popular music. The consistent twaddle that he is in any way stupid or inept is just that. An engaging little man with a penchant for transforming the mundane into the magical, Starr may turn out to be the most subtly brilliant of the lot. A sparkly-bearded Buddha playing out this incarnation with humor and compassion.

This book of collected interviews with the Fabs and friends is the end result of over twenty-five years of peeking in on the Beatles' turbulent lives through any window I could find. A strange way to spend the better part of one's youth, I know, but what's done is done. I just hope it helps the people who sincerely love them to gain a little insight into what it all really means.

As for me, I've traveled down that road about as far as I can. Anyone who wants to carry on will just have to make it on his own. Anyway, let me know how you get on and do enjoy the book. Beatles forever!

All you need is love. Give peace a chance. Power to the people. The farther one travels—the less one knows.

GEOFFREY GIULIANO
"Skyfield Manor"
Western New York
November 1994

ACT ONE

WHERE GIANTS WALK

*The Gospel of John, Paul,
George, and Ringo*

ROCK GROUP AT NESTON INSTITUTE

June 11, 1960

A Liverpool rhythm group The Beatles, made their debut at Neston Institute on Thursday night when north-west promoter, Mr. Les Dodd, presented three and a half hours of rock'n'roll.

The five strong group, which has been pulling in capacity houses on Merseyside, comprises three guitars, bass and drums.

John Lennon, the leader, plays one of the three rhythm guitars, the other guitarists being Paul Ramon and Carl Harrison. Stuart Da Stael plays the bass and the drummer is Thomas Moore. They all sing, either together, or as soloists.

Recently they returned from a Scottish tour, starring Johnny Gentle, and are looking forward to a return visit in a month's time.

Among the theaters they have played at are the Hippodrome, Manchester; the Empire, Liverpool and Pavilion, Aintree.

—Birkenhead News and Advertiser

THE BEATLES

Paris, 1963

QUESTION*: This afternoon we're visiting with four young men, and if I mention their first names—Paul, George, Ringo and John—I doubt you'd know about whom we're speaking. But if I said we're here this afternoon with the Beatles and if we were in England, I think we'd get a great big rousing hurrah, wouldn't we, boys?

PAUL: I don't know.

QUESTION: Now, Paul, tell us, how did the Beatles get going? How did you start?

PAUL: It's a funny story really. It was back in the old days. We were all at school together, we grew up at school as teenage buddies. It developed from there.

QUESTION: Did you sing together around school?

PAUL: Yeah. George and I were at school together, John was next door, and Ringo was at Butlins. We just started playing guitars and things. It went on from there, as far as I'm concerned.

---

*For the purposes of this work, interviews conducted personally by Geoffrey Giuliano will be identified by the use of the author's first name in the transcript in question. Interviews conducted by others will be signified by the generic term "question" within the body of that particular interview. Specific credits of other journalists contributing to this book, where applicable, are listed in the acknowledgements.

QUESTION: You say those were the olden days. Within the past year you have mushroomed tremendously in popularity. What levered this great rage for the Beatles?

PAUL: Well, it's funny really. I think it was the Palladium show, the television show in England. Then following hot in the footsteps we had the Royal Variety Command Performance for the Queen Mother and it all went from there, really. The national newspapers got hold of it and they got hold of Ringo, you know. A lot of columnists got onto the idea and started calling it Beatlemania.

QUESTION: George, what is the status of rock'n'roll in England today? Is that what you call your music?

GEORGE: No, not really. We don't like to call it anything. The critics and the people who write about it have to call it something. They didn't want to say it was rock'n'roll because rock was supposed to have gone out about five years ago. They decided it wasn't really rhythm and blues, so they called it the Liverpool Sound, which is stupid, really. As far as we were concerned, it's the same as the rock from five years ago.

QUESTION: Can you describe the Liverpool Sound?

GEORGE: Oh, it's more like the old rock, but everything's just a bit louder. More bass and bass drum and everybody sort of sings loud and shouts, that's it.

QUESTION: Is the Liverpool Sound then, *the* sound in the UK today?

GEORGE: Yeah, everybody's making records in that style.

QUESTION: Well, let's ask Ringo here. You're the drummer. We caught your act at the Olympia the other evening. How long have you been beating those skins?

RINGO: About five years now. I've been with the boys about eighteen months and with other groups before that.

QUESTION: Since you boys have gained your current popularity, have there been many other organizations trying to imitate you or perhaps take the thunder away from you? Let's ask John Lemon* this.

JOHN: Well, I suppose a couple of people have jumped on the bandwagon, but it really doesn't matter because it promotes the whole idea

---

*The interviewer is obviously so unfamiliar with both John and the Beatles that he mispronounces John's surname as "Lemon."

of us if we're away. There's a few little Beatles still going to remind people of us.

QUESTION: Paul, let's go back to you for a moment. When anyone sees your picture, the first thing that strikes them, naturally, is your hairdo. Some people have written that you have a "sheepdog" cut or, perhaps, an "early Caesar." What do you call it?

PAUL: To us, it just sort of seems a natural thing. We came out of the swimming baths one day and, you know how it is, your hair sort of flops about afterwards. It stayed that way, you see. Then the papers got hold of it and they called it the Beatle style. I suppose we go along with them now.

QUESTION: Do you go to the barber at all?

PAUL: Now and then. Do and don't.

QUESTION: Just to keep it trimmed?

PAUL: Yeah, but sometimes we do it ourselves. The thing is, it's really only our eyebrows that are growing upwards.

QUESTION: We've been told that in England today, there's this Beatlemania going on. What would you say Beatlemania is? All the girls scream whenever they see you and perhaps faint waiting in line. Let's be immodest a moment, what's the big attraction?

JOHN: I think it's like a dressing gown. George's dressing gown is definitely a big attraction.

PAUL: I don't think any of us really know what it is. We've been asked this question an awful lot of times, but we've never been able to come up with an answer. I think it's a collection of so many different things like: happening to be there at the right time, a little bit of originality in the songs, a different sound. Maybe the gimmick of the haircut as well, the look, getting into the national press at the right time.

JOHN: All these things and more fab listeners.

QUESTION: I understand you boys write your own material.

PAUL: John and I write them. This is Paul speaking.

QUESTION: Do you get together regularly or does an idea pop in your mind and you say, let's sit down and do it?

PAUL: If an idea does pop in your mind, then you do sit down and say let's do it, yeah. If there are no ideas and say we've been told we've got a recording date in about two days' time, then you've got to sit down and sort of slug it out. You normally get just a little idea which doesn't seem bad and you go on and it builds up from there. It varies every time.

QUESTION: Paul, we've seen you here at the Olympia. Can you compare the French audiences with what you're familiar with back in England?

PAUL: There's a lot of difference because in England, you see, the audiences are seventy-five percent female, here it's seventy-five percent male. That's the main difference, really. You're still appreciated, but you don't get the full noise and atmosphere of a place.

JOHN: No screams.

QUESTION: Why is it seventy-five percent boys?

GEORGE: I think they don't let the girls out at night in France.

JOHN: I think it's your dressing gown.

GEORGE: Somebody said that they still have chaperons, a lot of them, you see. Whereas in England, they're out. It's the same in Germany—all the boys like rock. It's usually the same on the Continent. I don't really know why.

QUESTION: Paul, we see "I Want to Hold Your Hand" is number one on the Hit Parade. How did you come to write that?

PAUL: Let's see, we were told we had to get down to it. So we found this house when we were walking along one day. We knew we had to really get this song going, so we got down in the basement of this disused house and there was an old piano. It wasn't really disused, it was rooms to let, we found this old piano and started banging away.

JOHN: And there was a little old organ.

PAUL: Yeah, there was a little old organ too. So we were having this informal jam and we started banging away. Suddenly, a little bit came to us, the catch line. So we started working on it from there. We got our pens and paper out and just wrote down the lyrics. Eventually we had some sort of a song, so we played it for our recording manager and he seemed to like it. We recorded it the next day.

QUESTION: Do all of your songs have a basic theme or message?

PAUL: No, they don't, but there's one thing that nearly always seems to run through our songs. People point it out to us. It's that I, You, Me always seem to be in the title. "I Want to Hold Your Hand," "She Loves You," "Love Me Do," and things like this. I think the reason for that is that we try and write songs which are a bit more personal than others, you see. I, Me, and You in the titles make the songs more personal, but that's the only basic message that runs through our songs.

QUESTION: And you coined this "Yeah, yeah, yeah." Isn't that sweeping England right now?

JOHN: Well, yeah. That was sort of the main catch phrase from "She Loves You." We'd written the song and then suddenly we needed more so we added yeah, yeah, yeah. It caught on, so now they use it if they're trying to be "with it" or "hip."

QUESTION: Paul, what do you think of your trip to the States? I understand in about a week you're going to be on *The Ed Sullivan Show*.

PAUL: Yeah, that's right. We're going to do the show in New York and we're taping one for later release. Then we go down to Miami, I can't wait, and we do another Sullivan show there. Before that, we do Carnegie Hall, don't we?

QUESTION: How were you selected for Ed Sullivan? Was he in England and caught your act or something?

GEORGE: We were arriving from Stockholm into London airport and at the same time the Prime Minister and the Queen Mother were also flying out, but the airport was overrun with teenagers, thousands of them waiting for us to get back. And Ed Sullivan was supposed to have arrived at that time and wondered what was going on. Also our manager went over to the States with another singer called Billy J. Kramer and he did a couple of TV shows over there. While he was there our manager got the bookings with Ed Sullivan, but he'd also heard of us from this London airport thing.

QUESTION: Is there a movie in the future?

PAUL: Yeah. We've been asked by United Artists to do a feature.

QUESTION: Will it be dramatic or just wrapped around your singing?

PAUL: We don't know yet what it's going to be like. I don't think we'll do an awful lot of acting. I think it will be written around the sort of people we are. There'll be four characters in it, very like us.

QUESTION: Do you plan to compose two or three songs specifically for the film?

GEORGE: Actually, we have to compose six songs specifically for the film.

PAUL: We've got to get down to that too. That's a job.

QUESTION: Then you boys haven't really had much of a chance to see Paris, have you?

GEORGE: Not really, no.

QUESTION: How about the French girls compared to the British girls.

RINGO: We haven't seen any yet.

JOHN: Well, I'm married. I didn't notice them.

QUESTION: We'll go back to Paul then. You're single.

PAUL: Yeah. I think the French girls are fabulous.

GEORGE: We have seen more French boys than French girls so, I mean, we can't really tell.

QUESTION: Perhaps when you get to *The Ed Sullivan Show* there'll be more girls for you.

PAUL: I hope so, yeah.

QUESTION: Any of you been to America before?

GEORGE: Yeah, me. I went in September, just for a holiday. For three weeks.

QUESTION: Well, I see our time is up boys. Thank you, Beatles, for being our guests this afternoon.

THE BEATLES

Paris, January 14, 1964

QUESTION: How important is it to succeed here?

PAUL: It is important to succeed everywhere.

QUESTION: The French have not made up their minds about the Beatles. What do you think of them?

JOHN: Oh, we like the Beatles. They're gear.

QUESTION: Do you like topless bathing suits?

RINGO: We've been wearing them for years.

QUESTION: Girls rushed toward my car because it had press identification and they thought I met you. How do you explain this phenomenon?

JOHN: You're lovely to look at.

QUESTION: What about your future?

RINGO: None of us has quite grasped what it is all about yet. It's washing over our heads like a huge tidal wave. But we're young. Youth is on our side. And it's youth that matters right now. I don't care about politics, *just people*.

GEORGE: I wouldn't do all this if I didn't like it. I wouldn't do anything I didn't want to, would I?

QUESTION: Is it true you're only in this for the money?

PAUL: Security is the only thing I want. Money to do nothing with, money to have in case you wanted to do something.

JOHN: People say we're loaded with money, but by comparison with those who are supposed to talk the Queen's English that's ridiculous. We're only earning. They've got real capital behind them and they're earning on top of that. The more people you meet, the more you realize it's all a class thing.

THE BEATLES

Washington, DC, February 11, 1964

QUESTION: Do any of you have any formal musical training?

JOHN: You're joking.

QUESTION: What do you think of President Johnson?

PAUL: Does he buy our records?

QUESTION: What do you think of American girls and American audiences?

JOHN: Marvelous.

QUESTION: Here I am, surrounded by the Beatles, and I don't feel a thing. Fellas, how does it feel to be in the United States?

JOHN: It's great.

QUESTION: What do you like best about our country?

JOHN: You!

QUESTION: I'll take that under advisement. Do you have any plans to meet the Johnson girls?

JOHN: No. We heard they didn't like our concerts.

QUESTION: Are they coming to your performance tonight?

PAUL: If they do, we'd really like to meet them.

QUESTION: You and the snow came to Washington today. Which do you think will have the greater impact?

JOHN: The snow will probably last longer.

QUESTION: One final question. Have you ever heard of Walter Cronkite?

PAUL: Nope.

JOHN: *NBC News*, is he? Yeah, we know him.

QUESTION: Thanks, fellas. By the way, it's *CBS News*.

GEORGE: I know, but I didn't want to say it as we're now on ABC.

QUESTION: This is NBC, believe it or not.

JOHN: And you're Walter?

QUESTION: No, I'm Ed.

JOHN: What's going on around here?

QUESTION: What do you think of your reception in America so far?

JOHN: It's been great.

QUESTION: What struck you the most?

JOHN: You!

RINGO: We already did that joke when we first came in.

GEORGE: Well, we're doing it again, squire!

QUESTION: Why do you think you're so popular?

JOHN: It must be the weather.

QUESTION: Do you think it's your singing?

PAUL: I doubt it. We don't know which it could be.

QUESTION: Where'd you get the idea for the haircuts?

JOHN: Where'd you get the idea for yours?

PAUL: We enjoyed wearing our hair this way, so it's developed this way.

QUESTION: Well you save on haircutting at least.

PAUL: Roar . . .

JOHN: I think it costs more to keep it short than long, don't you?

PAUL: Yeah, we're saving our money.

QUESTION: Are you still number one in Europe?

GEORGE: We're number one in America.

QUESTION: Where else are you number one then?

JOHN: Hong Kong and Sweden . . .

PAUL: Australia, Denmark, and Finland.

QUESTION: And you haven't any idea why?

RINGO: We just lay down and do it.

JOHN: In Hong Kong and these other places, suddenly you're number one years after putting out your records. Even here, we've got records we've probably forgotten.

QUESTION: You call your records "funny records"?

JOHN: "Funny," yeah, the ones we've forgotten.

GEORGE: It's unusual because they've been out in England for over a year. Like "Please, Please Me" is a big hit over here now, but it's over a year old.

QUESTION: Do you think they're musical?

JOHN: Obviously they're musical because it's music, isn't it! We make music. Instruments play music. It's a record.

QUESTION: What do you call it, rock and roll?

PAUL: We try not to define our music because we get so many wrong classifications off it. We call it music even if you don't.

QUESTION: With a question mark?

GEORGE: Pardon?

JOHN: We leave that to the critics.

QUESTION: Okay, that's it. Have a good time in America.

JOHN: Thank you. Keep buying them records and look after yourself.

THE BEATLES

New York, February 12, 1964

QUESTION: John, is the reaction to the group the same here as in England?

JOHN: I find it's very similar, only over here they go wilder quicker, you know.

QUESTION: Will you sing a song for us?

JOHN: No. Sorry, we need money first.

QUESTION: How much money do you expect to make here?

JOHN: About half a crown. Depends on the tax. How much have you got?

QUESTION: Some of your detractors allege that you are bald and those haircuts are wigs. Is that true?

JOHN: Oh, we're all bald. Yeah. And deaf and dumb too.

QUESTION: What is the Beatle sound?

JOHN: Well, as far as we are concerned, there's no such thing as a Liverpool or even a Beatles sound. It's just a name that people tag on.

QUESTION: One of your hits is "Roll Over Beethoven." What do you think of Beethoven as a composer?

RINGO: He's great. Especially his poems.

QUESTION: Are these your real names?

PAUL: Yeah, except Ringo. His name's Richard Starkey. He's called Ringo because of his rings, you know. And Starr, he didn't like Starkey.

QUESTION: Do all the Beatles write songs?

JOHN: Paul and I do most of the writing. George has written a few. Ringo hasn't, because it's hard to write something on the drums, isn't it?

RINGO: Yes.

QUESTION: How do you account for your fantastic success?

PAUL: Wish we knew.

JOHN: Good press agent.

QUESTION: Why do millions of Beatles fans buy millions of Beatles records?

JOHN: If we knew, we'd form another group and become their managers.

QUESTION: What do you think of American girls compared to British girls?

PAUL: The accents are different, of course. In films American women always seem to be bossing the men, being superior in big business and things. But from what I've seen, they're not. They're very similar to British women, just ordinary people, very nice.

QUESTION: Where did the name "Beatle" come from?

GEORGE: We were just racking our brains and John came up with the name Beatle. It was good because it was the insect and it was also a pun, you know, "beat," on the beat. We liked the name and we kept it.

QUESTION: Have you been influenced by any one American artist?

GEORGE: In the early days, it was Elvis Presley, Carl Perkins, Chuck Berry, Little Richard, and Buddy Holly. But there's no one we tried to copy.

QUESTION: Why do you wear your hair in such an unusual style?

GEORGE: Well, I went to the swimming baths and when I came out my hair dried and it was just all forward like a mop. I left it like that. When Ringo joined the group we got him to get his hair like this because by then people were calling it the Beatle cut.

QUESTION: Do you contemplate becoming permanent residents of the US?

GEORGE: I love the States, but if we came to live over here everybody would go mad. It's like Elvis, if he went to, say, Australia and then suddenly decided to live there. What would all the American people think?

QUESTION: Paul, what are your ambitions?

PAUL: We used to have lots of ambitions. Like number one records; *Sunday Night at the Palladium; The Ed Sullivan Show*; to go to America. A thousand ambitions like that. I can't really think of any more. We've lived an awful lot of them.

QUESTION: Paul, what is your aim in life?

PAUL: To have a laugh, you know, to be happy.

QUESTION: John, is it a fad?

JOHN: Obviously. Anything in this business is a fad. We don't think we're going to last forever. We're just going to have a good time while it lasts.

THE BEATLES

Blokker, The Netherlands, June 6, 1964

REPORTER: Here they are in the bar sitting behind me, the Beatles!

JOHN: *Yeah* . . .

QUESTION: First of all, introduce yourself.

JOHN: George Harrison, Paul McCartney, John Lennon, Jimmy Nichol.*

QUESTION: You want to get married?

PAUL: No good . . . no good, marriage.

JOHN: Good!

PAUL: I don't know yet, maybe when I got some more money.

QUESTION: You got money?

JOHN: You got more!

QUESTION: What do you think of the Dutch girls?

PAUL: Great, yeah.

QUESTION: They're good? Why?

---

*Suffering from an acute attack of tonsillitis, Ringo was unable to accompany the Beatles on this leg of their current tour. Session drummer Jimmy Nichol was brought in as a temporary replacement by Brian Epstein, much to the chagrin of George Harrison, who felt that the Beatles couldn't possibly be the Beatles without Ringo on board. Quite right too. Following Nichol's short-lived stint with the group, he faded into immediate obscurity.

PAUL: Well, all girls are good actually.

QUESTION: What makes a girl good?

PAUL: I don't know, do you?

JOHN: I know, I'm just helping him.

QUESTION: You're on, Jimmy. Do you find it difficult to take over the role of Ringo?

JIMMY NICHOL: No, not really, no. Because Ringo I can never replace. I can never make up for what Ringo is, you know.

QUESTION: How long will you be doing this?

JIMMY: Until next Thursday.

QUESTION: How is Ringo, by the way?

GEORGE: He's ill!

QUESTION: Do you consider the records you made with Tony Sheridan in the Star Club in Hamburg real Beatles records?

GEORGE: No, no, because on most of it Tony Sheridan sings and it's two years ago, you know. Anyway, it's not a very good record.

QUESTION: Do you play any other instrument besides the guitar and drums?

JOHN: I play mouth organ and a little piano.

PAUL: I play a little piano, about that big, a very *little* piano. I think we all play a little bit on other instruments.

QUESTION: Who mends your stockings when you're on your travels?

GEORGE: Stockings? Socks! Nobody, we just have them washed.

QUESTION: Do you think all the hysterics are necessary for your act?

PAUL: No, not necessary. But it helps give a good atmosphere, we don't mind. It's nice when there's a lot of noise about. It's like a football match with a lot of noise going on. It produces a good feeling.

JOHN: Goal! Goal!

QUESTION: But why is it always the girls?

JOHN: If it was all just boys, it would be a bit funny, wouldn't it?

QUESTION: I want to ask you whether you will go ahead with any musical change in direction?

PAUL: You never know. People always say we've changed, but we can't notice. So we probably will change our records. We wouldn't do anything drastic, like sing with a big band or anything, you know, because we don't enjoy that kind of music.

QUESTION: You do this kind of music because you enjoy it?

PAUL: We love it, you know, that's the main reason. If we didn't, we'd give it up tomorrow.

THE BEATLES

Adelaide, Australia, June 12, 1964

QUESTION: Paul, what do you expect to find here in Australia?

JOHN: Australians, I should think.

QUESTION: Do you have an acknowledged leader of the group?

JOHN: No, not really.

QUESTION: We heard that you stood on your head on the balcony outside, is that right?

PAUL: I don't know where you hear these rumors.

QUESTION: John, has the Mersey Beat changed much since you've been playing it?

JOHN: There's no such thing as Mersey Beat. The press made that up. It's all rock'n'roll.

QUESTION: Do you play the same way now as you did?

JOHN: It's only rock'n'roll. It just so happens that we write most of it.

QUESTION: Did Buddy Holly influence your music?

JOHN: He did in the early days. Obviously he was one of the greats.

PAUL: So did James Thurber, though, didn't he?

JOHN: Yeah, but he doesn't sing as well, does he?

QUESTION: Have you been practicing up your Australian accents?

GEORGE: No, guvnor, not at all.

QUESTION: Do you think you will be writing any songs with Australian themes?

JOHN: No, we never write anything with themes. We just write the same rubbish all the time.

QUESTION: Do you play the kind of music you want to or the music you think people want to hear?

JOHN: Well, we've been playing this kind of music for five or six years, something like that. It's all just rock'n'roll. It just happens that we write it.

QUESTION: What do you think made the difference that put you up above other groups?

GEORGE: We had a record contract.

QUESTION: What record do you all agree is generally your best recording? Not the best seller, but rather the best musically.

JOHN: We always like the one we just made, don't we? So "Long Tall Sally."

GEORGE: I like "You Can't Do That," personally.

QUESTION: What about you, Jimmy? How do you feel being in with the Beatles? A newcomer standing in for Ringo?

JIMMY NICHOL: It's a good experience, man.

QUESTION: How is Ringo?

JIMMY: He's much better. He joins us on Sunday.

QUESTION: What do you do then?

JIMMY: I go back to London, where they're fixing up a band for me. I'll do some television . . .

JOHN: And he's away.

QUESTION: You're progressing pretty well with your Beatle haircut.

JIMMY: I've been growing it for about three months now.

QUESTION: How long does it take to get a magnificent mane like this?

JOHN: I can't remember being without it.

QUESTION: Do you ever go to the barber's, John?

JOHN: No. I haven't had my hair cut since the film. The woman on the film cut it. I don't trust anybody else.

QUESTION: This is the film, *Beatlemania*, is it?

JOHN: No, it's not called that. That's another one. *A Hard Day's Night* it's called.

QUESTION: Are you satisfied with the finished product?

JOHN: Well, it's as good as it can be with anybody that can't act.

THE BEATLES

Melbourne, June 15, 1964

QUESTION: How do you feel about your responsibilities? I mean teenagers dwell on your every comment and action. Do you feel very responsible towards this?

PAUL: We never used to believe it. We used to open a magazine and it would say so-and-so doesn't drink, doesn't smoke. We just act normally and hope other people don't think we act funny.

QUESTION: I know you say you act normally, but how can you when you're getting so much money? When everywhere you go people go so crazy you can't see anything.

JOHN: Normal in the environment that surrounds us.

QUESTION: John, you started in something called a skiffle group. Now, does this automatically grow into what now is the Beatles or did this come about over a period of years?

JOHN: Over a period of time. See, I met Paul first and he sort of joined us. Then George. It was just us three.

QUESTION: What did you think of the Adelaide reception?

PAUL: It was good.

QUESTION: Was it like anything you've ever had before?

BEATLES: No.

QUESTION: Do you think it was well conducted?

JOHN: Yes, everyone was well behaved.

QUESTION: Do you ever get this feeling that someone's going to knock you off or something?

PAUL: Nah.

QUESTION: How long do you rehearse a new number when making up a new song?

PAUL: Normally with new numbers we don't rehearse them until we record them.

QUESTION: John, I remember the launching of the careers of Frank Sinatra and Johnny Ray, Elvis Presley, but this to my mind is unprecedented by the fantastic buildup and publicity and all the press agents. I'm not detracting in any way from the talent that you obviously have. How much do you attribute to Brian Epstein and his public relations men? And how many are there to your knowledge?

JOHN: We've never had more than one PR guy and Brian's only got one to each client he's got. So they have their own and they don't work together. We've only ever had one. We didn't even have that one until about six months ago.

QUESTION: Do you think Brian Epstein is going to wave his magic wand sometime and include you as a fifth Beatle or a stand-in drummer for Ringo permanently?

JIMMY: That I don't know.

QUESTION: Have any of you ever been involved in any zany publicity stunts?

JOHN: No. We've never had to, actually.

PAUL: When we first started up we didn't have a manager or anything, so we sat around trying to think of them.

QUESTION: What would be your most exciting moments in show business?

GEORGE: I can't remember, there's so many ever since last September. Everything's been exciting. I think when we had got to America and found that they'd gone potty on us. And when we'd got back to Britain last October we'd been touring Sweden and when this Beatlemania thing started. We hadn't heard about it because we were away. We just landed in London and everyone was there smashing the place up.

QUESTION: In your wildest dreams did you ever think you'd reach the state you have reached now?

JOHN: No. Nobody imagined anything like this.

QUESTION: What about your act tonight, at the Centennial Hall. How long will it last, your particular segment?

PAUL: Thirty minutes, each house.

QUESTION: Are you constantly changing your act?

JOHN: Well, depending on what city or state and which song is more popular. Sometimes we change the order.

QUESTION: What about when you played the Royal Variety Performance for Her Majesty? Same act as always?

PAUL: Yeah.

QUESTION: Do you get nervous before any shows?

JOHN: All of them.

QUESTION: Any trouble with the hordes of screaming fans outside of the hotel. Do you sleep through all that sort of thing?

JOHN: They never stay out there all night screaming.

THE BEATLES

Sydney, June 18, 1964

ANNOUNCER: Any minute now the Beatles will appear. Wait a minute, here comes someone. Here comes the Beatles! You can't hear them over the screech of the crowd. This is what they've all been waiting for!

JOHN: Hey!!

SCREAMS

JOHN: How are you?

SCREAMS

GEORGE: There's a camera!

SCREAMS

JOHN: We love you.

SCREAMS

ANNOUNCER: Well, you've just seen the Beatles. The crowds are subdued now and safely on their way home.

QUESTION: It's very brave to bring us the original Ringo Starr.

PAUL: Very brave, so brave.

JOHN (TO RINGO): I've seen your dad on TV, you know.

RINGO: Oh yeah? What was he doing?

QUESTION: Are you still ill?

RINGO: I'm better now.

QUESTION: I hear you had quite a reception when you came in to Melbourne.

JOHN: It's as wild as Adelaide. I think that makes them equal. That's about the wildest one we've ever seen.

PAUL: I think Australia's pretty wild all around.

QUESTION: Were you worried about what you saw?

PAUL: We get worried when it stops, you know.

QUESTION: John, didn't you bring some of your family over here with you?

JOHN: My auntie and she's in New Zealand. Yes, that's why she came. She's got relatives there that's related to her. She came back here to get fresh air.

QUESTION: There's so much noise at your shows, are you miming your songs?

JOHN: Wouldn't that be cheating?

QUESTION: Do you enjoy press conferences?

JOHN: Yes, depending on the intelligence of the questions.

I READ THE NEWS TODAY ...

BRITISH GROUP INVADES US

"A plague has swept the land, but we have been left whole" was the way one writer reviewed the first invasion of the Beatles, England's mop haired rock'n'roll sensation. Like most, the writer felt the idols were a fad among teenagers which would pass as quickly as it arrived. How wrong he was!

The Beatles returned in August, stronger than ever. Motel owners found their doors denuded of knobs because adolescent girls believed "the Beatles had touched them." An attendant found himself driving an ambulance through seething streets and hidden in the back were the Beatles. "If those kids had caught them, they'd really have needed an ambulance," he said. Some fans did require medical aid, one burst blood vessels in the neck, she screamed so hard; another fell and was used as a vantage point by spike-heeled fellow fans.

Some people profited, such as the entrepreneur who bought sheets from the Beatles' hotel beds, and sold them at $1 per square inch!

How did the Beatles take to America? "Can't say," Ringo admitted. "Didn't see much. Luv-ed the money, though." He was referring to the $2,112,000 the Beatles took home with them.

—Associated Press

THE BEATLES

San Francisco, August 19, 1964

QUESTION: How was your trip?

JOHN: Like any plane trip, boring.

RINGO: We've been going seventeen hours now.

QUESTION: Did you see more of this town than you did last time?

RINGO: I only saw the airport.

QUESTION: Who is your tailor?

PAUL: A fellow called Dougie Millings of London.

QUESTION: Do you know his address?

PAUL: Great Portney Street in London.

JOHN: He keeps moving with all the profit he makes.

QUESTION: How frightened were you when you looked at the cage you were to be photographed in upon your arrival?

JOHN: It wasn't bad because somebody had been up there and tested it out.

RINGO: In fact, all the press went up and tested it.

QUESTION: Why did you leave so soon?

RINGO: It got cold.

JOHN: Some people said climb up on the thing and wave and then they said get off. So we came down.

PAUL: We're very obedient.

QUESTION: Why did you start the tour in San Francisco?

RINGO: You'll have to ask someone else. We're never told.

JOHN: We don't plan the tours, they're planned for us, you see. We just say we don't want to go to say, Bobboobooland. We leave the rest of the world open and it's all planned for us.

QUESTION: How do you like not having any privacy?

PAUL: We do have some.

JOHN: We just had some yesterday, didn't we, Paul? Tell them.

PAUL: Yes, yes.

QUESTION: Ringo, you didn't look too happy when you got off the airplane. Was there any reason?

RINGO: If you'd been on it fifteen hours, how would you look?

JOHN: How would he look, Ringo?

RINGO: I don't know. Look at him now.

GEORGE: A bit of a fried face, if you ask me.

QUESTION: Where are your cameras? Do you still take pictures?

RINGO: Well, John hasn't sold his. I just forgot mine. They got me up too early.

QUESTION: Which one is married?

RINGO: John is married. We'll all get married in the end.

PAUL: We will, in the end?

JOHN: You mean, you're not *funny* like the rumor says?

RINGO: Two or three years, plenty of time.

PAUL: Lots of rumors in America.

QUESTION: Have you been writing now?

JOHN: Yes. I wrote all the way over on the plane.

QUESTION: Now that you've made a movie, do you dig the acting bit?

JOHN: We don't profess to be actors.

PAUL: It's Americans that "dig."

JOHN: Dig?

PAUL: Dig your baby, daddy!

JOHN: Oh, I get it.

PAUL: "With it."

QUESTION: In America, the current slang is: "tough," "boss," and "dig."

PAUL: They change all the time.

QUESTION: What are some of your hip words in England?

JOHN: They're ever changing, you know, madam. "Alec Douglas," that's a big one. "Wilson," everybody does it.

PAUL: "Harold Wilson."

GEORGE: Always.

PAUL: "Barry Goldwater."

JOHN: That's a new one over there. It means "drag."

QUESTION: What does it mean over there?

JOHN: It means "happy days are here again."

QUESTION: Ringo, how do you feel about the "Ringo for President" campaign?

RINGO: It's marvelous.

QUESTION: If you were president, what political promises would you make?

RINGO: I don't know. I'm sort of politically weird.

JOHN: Are you?

RINGO: No, John, believe me.

PAUL: I think you should be president, Ringo.

QUESTION: How about you other guys, how do you feel about Ringo being nominated for president?

JOHN: We think he should win. Definitely in favor.

GEORGE: Yes.

QUESTION: Would you make them part of your cabinet?

RINGO: I'd have to, wouldn't I?

GEORGE: I could be the door.

RINGO: I'd have George as treasurer.

JOHN: I could be the cupboard.

RINGO: George looks after the money.

QUESTION: Are you going to Miami this year?

GEORGE: No. We're going to Florida to do a show in Jacksonville at the Gator Bowl.

QUESTION: What sports do you like?

JOHN: We don't like any sports except swimming. We all swim.

QUESTION: When are you going to work on your next book?

JOHN: All the time.

QUESTION: Do you keep little notes?

JOHN: Yes, here and there.

QUESTION: Ringo, can you show us your rings?

PAUL: Go, go.

JOHN: Show him.

RINGO: Anybody want to see these? And don't keep saying I change them.

QUESTION: What do you boys plan to do in San Francisco other than sleep?

RINGO: Just play the Cow Palace, that's about it.

QUESTION: You're not going to see the town?

RINGO: No, we're not going to see your beautiful city that we've heard so much about.

QUESTION: Why not?

GEORGE: It would take too much organization, wouldn't it?

RINGO: You won't see anything just speeding along in a car.

QUESTION: I started this whole campaign of you running for President . . .

RINGO: It's very nice, but I don't think I'll win.

QUESTION: We think it would be good relief to have you over here.

RINGO: Okay, you get me in and I'll come over here and we'll sort it all out.

THE BEATLES

Seattle, August 21, 1964

QUESTION: Are you people disappointed with the reception you got in Seattle compared to the other cities in the United States?

PAUL: No, very nice.

QUESTION: How do you enjoy being mobbed?

JOHN: It's okay if you got the police.

PAUL: We've never actually been mobbed. In New Zealand, though, they got us.

QUESTION: Your film [A *Hard Day's Night*] received very good reviews right across the country. Are you pleased?

PAUL: Yes, of course. What could we say to that—no?

QUESTION: Somebody said that you're like the Marx Brothers. Can you follow that in the film?

PAUL: I'd say Ringo is like Groucho.

QUESTION: Do you wish you'd made your success more on how you look?

JOHN: We did originally. I mean, when you make a record it first gets heard on the radio before they see you.

QUESTION: Do you wish they'd be quiet and let you sing sometimes?

JOHN: Why? They've got the records.

PAUL: They paid to come in and if they want to scream, well, they paid.

GEORGE: And it's part of the atmosphere now.

QUESTION: It was said in Las Vegas and Frisco that your performance couldn't be heard because of the noise. Do you consider it might hurt your future concerts?

JOHN: It's been going on for years.

QUESTION: How many more years do you think it will go on?

PAUL: Don't know.

JOHN: We're not there yet.

QUESTION: Have you any idea, three, four? What do you think?

GEORGE: Till death do us part!

QUESTION: Do you ever get tired of all this and just want to go some place and relax?

PAUL: When you see us we're on tour, but we're not always on tour.

QUESTION: Ringo, how are you feeling?

RINGO: Fine, thank you.

PAUL: Originally, dangerously ill.

QUESTION: Haven't had any more throat trouble?

RINGO: No, not yet.

QUESTION: There was a report, Ringo, that you were married. Are you?

RINGO: No.

QUESTION: Any plans?

RINGO: Nope.

QUESTION: John, how does your wife like all these girls making all this fuss over you?

JOHN: She doesn't see them.

QUESTION: Ringo, why do you get the most fan mail?

RINGO: Do I?

QUESTION: You do in Seattle.

RINGO: I don't know. Perhaps it's because more people write me.

QUESTION: John, somebody said you borrowed your bathtub scene in the film from Cleopatra. Is that true?

JOHN: I haven't seen Cleopatra.

RINGO: She used milk, though, didn't she?

QUESTION: Paul, what are your plans once your notoriety as a Beatle diminishes?

PAUL: We never made any plans as a group. None of us has ever bothered planning. We'll just wait and see what happens.

QUESTION: What would you like to do after you're through singing?

PAUL: I don't know. Probably John and I will carry on songwriting.

JOHN: I'm not doing it with you.

PAUL: Aren't you? Are the Beatles breaking up? I don't know.

QUESTION: Ringo, what do you plan to do?

RINGO: I haven't thought of it yet.

QUESTION: How far booked ahead are you, gentlemen?

GEORGE: A few months, I think.

QUESTION: Another American swing in mind?

JOHN: We've got nothing to do with it. We just say, where are we?

QUESTION: Is there one particular artist or type of music that you fellas follow more closely?

JOHN: Just rock'n'roll, really.

QUESTION: Who are the previous groups you most like?

PAUL: Buddy Holly had a good group.

QUESTION: Did you ever meet him?

JOHN: No.

QUESTION: I understand you took a junket on the way up. Did you take a look at Boulder Dam?

PAUL: So that's what it was.

GEORGE: I heard about that in school.

QUESTION: Of all your imitators, which one do you have the most re-spect for, or give the biggest chance of making it?

JOHN: None of the imitators have really done anything at all.

PAUL: There's two groups, but they're not imitating really. They're just people who've got longer hair in England now. They're not imitating us, they had long hair before us. Especially in prehistoric days.

QUESTION: Who would be the biggest American stars in Great Britain now?

JOHN: Elvis.

QUESTION: John, have you written a poem after you got back to the United States?

JOHN: No, I never write anything like that.

PAUL: Don't you?

JOHN: Oh, no. I never do, you know.

PAUL: I wish you would.

QUESTION: Ringo, is there a story behind all the rings on your fingers?

RINGO: That's from me mother, that's from me grandfather. It's a wedding ring, but I'm not married. And these are from two different girls. I've had these on for three years now.

QUESTION: Could you tell us how much you make . . .

JOHN: A lot.

QUESTION: Do you like Donald Duck?

RINGO: No.

QUESTION: Why?

RINGO: I can't understand him.

PAUL: I can't either.

THE BEATLES

New York, August 28, 1964

QUESTION: How do you like this welcome?

RINGO: So this is America. They all seem out of their minds.

QUESTION: Why are your speaking voices different from your singing voices?

GEORGE: We don't have a musical background.

QUESTION: Do you like fish-and-chips?

RINGO: Yes, but I like steak-and-chips better.

QUESTION: How tall are you?

RINGO: Two feet, nine inches.

QUESTION: Paul, what do you think of columnist Walter Winchell?

PAUL: He said I'm married and I'm not.

GEORGE: Maybe he wants to marry you!

QUESTION: How did you find America?

RINGO: We went to Greenland and made a left turn.

QUESTION: Is it true you can't sing?

JOHN (POINTS TO GEORGE): Not me. Him.

QUESTION: Why don't you smile, George?

GEORGE: I'll hurt my lips.

QUESTION: What's your reaction to a Seattle psychiatrist's opinion that you are a menace.

GEORGE: Psychiatrists are a menace.

QUESTION: What's this about an annual illness, George?

GEORGE: I get cancer every year.

QUESTION: Where would you like to go if all the security wasn't necessary?

JOHN: Harlem.

QUESTION: How do you feel about other Beatle-type groups?

JOHN: The Rolling Stones are personal friends of ours. They are most creative and beginning to write good songs.

QUESTION: Do you plan to record any antiwar songs?

JOHN: All our songs are antiwar.

QUESTION: When you do a new song, how do you decide who sings the lead?

JOHN: We just get together and whoever knows most of the words sings lead.

QUESTION: How does it feel putting on the whole world?

RINGO: We enjoy it.

PAUL: We aren't really putting you on.

GEORGE: Just a bit of it.

JOHN: How does it feel to be put on?

QUESTION: What's your reaction to composer Aaron Copland, who found the Beatles' music interesting, and Richard Rodgers, who found it boring?

PAUL: I like anyone who says he likes our music. I don't mind Richard Rodgers saying he finds it boring, but I must add that I find Richard Rodgers's music boring. And I'm not being nasty, Richard.

QUESTION: George, how do you feel about the nightclub, Arthur, named after your hairstyle?

GEORGE: I was proud, until I saw the nightclub.

QUESTION: What do you consider the most important thing in life?

GEORGE: Love.

PAUL: I once knew a fellow on the Dingle who had two dads. He used to call them Number One Dad and Number Two Dad. Now apparently Number One Dad wasn't nice. He used to throw the boy on the fire, which can develop a lot of complexes in a young lad.

RINGO: I remember my uncle putting a red-hot poker on me, and that's no lie. He was trying to frighten me.

PAUL: Tell me, Ringo, do all your relatives go round applying red-hot pokers to you?

JOHN: It's the only way they can identify them.

PAUL: You see, Ringo comes from a depressed area.

JOHN: Some people call it the slums.

RINGO: No, the slums are farther.

QUESTION: How important is politics to the Beatles?

JOHN: I get spasms of being intellectual. I read a bit about politics, but I don't think I'd vote for anyone. No message from any of those phony politicians is coming through to me.

QUESTION: Is it fun being the Beatles?

GEORGE: We've always had laughs. Sometimes we find ourselves hysterical, especially when we're tired. We laugh at soft remarks the majority of people don't get.

QUESTION: What frightens you most?

JOHN: The thing I'm afraid of is growing old. I hate that. You get old and you've missed it somehow. The old always resent the young and vice versa.

RINGO: I'd like to end up, sort of, unforgettable.

QUESTION: Ringo, why are you always so quiet?

RINGO: I don't like talking. It's how I'm built. Some people gab all day and some people play it smogo. I don't mind talking or smiling. I just don't do it very much. I haven't got a smiling face or a talking mouth.

QUESTION: What will you do when the Beatles disband?

JOHN: We're not going to fizzle out in half a day. But afterwards I'm not going to change into a tap-dancing musical. I'll just develop what I'm doing at the moment, although whatever I say now I'll change my mind next week. I mean, we all know that bit about, "It won't be the same when you're twenty-five." I couldn't care less. This isn't show business. It's something else. This is different from anything that anybody imagines. You don't go on from this. You do this and then you finish.

THE BEATLES

Milwaukee, September 4, 1964

QUESTION: How are you feeling tonight, fellas?

DEREK TAYLOR*: We're all ill, the lot of us.

QUESTION: Do you think the pandemonium you cause is ridiculous?

PAUL: Nothing's ridiculous when people enjoy themselves. We're not idols, you know. That's what the press makes us out to be, but it's all rubbish. We're just chaps.

QUESTION: Was there any need from a safety point to have avoided the fans at the airport?

PAUL: We don't think so, no. The police told us we couldn't go past them. It's mean not to let them have a wave. It's a lousy deal . . . a dirty trick.

QUESTION: But the police say it was your manager's decision to duck out.

PAUL: It's a lie. Our manager wasn't even on the plane.

GEORGE: It was a dirty lying policeman who said that.

CATHOLIC PRIEST: What deficiency in American youth are you supplying?

PAUL: There's nothing like that. They just like our records.

PRIEST: What is your appeal?

RINGO: Our appeal is that we're normal lads.

---

*Derek Taylor was, and is, a close friend to all of the Beatles and has worked for them on and off since the early days of Beatlemania.

PRIEST: What are you rebelling against?

PAUL: We're not rebelling against anything.

PRIEST: Don't you hate your parents?

PAUL: No.

PRIEST: Well, don't you think all teenagers rebel against their parents?

PAUL: Well, it's the thing to do at a certain age. Didn't you when you were young?

PRIEST: Do you hate the press?

PAUL: Not at all. They're chaps. They've got a job to do.

PRIEST: Do you enjoy putting the press on?

RINGO: We're not putting on the press. We're just being ourselves.

PRIEST: How do the Beatles keep their psychic balance?

GEORGE: There's four of us, so if one goes a little potty, it's all right.

THE BEATLES

Kansas City, September 17, 1964

QUESTION: Did you ever date a fan?

JOHN: Yes, I have done, honestly. What more can I say?

QUESTION: Do you fellas hear what you're playing when the screams get going and how do you keep together?

GEORGE: We've heard it all before.

JOHN: It sounds louder to people who haven't been to the shows. We're immune.

QUESTION: You have inspired Beatles hairdos. Do you appreciate seeing these styles on other people?

RINGO: It's quite good. We always change them when we see someone else with them.

QUESTION: Do you plan to change your hairstyle any time soon?

RINGO: Not our hair, just our clothes.

QUESTION: Are you concerned about a poll in Britain which indicates that a group called the Rolling Stones . . .

RINGO: There's many polls. They just won one of them . . .

GEORGE: They won that one last year as well.

JOHN: That's *their* poll. It doesn't make any difference.

RINGO: We don't read the papers.

QUESTION: With the recent antismoking campaign, are you trying to give up smoking?

JOHN: No, I never even thought of it. When you got to go, you got to go.

QUESTION: Have you written any new songs lately?

PAUL: John and I have written two since we've been here.

QUESTION: On the plane?

PAUL: In Atlantic City, actually.

QUESTION: What's the most annoying thing about this whole thing?

RINGO: Not being able to see the fans at the airport.

PAUL: Too much security.

RINGO: The plane goes to the far end of the field and we just get put in a car. Away we go, without seeing anybody.

JOHN: Away we go.

RINGO: They blame us. You see, it's not us, it's them.

QUESTION: George, what caused you to throw a Scotch-and-Coke at a reporter in Los Angeles?

GEORGE: He was a very nasty young man.

JOHN: Old man.

GEORGE: He'd been told to leave anyway, you see. He insisted on jumping around trying to take pictures and we couldn't see with somebody flashing us in front. So I thought I'd baptize him.

QUESTION: What do you plan to do after the breakup of the Beatles?

PAUL: No one's made any plans, but John and I will probably carry on songwriting and George will go into basketball.

GEORGE: Or roller skating. I haven't really decided yet.

QUESTION: Ringo, would you show us your gray hair?

RINGO: No. I don't want to be messing it all up as we're on television.

QUESTION: What do you do about the barber?

JOHN: We never go to one.

GEORGE: We don't do anything about them when we're not on tour.

QUESTION: What care does your hair get?

PAUL: Just a bit of combing and washing.

RINGO: Nothing special.

GEORGE: We never put any hair oil on it because it makes it go funny, you see.

QUESTION: It was rumored a couple of days ago you tried to get reservations at a hotel in Springfield and were turned down repeatedly.

JOHN: We don't make them anyway and the ones that have turned us down, well, that's their privilege.

QUESTION: What is the one question you would like to be asked at a press conference?

PAUL: I think everything's been asked.

QUESTION: George, what ever became of your car wreck in London? What kind of accident was it?

GEORGE: I only just tapped into some fella and knocked the headlamp in. But the further away you are, the worse the damage appears. Over here, I mean, the car was a write-off, but actually it wasn't.

QUESTION: Did you have to pay for anything?

GEORGE: No. The other fella's insurance paid because it was his fault. I'm a good driver.

QUESTION: Are you considering making America your home?

PAUL: We like the place, but not to live here.

QUESTION: Is there any other particular city you enjoyed visiting?

JOHN: New York.

PAUL: New York.

GEORGE: Hollywood.

RINGO: Hollywood.

QUESTION: Do you have any favorite entertainers?

JOHN: American soul.

PAUL: And Sophie Tucker.

QUESTION: We heard you play cards between performances. What kind do you like?

RINGO: Poker and crazy eights.

QUESTION: I'd like to ask Paul how his feud with Walter Winchell is doing?*

PAUL: It's not a feud, he's just soft. I give up talking to him.

QUESTION: How much hysteria do you feel is real and how much is pretended by the little girls that adore you?

JOHN: Doesn't matter.

---

*Syndicated U.S. columnist Walter Winchell was critical of McCartney in several of his columns. In those days, taking a few lightweight potshots at a Beatle guaranteed across-the-board coverage.

PAUL: There's a lot of it in the papers that's not real. There's also a lot, I think, that is.

QUESTION: John, how does your wife feel about girls screaming and running after you?

JOHN: She knows they never catch me.

QUESTION: Ringo, I heard you were having trouble with your throat. Is it all right now?

RINGO: Yes. It's fine. I haven't had any trouble for the last two months.

QUESTION: Have you ever measured your hair to see who's got the longest?

BEATLES: No!

GEORGE: I think mine is anyway, because it grows faster than the others'.

JOHN: I'm usually a close second.

QUESTION: Ringo, are you going to have your tonsils taken out and have you had that offer yet from a girl to send her the tonsils?

RINGO: We got the telegram, but I don't think I'm going to give them to her.

JOHN: We're going to auction them off.

PAUL: That's disgusting.

QUESTION: We'd like to know if there's any truth to the rumor, John, that you might leave the group?

JOHN: No. I don't know where it started, it just appeared somewhere.

RINGO: We can hardly get rid of him anyway.

QUESTION: Did you make any new records while you were in Hollywood?

PAUL: We did do an album for a souvenir, but it's not for general release. It was so terrible, that's why.

QUESTION: Paul, how do you feel about reports that say you are conceited?

PAUL: They're true.

QUESTION: Is there anything you wanted to do in Kansas City that you didn't get a chance to, anyone in particular you wanted to see? Mrs. Truman?

JOHN: Not particularly, no.

QUESTION: Have you bought any new clothes in the United States?

JOHN: A guy on the radio yesterday described this as a typical Liverpool outfit. I got it in Key West.

QUESTION: Do you ever wear a tie?

JOHN: Me? Yeah, when I find it.

GEORGE: I've got one of his suits.

JOHN: I can never find my stuff.

QUESTION: Which do you like more, the fans or the money?

JOHN: We'll still have the money and we'll miss the fans, they'll be the ones who'll have gone. The money will still be there, thankfully.

QUESTION: I can't find out who the opening acts are with you.

PAUL: The Exciters, Clarence Frogman Henry, The Bill Black Combo, and Jackie DeShannon.

QUESTION: Another English group is going to play Kansas City. The Dave Clark Five. Are you going to play with them?

RINGO: We know them.

QUESTION: How did they come out in the poll?

RINGO: *The Melody Maker*, you're talking about?

PAUL: They didn't win.

JOHN: It varies. Each little paper has its own readership, so the votes go one way or another every year.

QUESTION: Ringo, what do you do when you're confined to your hotel room?

RINGO: We just sit around, watch telly, radio . . .

JOHN: Watch the radio!

RINGO: . . . or play cards. Anything at all. We even talk to each other.

QUESTION: How much are the American tax authorities earning off you?

BEATLES: Nothing!

QUESTION: How about the British government?

JOHN: They're getting a lot.

RINGO: We'll end up with about $10 when they get through.

QUESTION: Is it true you all are writing books and if so, what's the subject matter?

PAUL: No, John's the only one who writes.

RINGO: We haven't learned how yet.

QUESTION: Since your return to America this time have you been asked to appear on Ed Sullivan's program?

DEREK: Yes, they were, but it hasn't been fitted in yet.

QUESTION: You were saying earlier that the two of you might continue on and the rest of you break up the act. Is there a date you are going to break up?

PAUL: If it's got to happen, John and I would probably carry on songwriting. We didn't mean singing.

QUESTION: How long do you think it will be before it does happen?

PAUL: No idea, really. It could happen tomorrow after the Kansas show.

QUESTION: When you were in Florida did you talk with Cassius Clay?*

JOHN: We only met him once with the kind of publicity stunt that he's best at.

PAUL: It was organized by the newspapers down there. They asked us. He's a good fella, isn't he? Big!

QUESTION: Do you like baseball?

JOHN: Not particularly, no.

GEORGE: Great game.

RINGO: Nice holiday, throw the ball, have a cigarette, and throw a ball, ten minutes later throw another ball.

QUESTION: Are you going to do another picture?

GEORGE: Next February, but nothing else has been decided.

QUESTION: No date, no title?

GEORGE: No date, no title, no script, no other people to act in it.

JOHN: No nothing, just us.

QUESTION: Would any of you care to give us your views—I don't mean to be smart by this—on religion or politics?

JOHN: We're not interested in either.

QUESTION: Is it being planned to do a movie of your whole life, school, the Cavern Club . . .

JOHN: They couldn't put that kind of thing on the screen. Not yet, anyway.

QUESTION: One of you said you didn't like politics—it was like beer, you didn't like the taste. And in Chicago you made the comment that if you were for anyone in the election, you'd be for LBJ.

JOHN: We said Eisenhower, actually.

QUESTION: What about in your own country? You're going back to a general election campaign.

---

*Heavyweight boxer Cassius Clay later, of course, changed his name to Muhammad Ali after his conversion to Islam.

RINGO: We're not going to vote over there.

PAUL: None of us do.

JOHN: If we can find out which one takes the least tax, I'll vote for them.

QUESTION: In New Orleans you met Fats Domino. Could you tell us how that came about?

JOHN: Frogman Henry said he'd try and arrange for us to meet him, we've always liked him. He brought him round with a friend, stayed about an hour, and had some shots taken for his kids.

JOHN: He's marvelous, we sang a song with him.

QUESTION: Paul, you lost your driver's license. How did you do it?

PAUL: I lost it a year ago. I just got it back actually. For speeding three times. If they catch you three times, you lose it. Got caught!

RINGO: He wasn't fast enough!

QUESTION: Why did you want to go to New Orleans?

JOHN: Well, it's the clubs and that, the sounds, man.

QUESTION: Ringo, what do you think of Jayne Mansfield?

RINGO: She's a drag.

PAUL: Ringo!

GEORGE: I second him.

DEREK: It's the word D - R - A - G and it means, simply, a bore.

JOHN: It's American.

QUESTION: What about Mamie Van Doren?

GEORGE: We never met her. Her publicist wasn't as good as Jayne Mansfield's.

QUESTION: What is your reaction to girls who come up to your hotel and tear up the sheets and anything you've discarded, like cigarette butts?

JOHN: If they do it after we leave, it's all right.

RINGO: Not if they're ripping them while we're still asleep.

QUESTION: With all these girls chasing you all over the world, who's the most exciting woman you've ever met?

JOHN: Ringo's mother was pretty hot. I'm only joking.

QUESTION: Do you smoke American cigarettes and if so, what kind?

GEORGE: Yeah, we like American ciggies and we smoke filters, but we're not advertising anybody's cigarettes unless they give us a few million free.

QUESTION: Do you do anything for free?

JOHN: Yeah, charity shows.

QUESTION: George, I heard that in the Lafayette Hotel a girl climbed eight stories up the side of the building and jumped in the window, grabbed you in your night clothes, and was then arrested.

GEORGE: No. It's untrue. I heard a noise in the next room and it was the policemen chasing her around. She jumped on Ringo, actually.

RINGO: That bird was running round the room and I was chasing her!

QUESTION: How many of your records have been sold?

JOHN: We were told eighty-three . . .

RINGO: Eighty-five.

JOHN: Eighty-five, sorry.

QUESTION: Million?

JOHN: Yes.

Dallas, September 18, 1964

QUESTION: Although you haven't seen much of Dallas, how do you like it?

PAUL: Well, it's mighty fine, partner. Mighty fine.

QUESTION: Ringo, do you have any political affiliations?

RINGO: No, I don't even smoke.

QUESTION: What kind of girls do you prefer?

RINGO: My wife.

QUESTION: What kind of girl is she?

RINGO: A nice girl.

QUESTION: What kind of girl do you like, Paul?

PAUL: John's wife.

JOHN: Nobody likes a smart aleck.

QUESTION: Do you have any books coming out?

RINGO: John's the one with the books.

JOHN: I've got one coming out next year, but I haven't written it yet.

QUESTION: What's the name of it?

JOHN: I don't know. I haven't written it.

QUESTION: What kind of books do you like to do?

JOHN: Ah . . . rubbish.

RINGO: I'm writing a detective novel.

JOHN: Yeah, he's writing a detective book.

QUESTION: Last night, you had a lot of trouble getting into the Cabana. Did any of you get hurt at all?

GEORGE: I got punched in me face a few times. But, I mean, that's part of life, isn't it?

QUESTION: One of the reviews of your book [*In His Own Write*] says that you're being an anarchist. Would you say you are?

JOHN: I don't even know what it means.

QUESTION: Comparing the receptions you've received all over the United States and taking into consideration the time of night, how was the reception here in Dallas?

PAUL: It was hectic but nice.

QUESTION: Do you like your cowboy hats?

JOHN: Hey, sure do!

QUESTION: Ringo, in California the girls ate some grass you walked on. How do you feel about that?

RINGO: I just hope they don't get indigestion.

QUESTION: What is your opinion of Mods and Rockers?

JOHN: They should be locked up.

QUESTION: How does it feel to make over a thousand dollars a minute?

GEORGE: It's one of the very best feelings in life.

QUESTION: What do you think of American girls?

RINGO: Well, there's sure lots of them.

QUESTION: Which one of you is most anxious to get home?

JOHN: Probably me, I'm married.

QUESTION: Is there ever any jealousy between you during the act happening on stage?

RINGO: No, not yet.

QUESTION: How do you like Texas?

JOHN: Swell.

QUESTION: Have you ridden a horse yet?

PAUL: No, but we plan to. Don't worry.

QUESTION: George, are you trying to make your black curl a youth symbol like Ringo's rings or Paul's eyes?

GEORGE: Yeah, that's why I'm wearing one now.

QUESTION: When do you have time to write your songs?

JOHN: We write them in hotel rooms after the show sometimes.

QUESTION: Have you had any fish-and-chips since you've been in the States?

PAUL: No, not even a cup of tea.

QUESTION: How long y'all gonna to sing for us tonight?

JOHN: We do about thirty minutes, cousin.

QUESTION: Are you disappointed in your American tour because you've been forced to spend so much time in seclusion because of your fans?

GEORGE: We expect any tour we do to be secluded and not having much of a chance to see the cities and things . . .

JOHN: Because we're here to work.

THE MBE AFFAIR

June 11, 1965

Queen Elizabeth has included The Beatles in her birthday honors list, naming them members of the Most Excellent Order of the British Empire. They are the first group of pop singers to make the honors list. Henceforth, they may use the initials MBE after their name.

—*Daily Mail*

THE BEATLES

London, Summer, 1965

QUESTION: Well, gentlemen, first of all, many congratulations on receiving your MBE. The whole country seems very delighted indeed. How do you feel about it, Paul?

PAUL: Delighted, indeed. I'm delighted everyone's delighted. I love it.

QUESTION: Is it fun for you?

PAUL: Yeah. Of course, it would be for you too, wouldn't it? My uncle woke up one morning and said, "Mmm Bbb Eee." You know, it's great.

QUESTION: Ringo, how did you first hear about it?

RINGO: Um, well, we heard about it six weeks ago. We got the forms to fill in and then we knew we were going to get it two days ago.

QUESTION: How did these forms come? Straight through the post, or what?

RINGO: Just in brown envelopes delivered by hand, I think, to one of Brian's secretaries.

GEORGE: I'll tell him. They were sent from the Prime Minister at 10 Downing Street to our manager's office; and they were delivered from there to Twickenham, where we were filming.

JOHN: *Help!*

GEORGE: A day later, when we found them we thought we were being called up for the army and then we opened them and found out we weren't.

QUESTION: Why is the MBE awarded?

PAUL: I don't know. In fact I know nothing about it, just that we've got it and it's very nice to have. I don't think about it. Maybe people may think of it. But it doesn't make me any more respectable. I'm still a scruff.

QUESTION: I was wondering about that, Ringo. How do you feel about going to the palace in your morning suit and all that?

RINGO: I don't mind. It'll be all right, when I buy one.

QUESTION: You haven't got one, then?

RINGO: No, not yet. I've got an evening suit. If that will do.

QUESTION: Oh, I don't think it will.

HECTOR DUPUIS

June 14, 1965

Hector Dupuis, a member of the Canadian House of Commons representing a Montreal district, has announced he is returning his MBE medal because the Queen has awarded one to The Beatles. He claimed English royalty has placed him on the "same level as vulgar nincompoops." Mr. Dupuis received his medal for his work as director of the selective service in Quebec.

—*Montreal Gazette*

THE BEATLES

London, 1965

QUESTION: What was your reaction when you heard the news about your MBEs?

RINGO: There's a proper medal as well as the letters, isn't there? I will keep it to wear when I'm old. It's the sort of thing you want to keep.

JOHN: I thought you had to drive tanks and win wars to get the MBE.

GEORGE: I didn't think you got this sort of thing for playing rock'n' roll.

PAUL: I think it's marvelous. What does this make me dad?

QUESTION: What do you say about Hector Dupuis turning in his medal?

GEORGE: If Dupuis doesn't want the medal, he had better give it to us. Then we can give it to our manager, Brian Epstein. MBE really stands for "Mr. Brian Epstein."

QUESTION: Why do you think you got the medal?

JOHN: I reckon we got it for exports, and the citation should have said so. Look, if someone had got an award for exporting millions of dollars' worth of fertilizer or machine tools, everyone would have applauded. So why should they knock us?

THE ROYAL INVESTITURE

Buckingham Palace, October 26, 1965

THE QUEEN (TO PAUL): How long have you been together now?
PAUL: Oh, for many years.
RINGO: Forty years.
THE QUEEN (TO RINGO): Are you the one who started it?
RINGO: No, I was the last to join. I'm the little fellow.
THE QUEEN (TO JOHN): Have you been working hard lately?
JOHN: No, we've been on a holiday.

THE BEATLES

Outside Buckingham Palace, October 26, 1965

PAUL: We've played many palaces including Frisco's Cow Palace. But never this one before. It's a keen pad and I liked the staff. Thought they'd be dukes and things, but they were just fellas.

QUESTION: What about the Queen?

PAUL: She's lovely, great. She was very friendly. She was just like a mum to us.

QUESTION: Were you nervous?

JOHN: Not as much as some of the other people.

QUESTION: How did the other medal recipients act towards your award?

JOHN: One formally dressed middle-aged winner walked up to us after the ceremony and said, "I want your autographs for my daughter, but I don't know what she sees in you." So we gave him our autographs.

QUESTION: How did you know what to do during the ceremony?

JOHN: This big fellow drilled us. Every time he got to Ringo he kept cracking up.

QUESTION: What will you do with your medals?

PAUL: What you normally do with medals. Put them in a box.

THE BEATLES

Toronto, August 17, 1965

QUESTION: What do you think about your fans reading *Playboy?*
RINGO: Our young fans aren't supposed to read *Playboy.*
JOHN: It's you, their fathers, who should hide it from them.
RINGO: If their fathers read it, send us the back issues.
QUESTION: Everybody has a theory on why you affect crowds the way you do. Do you have one?
PAUL: No, not at all.
QUESTION: Does marriage agree with you?*
RINGO: Yes, it does.
JOHN: Yes.
QUESTION: How did you propose to your wife?
RINGO: Same as anybody else. Are you married? If you're not, you'll find out.
QUESTION: I want to get married and I want to do it right.
RINGO: You want to do it *right?*
QUESTION: How do I do it?
JOHN: Use both hands.
QUESTION: Ringo, would you still like to be a disc jockey?
RINGO: Oh yeah, yeah.

---

*On February 11, 1965, Ringo Starr married his Liverpool sweetheart, Maureen.

QUESTION: I'd like to ask Mr. Lennon why he took up writing and who's your biggest influence in that field?

JOHN: I don't know why I took it up and I haven't got a hero. Well, I suppose maybe Lewis Carroll.

QUESTION: Which film did you enjoy doing more. *Help!* or *A Hard Day's Night?*

GEORGE: We enjoyed both of them actually. I think the new one we liked a bit more because we knew more about the film business, you see.

QUESTION: Do you prefer the shorter tour this year as opposed to last? Does it give you more time to rest?

RINGO: Yes.

QUESTION: What kind of shampoo do you use?

RINGO: Anything we can borrow.

QUESTION: I'd like to know what happened to the color of John Lennon's hair.

JOHN: It's covered in sweat, you see, so it looks darker than it is.

QUESTION: Recently, on the Musical Express winners' concert and at Shea Stadium, you wore military type uniforms. Did you design them yourselves?

PAUL: No, we were in the Bahamas and I had nothing to wear, so I borrowed a soldier's outfit off the film and somebody said, "Wow, that's okay." So I said, "Right."

JOHN: That's how it happened.

GEORGE: Then we had them made.

QUESTION: Would you boys ever like to do a tour with completely English acts over here?

RINGO: We usually do in Britain. There's quite a lot of them over there.

QUESTION: Do you think that traveling with women companions hurts your image?

PAUL: We're not traveling with women companions and, anyway, we haven't got an image.

QUESTION: Of all the countries you've traveled, which audience has been the most responsive?

JOHN: Gravelbede!

QUESTION: Where?

PAUL: America actually, because there's more people. It's the biggest place.

QUESTION: Paul, are you planning to marry Jane Asher?*

PAUL: I haven't got any plans. That's all there is, but everyone keeps saying I have. So maybe they know more than me.

QUESTION: Would you like to visit Niagara Falls?

GEORGE: We've seen the photographs.

QUESTION: What was your reaction to your greeting in Rome?

JOHN: We had a good greeting, contrary to rumors over here. There was nobody at the airport because we arrived at five in the morning, but the show was a sellout. So sit down!

QUESTION: Did you boys have any difficult moments during the filming of *Help!*?

GEORGE: Only trying to get to the studio on time.

QUESTION: Have you had a chance to enjoy your success?

RINGO: Yeah, all the time, ha-ha.

QUESTION: Are you bored with this life, or do you still find it exciting?

JOHN: We still like it or we wouldn't be touring.

QUESTION: Are you going to have any more Beatles' Christmas shows?

JOHN: Ask Mr. Christmas Epstein.

GEORGE: Mr. Epstein may have a Mr. Epstein Christmas show?

JOHN: It'll give him something to work on.

QUESTION: Do you plan to continue writing and if so, do you have a medium in mind?

JOHN: Yeah, because I think we're under contract now, but I've got nothing in mind. It will be the same stuff, only backwards.

RINGO: Nothing in his mind, you get that?

QUESTION: Individually, how do you like being the Beatles?

RINGO: Simply wonderful to be here.

JOHN: We like it or we'd be the Rolling Stones.

QUESTION: How long do you plan to continue doing concert tours?

PAUL: It's up to Brian and the people who buy the tickets.

JOHN: Until people stop coming to see us.

QUESTION: Will Paul tell us a little bit about his marriage plans?

---

*Jane Asher was Paul McCartney's picture-perfect fiancée during the heady days of Beatlemania. They parted company forever shortly after he took up with Linda Eastman in 1969.

PAUL: You've just asked me. The thing is, you see, everyone keeps saying I'm married or I'm divorced or I've got fifty children, but I haven't . . .

RINGO: You've only got forty.

PAUL: I haven't said anything, people keep making it up, so if you'd like to make it up, I'll sue you.

QUESTION: Have any of you boys had a mental block on stage?

JOHN: It happens, yes.

PAUL: What?

JOHN: I didn't know what key I was in last night.

QUESTION: Ringo, Gerry Shotberg, the photographer, questioned whether or not you were still taking pictures. You said, "No, because I'm bored and all I can take pictures of is hotel rooms." Do you feel you boys have to stay in too much?

RINGO: The question is, why have I really stopped taking photographs!

QUESTION: Well, I realize it just gets boring staying in the hotel room.

RINGO: It's not boring staying in the hotel room, it's boring taking photos in a hotel room.

QUESTION: We realize that John and Paul are both prolific songwriters and we get the impression that their songs are written very quickly. How far in advance do you compose them?

PAUL: It depends. If we feel like writing a lot, then we'll get ahead of what we've got to do, but mainly we just write to order if we're doing a new film or LP. Brian makes us work.

QUESTION: Do you mind that you can't hear yourself think when you're singing?

JOHN: How do you know we can't hear ourselves think? You weren't in our minds, were you? We can hear ourselves think or we would forget what we were doing.

PAUL: The thing about singing, it doesn't matter because people pay to come in and know what they want. They don't pay to come in and do what other people want them to do. They're having a good time, so leave them alone. Up with the workers!

QUESTION: Do you call what they do having a good time?

PAUL: Why not? It's only *you* who don't!

JOHN: They must be or they wouldn't be coming again and again. If they were having a bad time like you, they wouldn't come.

QUESTION: Do you realize a lot of English groups are stealing your limelight?

JOHN: Yeah, it's terrible.

QUESTION: Ringo, are you Jewish?

RINGO: Stand up that man or woman!

JOHN: He's having his bar mitzvah tomorrow.

RINGO: No, I'm not Jewish.

QUESTION: If there had been national service in England, would the Beatles have existed?

RINGO: No, because we would have all been in the army.

PAUL: Unless we all got in the same hut.

QUESTION: Would Ringo consider changing his hairstyle?

RINGO: For what? I'm quite happy.

QUESTION: What do you think of the news media keeping you in front of the public?

JOHN: They're doing very well and without them people wouldn't know what we're doing, so that's it.

QUESTION: I was talking to Bill Haley at the start of this show and he was mentioning getting a gig together via TelStar with all the English and American groups. Who do you think would win such a challenge?

JOHN: By the fans at the moment the English would win. But if we judged it, the Americans would probably win.

THE BEATLES

Somewhere in North America, 1965

QUESTION: Were you worried about the oversized roughnecks who tried to infiltrate the airport crowd on your arrival?

RINGO: That was us!

QUESTION: How do you add up success?

BEATLES: Money.

QUESTION: What will you do when Beatlemania subsides?

JOHN: Count the money. I don't suppose I think much about the future. I don't really give a damn. Though now we've made it, it would be a pity to get bombed. It's selfish, but I don't care too much about humanity; I'm an escapist. Everybody's always drumming on about the future, but I'm not letting it interfere with my laughs, if you see what I mean.

QUESTION: What is your opinion on the atom bomb?

PAUL: It's disturbing that people should go around blowing up, but if an atom bomb should explode I'd say, "Oh well." No point in saying anything else, is there? People are so crackers. I know the bomb is ethically wrong, but I won't go around crying. I suppose I could do something like wearing those "Ban the Bomb" things, but it's something like religion that I don't think about. It doesn't fit in with my life.

QUESTION: Are you ever in any danger during your concerts?

PAUL: I was got once by a cigarette lighter. Clouted me right in the eye and closed my eye for the stay. In Chicago a purple-and-yellow stuffed animal, a red rubber ball, and a skipping rope were plopped up on stage. I had to kick a carton of Winstons out of the way when I played. And I saw a cigarette lighter go flying past me in Detroit's Olympia Stadium.

QUESTION: Don't you worry about all that?

PAUL: It's okay, as long as they throw the light stuff, like paper.

QUESTION: Would you ever accept a girl in your group if she could sing, play an instrument, and wear the Beatle haircut?

RINGO: How tall is she?

QUESTION: Beatle-licensed products have grossed millions and millions of dollars in America alone. Beatle wigs, Beatle hats, Beatle T-shirts, Beatle egg cups, Beatlenut ice cream . . .

RINGO: Any time you spell beetle with an "a" in it, we get some money.

QUESTION: What are your favorite programs on American television?

PAUL: *News in Español* from Miami. *Popeye, Bullwinkle.* All the cultural stuff.

JOHN: I like American TV because you can get eighteen stations, but you can't get a good picture on any one of them.

QUESTION: George, is the place you were brought up a bit like Greenwich Village?

GEORGE: No. More like the Bowery.

QUESTION: Do you get much fan mail?

RINGO: We get two thousand letters a day.

JOHN: And we're going to answer every one of them.

QUESTION: Do any of you have ulcers?

GEORGE: None that we've noticed.

QUESTION: How come you were turned back by immigration?

JOHN: We had to be deloused.

QUESTION: Who in the world would the Beatles like to meet more than anyone else?

RINGO: Santa Claus.

QUESTION: Paul, you look like my son.

PAUL: You don't look a bit like my mother.

QUESTION: Why aren't you wearing a hat?

GEORGE: Why aren't you wearing a tie?

QUESTION: Is it true that on one flight the stewardess broke up a pillow fight among you guys and got clobbered on the head?

GEORGE: I'm not really sure where she got hit. She did make us break it up, though. Remember that house we stayed in at Harlech?

PAUL: No. Which one?

GEORGE: Yes, you do! There was a woman who had a dog with no legs. She used to take it out in the morning for a slide.

QUESTION: Do teenagers scream at you because they are, in effect, revolting against their parents?

PAUL: They've been revolting for years.

JOHN: I've never noticed them revolting.

QUESTION: Do you have any special messages for the Prime Minister and your parents?

JOHN: Hello, Alec.

GEORGE: Hello, Mudda.

RINGO: Hello, fellas.

QUESTION: Did you really use four-letter words on the tourists in the Bahamas?

JOHN: What we actually said was, "Gosh."

PAUL: We may have also said, "Heavens!"

JOHN: Couldn't have said that, Paul. More than four letters.

QUESTION: Why don't all four of the Beatles ever sing together?

GEORGE: Well, we try to start out together, anyway.

QUESTION: What does each Beatle consider his most valued possession?

JOHN: Our lives.

QUESTION: What do you do with your money?

RINGO: We bury it.

GEORGE: We hide it.

PAUL: We don't see it. It goes to our office.

JOHN: We pay a lot of taxes.

QUESTION: What are your feelings on the "hints of queerness" American males found in the Beatles during the early days of your climb to popularity?

PAUL: There's more terror of that hint of queerness—of homosexuality—here than in England, where long hair is more accepted. Our whole promotion made us look silly, but we've had a chance to talk to people since then and they can see we're not thick little kids.

QUESTION: Do you wear wigs?

JOHN: If we do, they must be the only ones with real dandruff.

QUESTION: How do you feel about teenagers imitating you with Beatle wigs?

JOHN: They're not imitating us because we don't wear Beatle wigs.

QUESTION: Where did you get your hairstyle?

PAUL: From Napoléon. And Julius Caesar too. We cut it any time we feel like it.

RINGO: We may even do it now.

QUESTION: Are you wearing wigs or real hair?

RINGO: Hey, where's the police?

PAUL: Take her out!

GEORGE: Our hair's real. What about yours, lady?

QUESTION: What would happen if you all switched to crew cuts?

JOHN: It would probably be the end of the act.

QUESTION: What do you think of the Vietnam War?

JOHN: We think of it every day. We don't like it. We don't agree with it. We think it's wrong. But there is not much we can do about it. All we can do is say we don't like it.

QUESTION: What is your opinion of Americans who go to Canada to avoid the draft?

JOHN: We're not allowed opinions.

PAUL: Anyone who feels that fighting is wrong has the right not to go in the army.

JOHN VS JESUS VS THE WORLD

1966

"In the only popularity poll in Jesus' time, he came out second to Barabbas . . ."

The Rt. Rev. Kenneth Maguire, Anglican Bishop of Montreal

"Christianity will go. It will vanish and shrink. I needn't argue about that; I'm right and will be proved right. We're more popular than Jesus now; I don't know which will go first, rock'n'roll or Christianity. Jesus was all right, but his disciples were thick and ordinary. It's them twisting it that ruins it for me."

John Lennon

"John Lennon's remarks were taken out of context and did not accurately reflect the article or the subject as it was discussed. What actually occurred was a lengthy conversation between me and John in which the subject of Christianity was discussed. He observed that the power of Christianity was on the decline in the modern world and that things had reached such a ridiculous state that human beings—such as the Beatles—could be worshipped more religiously by people than their own religion. He did not mean to boast about the Beatles' fame."

Journalist Maureen Cleave

"Beatle-burning teenagers, joined by a surprising number of adults, turned a huge pile of Beatle lore, records and pictures into a pile of ashes near Radio Station KLUE Friday night. Tony Bridge, station owner, joined the campaign along with staff members. Lowell Wolfe, station manager, aided Donna Woods, of Longview, at the bonfire, spreading kerosene on the pile."

The Longview, Texas, Morning Journal, 1966

"I've nothing really against the ideas of Christianity and their ways. I suppose I wouldn't make that Jesus remark today. I think about things differently. I think Buddhism is simple and more logical than Christianity, but I've nothing against Jesus."

John Lennon

"I will revoke the membership of any member of my church who agrees with John Lennon's remarks about Jesus."

Reverend Thurman Babbs, Cleveland, Ohio

"Deport the Beatles. They are unworthy of a decent American reception. They should be fumigated. They are undesirables and enemy agents to the Christian cause. They have been a corrupting influence. Parents in our country have no time for their lousy, low and lewd forms of so-called entertainment. Let them go back to Britain!"

Carl L. Estes, newspaper publisher

"I'll let Julian* learn all about Jesus when he goes to school, but I'll also tell him there have been lots of other Jesuses. I'll tell him about the Buddhist ones; they're good men as well."

John Lennon

"When I heard in *Datebook* that John Lennon was playing the role of Christ in *The Jesus Saga*, I nearly died. I have always admired the Beatles, but this has shaken my loyalty to the core. It was shocking enough to hear John announce that heaven-shaking boast that the

---

*John Charles Julian Lennon was born in Liverpool on April 8, 1963. He was John and Cynthia's only child.

Beatles were bigger than Jesus, but now to hear that that hypocrite is actually playing the role of the greatest man on Earth, well, it's enough to make the angels wipe their glasses and clean out their ears! For John's sake I do hope John has repented that statement a million times."

Jennifer, Waco, Texas

THE "SAY SORRY"
PRESS CONFERENCE

1966

JOHN: Look, I wasn't saying the Beatles are better than God or Jesus. I said "Beatles" because it's easy for me to talk about Beatles. I could have said TV or the cinema, motor cars or anything popular and I would have gotten away with it. My views on Christianity are directly influenced by *The Passover Plot* by Hugh J. Schonfield. The premise is that Jesus' message had been garbled by his disciples and twisted for a variety of self-serving reasons by those who followed, to the point where it has lost validity for many in the modern age. The passage which caused all the trouble was part of a long profile Maureen Cleave was doing for the *London Evening Standard.* Then, the mere fact that it was in *Datebook* [magazine] changed its meaning that much more.

QUESTION: What was your own formal religious background?

JOHN: Normal Church of England, Sunday School and church. But there was actually nothing going on in the church I went to. Nothing really touched us.

QUESTION: How about when you got older?

JOHN: By the time I was nineteen, I was cynical about religion and never even considered the goings-on in Christianity. It's only in the last two years that I, all the Beatles, have started looking for something else. We live in a moving hothouse. We've been mushroom-grown, forced to grow up a bit quick, like having thirty- to forty-year-old heads in twenty-year-old bodies. We had to develop more sides, more attitudes. If you're a bus man, you usually have a bus man's attitude. But we had to be more than four mopheads up there on stage. We had to grow up or we'd have been swamped.

QUESTION: Just what were you trying to get across with your comments then, sir?

JOHN: I'm not anti-God, anti-Christ, or antireligion. I was not saying we are greater or better.

QUESTION: Mr. Lennon, do you believe in God?

JOHN: I believe in God, but not as one thing, not as an old man in the sky. I believe that what people call God is something in all of us. I believe that what Jesus, Mohammed, Buddha, and all the rest said was right. It's just that the translations have gone wrong.

QUESTION: Are you sorry about your statement concerning Christ?

JOHN: I wasn't saying whatever they're saying I was saying. I'm sorry I said it, really. I never meant it to be a lousy antireligious thing. From what I've read, or observed, Christianity just seems to me to be shrinking, to be losing contact.

QUESTION: Why did you subject yourself to a public apology in front of television cameras?

JOHN: If I were at the stage I was five years ago, I would have shouted we'd never tour again, packed myself off, and that would be the end of it. Lord knows, I don't need the money. But the record burning, that was a real shock, the physical burning. I couldn't go away knowing that I'd created another little pocket of hate in the world. Especially with something as uncomplicated as people listening to records, dancing, and enjoying what the Beatles are. Not when I could do something about it. If I said tomorrow I'm not going to play again, I still couldn't live with somebody hating me for something so irrational.

QUESTION: Why don't you tell your fans all this?

JOHN: But that's the trouble with being truthful. You try to apply truth talk, although you have to be false sometimes because this whole thing is false in a way, like a game. But you hope sometimes that if you're truthful with somebody, they'll stop all the plastic reaction and be truthful back and it'll be worth it. But everybody is playing the game and sometimes I'm left naked and truthful with everybody biting me. It's disappointing.

QUESTION: We've been hearing a great deal regarding your comments on God versus Jesus. Would you tell us what you really meant by that statement?

JOHN: I'll try and tell you. I was just talking to a reporter, who also happens to be a friend of mine and all of us at home. It was a sort of in-depth series she was doing and so I wasn't really thinking in terms of PR or translating what I was saying. It was going on for a couple of hours and I said it just to cover the subject. I didn't mean it the way they said it. It's just so complicated, it's gone way out of hand, you know. I wasn't saying that the Beatles were any better than Jesus, God, or Christianity. I never thought of any repercussions. I knew she was interviewing me, but I wasn't thinking that it meant anything.

QUESTION: What's your reaction to the repercussions?

JOHN: Well, when I first heard it I thought it can't be true. It's just one of those things like bad eggs in Adelaide. But when I realized it was serious I was worried stiff because I knew how it would go on. All the nasty things that would get said about it and all those miserable-looking pictures of me looking like a cynic. And they'd go on and on and on until it would get out of hand and I couldn't control it. I really can't answer for it when it gets this big, it's nothing to do with me now.

QUESTION: A disc jockey in Birmingham, Alabama, who actually started most of the repercussions has demanded an apology from you.

JOHN: He can have it: I apologize to him. If he's upset and he really means it, you know, then I'm sorry. I'm sorry I said it for the mess it's made, but I never meant it as an antireligion thing, or anything. You know, I can't say any more than that. There's nothing else to say really, no more words. I apologize to him.

QUESTION: Do you really think Christianity is shrinking?

JOHN: It just seems to me to be shrinking. I'm not knocking it or saying it's bad. I'm just saying it seems to be shrinking and losing contact.

PAUL: And we deplore the fact that it is, you know, that's the point about it all.

JOHN: Nothing better seems to be replacing it, so we're not saying anything about that.

PAUL: If it is on the decline in any way and you say it is, then it must be helpful.

JOHN: It's silly going on saying, "Yes, it's all fine and we're all Christians.

Yeah, yeah. We're all Christians and we're all doing this," and we're not.

PAUL: We're going to get blamed for the rise and fall of Christianity now.

QUESTION: Mr. Lennon, are you a Christian?

JOHN: Well, we were all brought up to be. I don't profess to be a practicing Christian. And Christ was what he was and anything anybody says great about him I believe. I'm not a practicing Christian, but I don't have *un-Christian* thoughts.

QUESTION: Was there as much reaction to your statements throughout Europe and other countries around the world as there was here in America?

JOHN: I don't think Europe heard about it, but they will now! It was just England and I sort of got away with it there. In as much as nobody took offense and saw through me. Over here it's just as I said, it went this way.

QUESTION: Some of the wires this morning [UPI] said that Pan American Airlines had provided each of you with free Bibles.

JOHN: We never saw that.

QUESTION: If Jesus were alive today in a physical form, not a metaphysical one, he would find "Eleanor Rigby" a very religious song, a song of concern with human experience and need. I'm curious about your expression of that.

JOHN: Well, I don't like supposing that if Jesus were alive now, knowing what he'd like to say or do. But if he was the real Jesus, the Jesus as he was before, well, "Eleanor Rigby" wouldn't mean much to him, but if it did come across his mind, he'd think that probably.

QUESTION: There have been Beatle boycotts nationwide, record burnings, even threats against your life. Does this bother you?

PAUL: Well, it's bound to bother us, isn't it?

QUESTION: Mr. Lennon, do you feel you are being crucified?

JOHN: No, I wouldn't say that at all.

* * *

JOHN: I can't express myself very well, that's my whole trouble. I was just commenting, in my illiterate way of speaking. It was about how Christ's message had been garbled by disciples and twisted for various selfish reasons by those who followed, to the point where it lost validity for many today. Actually, if I am going to blame anyone, it's myself for not thinking what people a million miles away were going to say about it. I've just had a reshuffling of all the things pushed into my head. I'm more of a Christian than I ever was. I don't go along with organized religion and the way it has come about.

Jesus says one thing and then all the clubs formed telling their versions and the whole thing gets twisted. It's like a game of having six people in a line and I whisper something to the guy next to me, maybe "love thy neighbor" or "everything ought to be equal." By the time it gets to the end of the line it's altogether something else.

THE BEATLES

New York, August 23, 1966

QUESTION: How do you manage to have such a weird effect on teenagers?

GEORGE: Enthusiasm, I guess.

QUESTION: Do you worry about smoking in public? Do you think it might set a bad example for your younger fans?

GEORGE: We don't set examples. We smoke because we've always smoked. Kids don't smoke because we do. They smoke because they want to. If we changed, we'd be putting on an act.

RINGO: We even drink.

QUESTION: What careers would you individually have chosen had you not become entertainers?

RINGO: A hairdresser.

GEORGE: I had a short go at being an electrician's apprentice, but I kept blowing things up, so I got dumped.

PAUL: I don't know . . . maybe something with art in it.

JOHN: No comment.

QUESTION: Do you have any special message for the Dutch youth?

JOHN: Tell them to buy Beatles records.

QUESTION: What's it like being Beatles?

GEORGE: We've gotten to know each other quite well. We can stand each other better now than when we first met.

QUESTION: Has success spoiled the Beatles?

JOHN: Well, you don't see us running out and buying bowler hats, do you? I think we've pretty well succeeded in remaining ourselves.

PAUL: The great thing about it is that you don't have big worries anymore when you've got where we have only little ones, like whether the plane is going to crash.

QUESTION: Can we look forward to any more Beatle movies?

JOHN: Well, there'll be many more. But I don't know whether you can look forward to them or not.

QUESTION: Is your popularity beginning to taper off?

PAUL: I agree that our popularity has hit a peak. But I also agreed with a man who said the same thing last year. And we were both wrong.

QUESTION: How do you feel about bandleader Ray Bloch's statement that the Beatles won't last a year?

JOHN: We'll probably last longer than Ray Bloch.

QUESTION: Sorry to interrupt you while you are eating, but what do you think you will be doing in five years' time when all this is over?

JOHN: Still eating.

QUESTION: What will you do when the bubble bursts?

GEORGE: Take up ice hockey.

PAUL: Play basketball.

QUESTION: Aren't you tired of all the hocus-pocus? Wouldn't you rather sit on your fat wallets?

PAUL: When we get tired, we take fat vacations on our fat wallets.

QUESTION: What is the biggest threat to your careers, the atom bomb or dandruff?

RINGO: The atom bomb. We've already got dandruff.

QUESTION: How long will your popularity last?

JOHN: When you're going to go, you're going to go.

QUESTION: What do you think you've contributed to the musical field?

RINGO: Records.

GEORGE: A laugh and a smile.

QUESTION: Do you care what the public thinks about your private lives?

RINGO: There's a woman in the United States who predicted the plane we were traveling on would crash. Now, a lot of people would like to think we were scared into saying a prayer. What we did actually—we drank.

QUESTION: What do you think of space shots?

JOHN: You see one, you've seen them all.

QUESTION: What about the recent criticism of your lyrics?

PAUL: If you start reading things into them, you might just as well start singing hymns.

QUESTION: Why are you disinterested in politics?

JOHN: We're not. We just think politicians are disinteresting.

QUESTION: You've admitted to being agnostics. Are you also irreverent?

PAUL: We are agnostics, so there's no point in being irreverent.

QUESTION: How do you stand in the draft?

JOHN: About five feet, eleven inches.

QUESTION: Are you afraid military service might break up your careers?

JOHN: No. There's no draft in England now. We're going to let you do our fighting for us.

QUESTION: What do you think about the pamphlet calling you four Communists?

PAUL: Us, Communists? Why, we can't be Communists. We're the world's number one capitalists. Imagine us Communists!

QUESTION: What do you consider the most important thing in life?

GEORGE: Love.

QUESTION: What is your personal goal?

GEORGE: To do as well as I can at whatever I attempt. And someday to die with a peaceful mind.

QUESTION: But you really don't expect that to happen for a long time yet, do you?

GEORGE: When your number's up, it's up.

QUESTION: What about your future?

JOHN: It looks nice.

QUESTION: Are you scared when crowds scream at you?

JOHN: More so in Dallas than in other places, perhaps.

QUESTION: Would you like to walk down the street without being recognized?

JOHN: We used to do it with no money in our pockets. There's no point in it.

QUESTION: What would you do if the fans got past the police lines?

GEORGE: We'd die laughing.

QUESTION: If you could have any wish you wanted at this moment, what would it be?

JOHN: No more unscheduled public appearances. We've had enough. We're going to stay in our hotel except for concerts.

QUESTION: Won't this make you feel like caged animals?

JOHN: No. We feed ourselves.

THE BEATLES

Seattle, August 25, 1966

QUESTION: John, could you please tell me something about your new movie [*How I Won the War*]?

JOHN: I don't really know anything except that I'm in it and it's about the last world war.

QUESTION: Mr. McCartney, would you please confirm or deny reports of your marriage to Jane Asher in Seattle this evening?

PAUL: It's tonight, yeah.

QUESTION: What time and where?

PAUL: I can't tell you that, can I?

QUESTION: You are confirming the report then?

PAUL: No, I'm not really. It was a joke. Who started this, anyone know? I just got in and found out I was getting married this evening. No, she is not coming in tonight as far as I know. And if she is, we are going out anyway. So we'd miss her.

QUESTION: Do you believe you represent a different type of morality than, say, a group like the Rolling Stones or the other protest groups?

PAUL: No, we don't represent anything like that.

JOHN: Are the Stones a protest group? I thought it was the Circle.

QUESTION: I'd like to know if your motivation in this is money? I'd like to think you're having as much fun as you seem when you're doing it.

JOHN: Well, when I look as though I'm having fun, I am. When I'm not, I'm not, usually.

QUESTION: I have a prediction that in twenty-five years, you're going to be a great writer.

JOHN: I don't know where I'll be in twenty-five years.

QUESTION: What about the Beatles' next movie? There's been a lot of stories, but nothing's confirmed.

JOHN: Somebody gave us a good idea, so we told him to go and turn it into a script. But we won't be able to tell whether or not we're going to make the film until we've read it.

QUESTION: The audience your music attracts has changed from say, thirteen-year-old girls to more the college age. Do you like it better that way?

GEORGE: I think it's probably gotten a bit older, but I don't know how old.

QUESTION: Paul, since you've denied the marriage rumors, what are you doing after the show?

PAUL: Marrying you, probably.

QUESTION: How is the attendance on this tour compared to past American tours?

PAUL: There's apparently been more people at the shows than in the past.

QUESTION: John and Paul, I'd like to know if all the songs written by Lennon/McCartney are composed by the two of you or do you ever write one by yourselves?

JOHN: We do them separately and together.

QUESTION: Your music used to be composed mostly of guitar backgrounds, but recently you've come around to using strings, harpsichords, and a lot of weird things like that. Is there any particular purpose in this evolution?

JOHN: No, just to use something besides guitar. It's not necessarily that we are coming around to them. It's finding them again.

QUESTION: George, where can people generally get a sitar?

GEORGE: In India.

QUESTION: Paul, you've said that sometimes you "have" to write. Could you explain what you mean by that?

PAUL: I just meant that when there's an LP due, we write songs. We do it like that more than write all the time. We write more to order. You know, if we've got fourteen tracks to fill, then we've got fourteen songs to write. That's what I meant.

THE BEATLES

Hollywood, August 28, 1966

QUESTION: How do you compare movie work to concert tours or recording sessions?

JOHN: We don't.

QUESTION: Would you rather play the Hollywood Bowl again instead of Dodger Stadium?

GEORGE: We don't really mind.

QUESTION: Maybe we can start another controversy here. One of your countrymen said on his arrival in England that he thought American women were out of style for not wearing miniskirts and as they didn't wear them their legs were ugly. I'd like to ask you what you think of American women's legs.

RINGO: Well, if they don't wear miniskirts, how does he know their legs are ugly?

QUESTION: Regarding your album jacket which was banned here,* whose idea was it and what was it supposed to mean?

---

*References are made here to the then controversial butcher cover, which was used on the American compilation LP *Yesterday and Today*. A panel from a larger photographic work by then Beatle photographer Robert Whittiker depicted the Beatles, wearing white butcher coats, surrounded by a few dismembered dolls and several prime cuts of beef. John Lennon later commented that the cover was a snide aside on the way the

JOHN: Ask the photographer who took it.

QUESTION: John, how did you decide to make *How I Won the War?*

JOHN: Because he [Richard Lester] asked me and I just said yes.

QUESTION: Do you consider that now, since you've been in the United States for almost a week, that this religious issue is answered once and for all?

JOHN: I hope so.

QUESTION: Would you clarify and repeat the answer you gave in Chicago?

JOHN: I can't repeat it because I don't know what I said.

QUESTION: Well, would you clarify the remarks that were attributed to you?

JOHN: You tell me what you think I meant and I'll tell you if I agree.

QUESTION: Some of the remarks attributed to you compared the relative popularity of the Beatles with Jesus Christ and intimated that the Beatles were more popular. This created quite a furor in this country, as you are aware.

PAUL: Did you know that, John? You created a furor!

QUESTION: Now, would you clarify the remark?

JOHN: I've clarified it about eight hundred times. I could have said TV or something. And that's just as clear as it can be. I used Beatles because I know about them a bit more than TV. I could have said any number of things, but it wouldn't have gotten as much publicity.

QUESTION: Do you think the controversy has hurt your careers or helped?

GEORGE: It hasn't helped or hindered, I don't think. I think most sensible people took it for what it was. It was only the bigots that thought it was on their side. They thought, "Ha-ha, here's something to get them for." But when they read it they saw there was nothing wrong with it really. They thought by John saying we were more popular than Jesus that he must be arrogant.

QUESTION: John, what stimulates you in your work?

JOHN: Just anything, you know.

QUESTION: What's your favorite group in the U.S.?

American record companies butcher their music by carving them up into cheesy packages for the ever Beatle-hungry American market.

JOHN: I've got a few. The Byrds, the Lovin' Spoonful, Mamas and Papas, I suppose.

PAUL: Beach Boys.

JOHN: The Miracles are the other side of it.

QUESTION: I was wondering if you still have an arrangement with the U.S. Internal Revenue Service to pay your taxes to England? How much money have you grossed on your current U.S. tour?

GEORGE: Money's got nothing to do with us.

PAUL: Brian does that.

GEORGE: And we don't particularly care about it.

JOHN: They just tell us what we get in the end, you know.

GEORGE: We pay tax, but we don't know how much we've made, because if we worried about that, we'd be nervous wrecks by now.

QUESTION: I'd like to direct this question to Messrs. Lennon and Mc-Cartney. A recent article in *Time* magazine put down pop music and referred to "Day Tripper" as being about a prostitute and "Norwegian Wood" as about a lesbian. I want to know what your intent was when you wrote them and what your feeling is about *Time*'s criticism of the music that is being written today?

GEORGE: We were just trying to write songs about prostitutes and lesbians. That's all.

QUESTION: Do you have any plans to work separately in the future?

GEORGE: All together probably.

QUESTION: Mr. Lennon, aren't you doing a picture alone?

JOHN: Yeah, but that's only in the holiday bit, in between Beatles.

QUESTION: I'd like to ask a question you've never been asked before.

JOHN: Go ahead, Fred.

QUESTION: What are you going to do when the bubble bursts?

JOHN: That's a personal "in" joke. He used to ask it at every press conference just to keep the party going.

QUESTION: Do you think we'll have another tour again next year?

GEORGE: Could be, Fred, Brian does that.

QUESTION: In Hollywood tonight, you had to arrive in an armored truck, which was swarmed by adoring fans. Do you ever have an opportunity to walk out on the streets without being recognized? Can you walk into a theater to see a movie by yourself?

JOHN: If you go in when the lights are down.

PAUL: We can do that in England. It's easier than it is here because we know England.

RINGO: Also it would be easier to do it if we weren't on tour. Because when we're on tour people know where we are and that's why we have a crowd.

QUESTION: Paul, many of the top artists in the pop field have said the Beatles have been a major influence on their music. Are there any artists who have had an important influence on you?

PAUL: Oh yes, nearly everyone. We pinch as much from other people as much as they pinch from us.

QUESTION: Ringo, do you carry wallet pictures of your baby with you?*

RINGO: I don't carry photos of anything.

QUESTION: May I ask about the song "Eleanor Rigby"? What was the inspiration for that?

JOHN: Two queers.

QUESTION: John, did you ever meet Cass of the Mamas and the Papas?

JOHN: Yes and she's great. I'm seeing her tonight.

QUESTION: Have you ever used Beatle doubles as decoys?

PAUL: No, we tried to get Brian Epstein to do it, but he wouldn't.

QUESTION: Ringo, how much did you contribute to "What Goes On"? And are you contributing to any other Lennon/McCartney compositions?

RINGO: About five words to "What Goes On." I haven't done a thing since.

QUESTION: I'd like to address this to John and Paul. You write a lot of stuff that other people steal from you and also purchase from you as with Ella Fitzgerald and the Boston Pops. How do you feel about your pieces being changed around?

JOHN: It depends how they do it.

PAUL: Once we've done a song and it's published anyone can do it. So whether we like it or not depends on if they've done it to our taste.

QUESTION: Then let's ask it this way: who do you think does it the best?

RINGO: Us!

QUESTION: For those of us who have followed your career from the early

---

*Ringo and Maureen's first child, Zak, was born September 13, 1965. Interestingly, he is now a top rock drummer just like his dad.

days of Liverpool and Hamburg and the pride in you being awarded the MBE and the dismay over the unwarranted adverse publicity of late, the question is: individually, what have been your most memorable occasions and what have been the most disappointing?

GEORGE: I think Manila was the most disappointing.

JOHN: And the most exciting is yet to come.

RINGO: Maybe the most disappointing.

QUESTION: Gentlemen, there was quite a ruckus when you went on the stock market with your stock. How is your stock doing?

JOHN: Fine, thank you.

RINGO: It went down, but it's coming up again.

GEORGE: It's gone down.

RINGO: It's the same as any other stock.

JOHN: It goes down every time the LPs drop out. They all think they're buying bits of records.

QUESTION: Leonard Bernstein likes your music. How do you like Leonard Bernstein's?

PAUL: Very good. He's great.

JOHN: One of the greatest.

QUESTION: George, before you left England you made a statement that you were going to America to be beaten up by Americans. Do you mean to say that you feel the American fan is more hostile than in Britain?

GEORGE: No, not at all. Actually, I said that when we were just back from Manila. They said, "What are you going to do next?" And I said, "We're going to rest up before we go get beaten up over there." Really, we just got shoved around. Jostled around in cars . . .

RINGO: It was a joke.

QUESTION: Do you think that's more an enthusiastic fan than a hostile fan? Would you say?

PAUL: If anyone beats us up, they're not really fans, are they?

GEORGE: I think they proved it themselves that there are a lot of fans who are great. And all the ones we've lost we don't really mind anyway, because if they can't make up their minds, who needs them!

QUESTION: How has your image changed since 1963?

GEORGE: An image is how *you* see us, so you can only answer that.

JOHN: You're the only one that knows.

QUESTION: Oh, I want to get your opinion. Is it a little tarnished now or more realistic? I know I have my opinion.

JOHN: Everybody attacks our opinion.

PAUL: We can't tell you our image. Our image is what we read in the newspapers and that's the same as you read. We know our real image which is nothing like our image. What I meant to say was . . .

RINGO: Take two bricks. . . .

QUESTION: Who is the young man with the lengthy haircut to your right?

JOHN: That's good old Dave, isn't it? That's Dave [Crosby] from the Byrds. A mate of ours. Ahoy, maties.

PAUL: He's shy.

QUESTION: Do you ever plan to record in the United States and why haven't you yet?

PAUL: We tried actually, but it's a financial matter. We had a bit of trouble over that one. We tried, but it didn't come out.

RINGO: It's all a bit of politics and dice.

JOHN: No comment.

QUESTION: Mr. Lennon, is it true you're planning to give up music for a career in the field of comparative religion?

JOHN: No. Is that another joke going around?

QUESTION: I'm sure you've heard about the many Beatle burnings and Beatle bonfires. Do you think American girls are fickle?

RINGO: All girls are fickle.

JOHN: The photos that we saw of them were of middle-aged DJs and twelve-year-olds burning a pile of LP covers.

QUESTION: This question is directed to Paul and John. You have written quite a few numbers for Peter and Gordon and I understand they don't like it because they think it's your writing the songs that makes them popular. Do you plan to write any more songs for them?

PAUL: They don't mind it. They like it, but people come up and say, "Ah, we see, you're just getting in on the Lennon/McCartney bandwagon." That's why they did that one with our names not on it, "Woman."* Because everyone thinks that's the reason they get hits. It's not true, really.

---

*At the time McCartney listed himself on the composing credits as Bernard Weff.

QUESTION: Gentlemen, what do you think would happen to you if you were to do an appearance without the armored truck and the police?

RINGO: We'd get in a lot easier.

JOHN: We wouldn't make it.

PAUL: It depends. Sometimes we could have made it much better without the armored truck. But today we probably wouldn't have.

QUESTION: Do you think you'd be physically harmed?

PAUL: Oh yeah, probably.

JOHN: What do you think?

QUESTION: The *New York Times Magazine* of Sunday, July third carried an article by Maureen Cleave in which she quotes one of the Beatles, not by name, as saying, "Show business is an extension of the Jewish religion." Would you mind amplifying that?

PAUL: Did she say that?

JOHN: I said that to her. No comment.

GEORGE: Ah, come on, John. Tell me what you meant.

JOHN: You can read into it what you like. It's just a little old statement. It's not very serious.

QUESTION: Paul, are you getting married? And if yes, to whom?

PAUL: Yes, but I don't know when. I've got no plans.

QUESTION: John, under what conditions did you write *In His Own Write?* Those sort of wild, kinky words, how did you piece them together?

JOHN: I don't know.

QUESTION: Do you have any more books coming out?

JOHN: Well, ah, yes and I can't answer that. It's just the way it happens.

PAUL: Any more books coming?

JOHN: I didn't think, "Now, how can I do this?"

PAUL: Just like an author.

QUESTION: I understand there's a suit pending against the Beatles by Peter Best* who claims to be a former member of the group. Is that true?

JOHN: I think he's had a few, but we don't bother with those.

QUESTION: Are all of your news conferences like this? I'm talking about all of the reporters or would-be reporters or semi-reporters that show up.

---

*Following his departure from the group, Pete Best was persuaded to file suit against his former band mates. The action was eventually settled very quietly some months later.

Are you besieged by these kind of people throughout your travel here in the United States?

JOHN: You can't always tell the would-bes from the real thing. So we never know.

QUESTION: Is it this way when you travel in Europe?

JOHN: Yes.

PAUL: But what's wrong with a crowd?

QUESTION: Nothing, I'm just wondering if you have this many reporters everywhere you go.

PAUL: No, not always.

GEORGE: Some of them are just onlookers.

QUESTION: "Tomorrow Never Comes" is the last cut on the second side of your latest LP, right?

GEORGE "Tomorrow Never Knows."

QUESTION: Could you give me a vague idea of some of the tape manipulations you used when your voice drops into the track. Is that sung backwards, by any chance, and then recorded forwards?

PAUL: No, it's not sung backwards.

GEORGE: It would be hard to do that, wouldn't it?

PAUL: It's recorded pretty straight. There's tape loops on it which are a bit different and the words are from *The Tibetan Book of the Dead*. So there.

GEORGE: There, nearly.

REMEMBERING *SGT. PEPPER*

Most songs [on *Sgt. Pepper*] we did we had to do as if we were recording live, like mono. We spent hours getting drum, bass, and guitar sounds, then balancing them and doing the take. That was in effect a backing track and then we later added overdubs. Nowadays you can overdub individually with each person having his own channel to record on. Then we'd have to think of all the instrumental overdubs, say, a guitar coming in on the second verse and a piano in the middle and then a tambourine. And we'd routine all of that, get the sound and the balance and the mix and do it as one performance. And if one person got it wrong we'd have to back up and do the entire overdub of all the parts again.

We had old microphones and pretty antiquated machines, but we'd find new meanings in old equipment, and I think that it was largely because of the times and the state of mind everyone was in that it was exciting to try and come up with ideas.

George Harrison

We were being influenced by avant-garde composers. For "A Day in the Life," I suggested we should write all but fifteen bars properly so that the orchestra could read it, but where the fifteen bars began we would give the musicians a simple direction: "Start on your lowest note and eventually, at the end of the fifteen bars, be at your highest note." How they got there was up to them, but it all resulted in a crazy crescendo. It was interesting because the trumpet players, always famous for their fondness for lubricating substances, didn't care, so they'd be there at the note ahead of everyone. The strings all watched each other like little sheep: "Are you going up?" "Yes." "So I am." And they'd go up. "A little more?" "Yes." And they'd go up a little more, all very delicate and cozy, all going up together. You listen to those trumpets. They're just freaking out.

Paul McCartney

John Lennon brought a television set because he felt that television was very important to him at this stage. I had thought they would bring teddy bears, things like that, but it went into a whole other dimension. There are a number of myths as a result. The flowers, for instance. My concept was that it was a municipal flower bed, so that you would have the letters spelled out in flowers like the Boy Scouts [logo] on the clock at Edinburgh.

There was a young boy helping who asked if he could do a guitar in hyacinths, and it was such a gentle sort of idea we said, "Yes, certainly," so the sort of white shape at the front of the cover is actually a guitar and one of the myths that arose is that you could read that as "PAUL?" When the stories that Paul died arrived, this was taken to be a sign that Paul had indeed died, but it was never intended to be Paul; it was simply a guitar.

Another myth is that the plants around the edge were marijuana plants and for a time I thought someone had played a joke on me and put some in, but they're not marijuana plants at all, just plants from a regular nursery.

Robert Fraser, a friend of the Stones, owned the gallery I was with. A cover for *Sgt. Pepper* designed by the Fool already existed and was very psychedelic—swirly orange and green and purple—there were a lot of others like it. Robert thought it would be interesting to have the first cover done by a fine artist as opposed to a record-cover designer. A certain amount had already been established: the concept of their being a band within a band, for instance. They'd had their uniforms made already. I think my contribution was to talk a great deal to them about the concept and try to add something visual to it. Paul explained that it was like a band you might see in a park. So the cover shot could be a photograph of them as though they were a town band finishing a concert in a park, playing on a bandstand with a municipal flower bed next to it. I think my main contribution was to decide that if we had the crowd a certain way the people in it could be anybody. I think that was the thing I would claim actually changed the direction of it: making a life-sized collage incorporating real people, waxworks, photographs and artwork . . .

All the figures you see behind the Beatles only filled a space about two feet deep and then there was a line of figures in front of them which were the waxworks. The actual Beatles stood on a platform about four feet deep. So that from front to back the whole thing was only about fifteen feet deep. People were asked to put in favorite objects. In a way this didn't work; maybe I didn't explain it well enough, so Paul, for instance, decided his favorite objects were musical instruments and hired a great number of them and came with a vanload of French horns and trumpets and beautiful things and I think that would have emphasized it too hard, so we only used one or two.

I couldn't be more thrilled to have worked on it. It was very exciting, of course it was.

Peter Blake*

[The Fool] hadn't somehow checked on the album size and their design was just out of scale. So they said, "Oh, okay, we'll put a border on it," so we now had this design which was too small and a border being added just to fill up space. I said to the fellows, "What are we selling here, a Beatles album or a centerfold with a design by the Fool which isn't even ready? Hadn't we better get a picture taken of the four of you and stick that in so we can see who you are?" So they posed for a picture and that went in the middle. The back took some time and had to be left till last because we were printing lyrics and they had to be designed and we had to have a running order and we couldn't have that

---

*Peter Blake is the London-based artist who designed the lauded *Sgt. Pepper* album cover.

until everyone decided on it. I remember Paul and I walking along, I think on Kingly Street in the West End, trying to work out some clever word using the initial letter of each song—the first would have to be S for Sgt. Pepper and then we'd try and get a vowel, say—but we couldn't get it right, so the running order was decided in another way. But it all worked out and we made it on time.

Neil Aspinall

One of the few opera triumphs of the recording century. They were giving an example around the world that guys can be friends. They had conveyed a realization that the world and human consciousness had to change.

After the apocalypse of Hitler and the apocalypse of the Bomb, there was here [in *Sgt. Pepper*] an exclamation of joy, the rediscovery of joy and what it is to be alive. . . . They showed an awareness that we make up our own fate, and they have decided to make a cheerful fate. They have decided to be generous to "Lovely Rita," or to be generous to "Sgt. Pepper" himself, turn him from an authority figure to a figure of comic humor, a vaudeville turn.

Remember, this was in the midst of the sixties; it was 1967 when some of the wilder and crazier radicals were saying "Kill the pigs." They were saying the opposite about old Sgt. Pepper. In fact the Beatles themselves were dressing up in uniforms, but associating themselves with good old-time vaudeville authority rather than sneaky CIA, KGB, MI5, or whatever. It was actually a cheerful look round the world . . . for the first time, I would say, on a mass scale.

Allen Ginsberg

It was six in the morning and we went down the King's Road to see Cass Elliott of the Mamas and Papas. We had the album with us, finished at last. She had a great sound system. Her flat was in a block of houses, back to back, really close together, and we put the system on a window ledge and the music blasted throughout the neighborhood. "We're Sgt. Pepper's Lonely Hearts Club . . ." It sounded great. All the windows around us opened and people leaned out, wondering. It was obvious who it was in a second. Nobody complained. A lovely spring morning. People were smiling and giving us the thumbs up. Then we piled on to a bus and went off. John had a new song in his head. I don't know which one, but he said he had a new sound. Nice.

Neil Aspinall

I knew there was some possible connection with cannabis in the studios—"smells" were noted—but I never pursued it. I had a pretty close relationship with the Beatles, largely because they were so successful. I knew them better than I did most of the pop artists and the situation developed when they were refused something by EMI's management, which was quite often—some disagreement about a minor thing maybe—Lennon and McCartney would come to me.

Just about the time the record [*Sgt. Pepper*] was issued I got an invitation and I went, rather unusually for me, to a dinner party with a very rich group of middle-class older ladies and I never met with such an atmosphere, they were absolutely thrilled with this record. Most of us sat on the floor for hours after dinner singing extracts from it. This to me was a new experience, the music had spread so widely.

Sir Joseph Lockwood, Chairman of EMI

JOHN BUYS A ROLLS

May 26, 1967

Beatle John Lennon took delivery of his rainbow colored Rolls yesterday.

His £11,000 car has been painted mainly yellow with bunches of flowers on the door panels, blue, red, green and white have been used in the color scheme. The car also has the sign of the zodiac on the roof.

The work was done by a firm of coach builders and paint sprayers at Chertsey, Surrey.

Mr. John Fallon, aged 50, the firm's managing director, said: "It took about five weeks to do."

He refused to reveal the cost.

—*Liverpool Echo*

THE BEATLES

London, 1967

RINGO: The four of us have had the most hectic lives. We have got almost anything money can buy. But when you can do that, the things you buy mean nothing after a time. You look for something else, for a new experience. We have found something now which fills the gap. Since meeting His Holiness, Maharishi Mahesh Yogi, I feel great.

PAUL: I now realize that taking drugs was like taking an aspirin without having a headache.

JOHN: If we'd met Maharishi before we had taken LSD, we wouldn't have needed to take it.

GEORGE: We haven't really started yet. We've only just discovered what we can do as musicians, what thresholds we can cross. The future stretches out beyond our imagination.

JOHN: The main thing is not to think about the future or the past, the main thing is just to get on with now. We want to help people do that with these academies. We'll make a donation and we'll ask for money from anyone we know with money, anyone that's interested, anyone in the so-called establishment who's worried about kids going wild and drugs and all that . . .

With Brian dying it was sort of a big thing for us. And if we hadn't had this meditation it would have been much harder to assess and carry on and know how we were going.

GEORGE: We've all come along the same path. We've been together a long time. We learned right from the beginning that we're going to be together.

JOHN: We'd dropped drugs before this meditation thing. George mentioned he was dropping out of it and I said: "Well, it's not doing me any harm, I'll carry on." But I just suddenly thought, I've seen all that scene. There's no point and what if it does do anything to your chemistry or brains? Then someone wrote to me and said that whether you like it or not, whether you have no ill effects, something happens up there. So I decided if I ever did meet someone who could tell me the answer, I'd have nothing to do it with.

GEORGE: There's still the craze. Usually the people who establish something that becomes a craze, well, they're usually very sincere people. It's just when all the publicity comes, then it turns bad.

JOHN: There's a big academy of this meditation scene out in California and if even just two hundred of them try it, just because of what we say, they'll turn the next two hundred on themselves as soon as they've done it, and that might have been worth all the Haight-Ashbury and all the dropouts. The point about how the English are taking it now seems to me to be better. It's not drop out, it's drop in and change it.

BEATLE, WIFE FLY TO LOS ANGELES ON VACATION

August 9, 1967

LOS ANGELES—Beatle George Harrison and his wife, Pattie Boyd, attired in the latest in psychedelic gear, arrived at Los Angeles International Airport from London Tuesday.

About 200 fans were at the airport when the couple's plane touched down, but airline officials drove the pair to the other side of the airport, away from the main terminal, to avoid a mob scene.

Harrison wore a flower print jacket, (mostly green), blue bell-bottom pants, purple shoes and sunglasses. His hair was shoulder length.

Mrs. Harrison wore a micro-miniskirt, 50 strands of beads around her neck, red knee-length wrap around Roman sandals and a leather tiara in her hair.

Harrison reportedly said he was here to attend Friday night's Hollywood Bowl presentation, an all-India music evening with Ravi Shankar, sitar player, and guest artists.

Harrison and his wife were met by friends, who whisked them away to an undisclosed vacation site.

—United Press International

THE BEATLES ON GOD AND GETTING HIGH

God is in everything, God is in the space between us. God is in the table in front of you.

Paul, 1967

My life belongs to Lord Krishna now. I'm just the servant of the servant of Krishna. I've never been so humble in all my life, and I feel great!

George, 1974

You're just left with yourself all the time, whatever you do anyway. You've got to get down to your own God in your own temple. It's all down to you, mate.

John, 1969

It is one of our perennial problems, whether there is actually a God. From the Hindu point of view each soul is divine. All religions are branches of one big tree. It doesn't matter what you call Him as long as you call. Just as cinematic images appear to be real but are only combinations of light and shade, so is the universal variety a delusion. The planetary spheres, with their countless forms of life, are naught but figures in a cosmic motion picture. One's values are profoundly changed

101

when he is finally convinced that creation is only a vast motion picture; and that not in, but beyond, lies his own ultimate reality.

George, 1973

With life and all I've been through, I do have a belief in goodness, a good spirit. I think what people have done with religion is personified good and evil, so good's become God with "o" out, and evil's become Devil with a "d" added. That's my theory of religion.

Paul, 1989

I still practice Transcendental Meditation and I think it's great. Maharishi only ever did good for us, and although I have not been with him physically, I never left him.

George, 1992

I won't go to funerals because I don't believe in them. I believe your soul has gone by the time you get into the limo. She or he's up there or wherever it is. I can't wait to go half the time.

Ringo, 1980

Through Hinduism, I feel a better person. I just get happier and happier. I now feel that I am unlimited, and I am more in control of my own physical body. The thing is, you go to an ordinary church and it's a nice feeling. They tell you all about God, but they don't show you the way. They don't show you how to become Christ-conscious yourself. Hinduism, however, is different.

George, 1972

Watching the wheels? The whole universe is a wheel, right? They're my own wheels, mainly. But watching myself is like watching everybody else. And I watch myself through my child, too. Then, in a way, nothing is real. As the Hindus or Buddhists say, it's an illusion, meaning all matter is simply floating atoms. The agreed-upon illusion is what we live and the hardest thing is facing yourself. It's easier to shout revolution or power to the people than it is to look at yourself and try to find out what's real inside you and what isn't. That's the hardest one.

I used to think the world was doing it to me and that the world owed me something. That either the conservatives, the socialists, fascists, communists, Christians, or the Jews were doing something to me; when you're a teenybopper, that's what you think. But I'm forty now and I don't think that anymore, because I found out it doesn't fucking work! The thing goes on anyway, and all you're doing is jacking off, screaming about what your mommy, daddy, or society did, but one has to go through that. Most assholes just accept what is and get on with it, right? But for the few of us who did question what was going on . . . I have found out *personally*—not for the whole world!—that *I* am responsible for it. I am part of them. There's no separation; we're all one, so in that respect, I look at it all and think, "Ah, well, I have to deal with me again in that way. What is real? What is the illusion I'm living or not living?" And I have to deal with it every day. The layers of the onion. But that is what it's all about . . . You make your own dream. That's the Beatles' story, isn't it? That's what I'm saying now, produce your own dream . . . I can't wake you up. I can't cure you. *You* can cure you.

It's fear of the unknown. The unknown is what it is. And to be frightened of it is what sends everybody scurrying around chasing dreams, illusions, wars, peace, love, hate, all that—it's all illusion. Accept that it's unknown and it's plain sailing. Everything is unknown—then you're ahead of the game. That's what it is. Right?

John, 1980

I keep [my religious beliefs] to myself unless somebody asks me about it. But I still feel the same as I felt back in the sixties. I lost touch with the Krishnas when Prabhupada died. I used to go and see the old master, A. C. Bhaktivedanta, quite a lot. He was real good. I'm still involved, but it's something which is more a thing you do inside yourself. You don't actually do it in the road. It's a way of just trying to get in touch with yourself. I still write songs with [Krishna] in there in little bits and pieces. Lots of songs that are unfinished say various things, but maybe I say it in different ways now. There's a song [on *Cloud Nine*] which is straight out of Yogananda, "Fish on the Sand" it's called.

George, 1990

I really didn't like that. Unfortunately, John was driftin' away from us at that point, so none of us actually knew. He never told us; we heard rumors and we were very sad. But he'd embarked on a new cause, which really involved anything and everything. Because John was that kind of guy—he wanted to live life to the full as he saw it. He would often say things like, "If you find yourself at the edge of a cliff and you wonder whether you should jump or not—try jumping."

Paul, 1986, discussing John's heroin use

Up until LSD, I never realized that there was anything beyond this normal waking state of consciousness. But all the pressure was such that, as Bob Dylan said, "There must be some way out of here." I think for me it was definitely LSD. The first time I took it, it just blew everything away. I had such an incredible feeling of well-being, that there was a God and I could see Him in every blade of grass. It was like gaining hundreds of years experience within twelve hours. It changed me and there was no way back to what I was before. It wasn't all good, though, because it left quite a lot of questions as well.

George, 1987

I know the only time we ever took drugs was when we were without hope. And the only way we got out of it was through hope. If we can sustain that, then we won't need drugs, liquor, or anything.

John, 1969

I don't recommend it [acid]. It can open a few doors, but it's not any answer. You go out and get the answers yourself.

Paul, 1968

[LSD] went on for years. I must have had a thousand trips. I used to just eat it all the time.

John, 1970

I'm a tidy sort of bloke, I don't like chaos. I kept records in the record rack, tea in the tea caddy, and pot in the pot box. This was the biggest stick of hash I have ever seen and obviously I'd have known about it if I'd seen it before. Those who think it's a low-down dirty thing to smoke pot will be further convinced they're right and we're wrong. But it will strengthen the others who follow us. We were once everybody's darlings. But it isn't like that anymore. They hate us.

George, 1969, discussing his arrest for possession of cannabis

We smoke pot. We like it. We think it's harmless. Just like drainpipe trousers used to be. I had a real suburban upbringing in Liverpool and I can see the other point of view, but it can't change the person I've become.

My dad didn't like it when I wore narrow trousers. Now his are sixteen inches and mine thirty inches. You can see what I'm getting at.

And I guess it'll be like that with drugs. I don't go round preaching the gospel, I just live my life quietly.

Paul, date unknown

THE HAPPY DREAM ENDS
WITH A TRAGEDY

August 27, 1967

The Beatles, mourning the death of their manager Brian Epstein yesterday, have cut short their weekend of meditation at Bangor and drove back to London early today. . . .

Before getting into the cars the Beatles and their companions were handed flowers by "disciples" of the Himalayan mystic Maharishi Mahesh.

A Scotland Yard spokesman said today that there are no suspicious circumstances surrounding the death yesterday of 32-year-old Beatle manager Mr. Brian Epstein, at his London home.

Mr. Epstein, the man who launched the Beatles on the road to fame, was found dead yesterday afternoon by his housekeeper who became worried when she could get no reply from his locked bedroom.

Since Friday the four Beatles, together with John Lennon's wife Cynthia, Pattie Harrison and her sister Jennie Boyd and Jane Asher had been meditating at the feet of the Maharishi Yogi.

Just before the news yesterday afternoon of Mr. Epstein's death, two of them described how much more relaxed they were after the result of their meditation.

Paul McCartney confirmed that the Beatles were no longer going to take drugs. "You cannot keep on taking drugs forever," he said. "You get to the stage where you are taking 15 aspirins a day without having a headache.

"We were looking for something more natural. This is it.

"It is not weirdy or anything, it is dead natural. Meditation will be good for everyone, it is something which one does normally anyway."

And Ringo Starr said: "I hope the fans will take up meditation instead of drugs."

Earlier, the four Beatles and their companions had all been initiated into the society. Paul said: "There is no black magic or anything like that about initiation.

"At the moment I am finding what I am searching for by meditation, I hope I will get more out of meditation, so that I will have no need for drugs. . . ."

And so Sunday afternoon there was a social call for Paul McCartney from his father, Mr. Jim McCartney, his stepmother and his seven-year-old stepsister, Ruth, who had travelled from Gayton.

—*Times*

YOKO IS NAMED IN DIVORCE BID

August 22, 1968

BEATLE John Lennon is being sued for divorce.

His wife, 27-year-old Cynthia Lennon, has filed a petition in which she alleges her husband has committed adultery.

The woman named in the petition is 34-year-old Japanese actress Yoko Ono.

Solicitors acting for both 27-year-old John and Yoko have entered an appearance denying Mrs. Lennon's allegations.

John and Cynthia were married in 1962 and have a five-year-old son.

Their home at St. George's Hill, Weybridge, Surrey is up for sale at £40,000.

Yoko is married to American film producer, Anthony Cox.

The hearing of the petition is expected to be before the end of the year. Meanwhile solicitors for John and Cynthia are negotiating financial settlements.

—*Times*

JOHN LENNON and PAUL McCARTNEY

New York, 1968

QUESTION: Why did you leave the Maharishi?*

JOHN: We made a mistake.

QUESTION: Do you think other people are making a mistake as well?

JOHN: That's up to them. We're human.

QUESTION: What do you mean, you made a mistake?

JOHN: That's all, you know.

PAUL: We thought there was more to him than there was, but he's human and for a while we thought he wasn't.

QUESTION: Could you tell us about your newest corporate business venture [Apple]?

JOHN: It's a business concerning records, films, and electronics and, as a sideline, manufacturing or whatever. We want to set up a system whereby people who just want to make a film about anything don't have to go on their knees in somebody's office, probably yours.

---

*The Maharishi Mahesh Yogi came to the West from India in the late fifties to establish his Transcendental Meditation movement. The Beatles first came in contact with the giggly guru via Pattie Boyd, who encouraged the group to go along and meet him personally on a visit to London. After practicing his meditational techniques for some time, the Beatles became disillusioned with the diminutive spiritual teacher, when, rumor had it, he made a pass at fellow meditator Mia Farrow.

PAUL: We really want to help people, but without doing it like charity or seeming like ordinary patrons of the arts. I mean, we're in the happy position of not really needing any more money, so for the first time the bosses aren't in it for the profit. If you come to see me and say, "I've had such and such a dream," I will say, "Here's so much money. Go away and do it." We've already bought all our dreams, so now we want to share that possibility with others. There's no desire in any of our heads to take over the world. That was Hitler. There, is, however, a desire to get power in order to use it for the good.

JOHN: The aim of this company isn't really a stack of gold teeth in the bank. We've done that bit. It's more of a trick to see if we can actually get artistic freedom within a business structure, to see if we can create nice things and sell them without charging three times our cost.

QUESTION: How will you run your new company?

JOHN: There's people we can get to do that. We don't know anything about business.

APPLE PRESS RELEASE

London, 1968

BEATLES TO RECORD FOR THEIR OWN APPLE LABEL

Apple Records, a branch of the music division The Beatles Apple Corps Ltd., announces that contracts have been signed between Apple and Capitol Records (for the USA and Canada) for Capitol to manufacture and distribute all record product for North America in New York and Los Angeles.

The deals were concluded this week after prolonged negotiations between The Beatles and their representatives and the heads of Capitol. The Beatles themselves will henceforth be released on their own label, "APPLE."

APPLE BOUTIQUE PRESS RELEASE

London, 1968

Paul McCartney says tonight:

We decided to close down our Baker Street shop yesterday and instead of putting up a sign saying "Business will be resumed as soon as possible" and then auction off the goods, we decided to give them away. The shops were doing fine and making a nice profit on turnover. So far, the biggest loss is in giving the things away but we did that deliberately. We're giving them away—rather than selling them to barrow-boys—because we wanted to give rather than sell.

We came into shops by the tradesman's entrance but we're leaving by the front door. Originally, the shops were intended to be something else, but they just became like all the boutiques in London. They just weren't our thingy. The staff will get three weeks pay but if they wish they'll be absorbed into the rest of Apple. Everyone will be cared for. The King's Road shop, which is known as Apple Tailoring, isn't going to be part of Apple anymore but it isn't closing down and we are leaving our investment there because we have a moral and personal obligation to our partner John Crittle who is now in sole control. All that's happened is that we've closed our shop in which we feel we shouldn't, in the first place, have been involved.

Our main business is entertainment, communication. Apple is mainly concerned with fun not frocks. We want to devote all our energies to records, films and our electronics adventures. We had to refocus. We had to zoom in on what we really enjoy, and we enjoy being alive, and we enjoy being Beatles.

It's 1968; already, it's 1968. Time is short. I suppose really what we're doing is Spring cleaning in mid-summer. The amazing thing is our giving things away. Well, the answer is that it was much funnier to give things away.

Well, it's just that The Beatles are The Beatles are the moptops and the moptops are The Beatles are the moptops . . . are whatever you see them to be, whatever you see us to be. Create and preserve the image of your choice. We are yours with love, John Lennon, Paul McCartney, George Harrison and Ringo Starr.

JOHN LENNON FINED £150 ON DRUG CHARGE

November 29, 1968

John Winston Lennon, aged 28, of The Beatles, was fined £150 with 20 guineas costs at Marylebone Magistrates Court yesterday when he pleaded guilty to the unauthorized possession of 219 grains of Cannabis resin found when detectives accompanied by dogs searched his flat at Montagu Square, Marylebone, on October 18.

Appearing with him on remand was Mrs. Yoko Ono Cox, aged 34, artist, of the same address, who denied charges of unauthorized possession of the drug and willfully obstructing Detective Sergeant Norman Pilcher when he was exercising his powers under the Dangerous Drugs Act.

She was discharged and Mr. Lennon was also discharged on a similar charge of obstructing the officer, which he denied. The prosecution offered no evidence on those three counts.

Mr. Roger Frisby for the prosecution told Mr. John Phipps, the Magistrate, that although the flat appeared to be in the joint occupation of the couple, Mr. Lennon had taken full responsibility for the drugs and said Mrs. Cox had nothing to do with it.

Mr. Frisby said that when the officers got into the flat and told Mr. Lennon that they had a search warrant they found a large quantity of

Feline lovers all, the Stankey family definitely adored their cats. Here's Mimi with one of her favorites. (GEOFFREY GIULIANO COLLECTION.)

Prehistoric Fabs outside the Cavern Club in Liverpool, 1960. (SOMA RASA SERVICES.)

The Beatles at their local, the Grapes on Mathew Street, Liverpool.
(SOMA RASASERVICES. THANKS TO EDDIE PORTER.)

George in Liverpool at the ripe old age of seventeen.
(SOMA RASA SERVICES.)

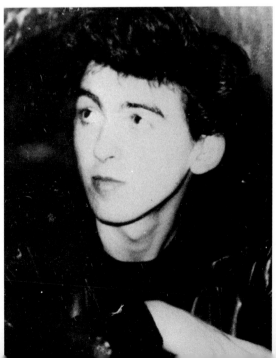

ABOVE: The Beatles pitch Vox amplifiers, 1963. (GEOFFREY GIULIANO COLLECTION)
BELOW: The Beatles...in the beginning. (GEOFFREY GIULIANO COLLECTION)

ABOVE: Four tightly cropped young Beatles in a gag photo from the early sixties. (GEOFFREY GIULIANO COLLECTION.) BELOW: The boys meet the press somewhere in America. (CHARLES ROSENAY, GOOD DAY SUNSHINE.)

ABOVE: The Fabs in 1964. (CHARLES ROSENAY, GOOD DAY SUNSHINE.) BELOW: Live on their second American tour. (CHARLES ROSENAY, GOOD DAY SUNSHINE.)

Four hairdos that shocked the world. (SQUARE CIRCLE ARCHIVES)

On telly in England. (SQUARE CIRCLE ARCHIVES)

John and Cynthia during Lennon's self-proclaimed "fat period."
(SQUARE CIRCLE ARCHIVES)

Mr. and Mrs. Richard Starkey following their 1965 nuptials. (SQUARE CIRCLE ARCHIVES)

ABOVE: Mr. and Mrs. Lennon, mach one. (SQUARE CIRCLE ARCHIVES) RIGHT: Hari's Son looking oh-so Indian after a high-flying trip to the Himalayas, 1966. (SQUARE CIRCLE ARCHIVES)

Cool John on stage. (SOMA RASA SERVICES.)

At the press launch of *Sgt. Pepper's Lonely Hearts Club Band*, 1967.
(SQUARE CIRCLE ARCHIVES.)

Starr on the moors filming
the Beatles' *Strawberry Fields*
promotional clip, 1967.
(SOMA RASA SERVICES.)

ABOVE: On location during the shooting of *Magical Mystery Tour*, 1967. (COURTESY PINK SHOES CAFE.) BELOW: EMI's Abbey Road Studios, #3 Abbey Road, St. John's Wood, London. (PHOTO BY SESA GIULIANO. COPYRIGHT INDIGO EDITIONS.)

ABOVE: Meeting the press in late 1965. (SQUARE CIRCLE ARCHIVES) BELOW: Starr posing for the ever-present paparazzi, 1969. (SQUARE CIRCLE ARCHIVES)

Producer Paul and protege Mary Hopkin in the studio, 1969.
(SQUARE CIRCLE ARCHIVES.)

ABOVE: John's gypsy caravan planted in the garden of the palatial Weybridge home he used to call his "mock Tudor shithouse" (SQUARE CIRCLE ARCHIVES.) BELOW: Pretty Mary Hopkin as she was back in her teen-queen Apple days. (SQUARE CIRCLE ARCHIVES.)

George and wife Pattie leave an Esher court after their arraignment on marijuana charges. (MORNING GLORY ARCHIVES.)

The world's first peek at John after finally shearing off his trademark long locks. (SQUARE CIRCLE ARCHIVES.)

drugs properly prescribed by Mr. Lennon's doctor. When asked if he had any he should not have, such as Cannabis, Mr. Lennon shook his head.

Mr. Frisby said a cigarette-rolling machine found on top of a bathroom mirror, a tin originally containing film found in a bedroom and a cigarette case all bore traces of Cannabis resin. In an envelope in a suitcase was found 27.3 grains of the drug and 19.8 grains were in a binocular case nosed out by a dog, on the mantel in the living room.

—Times

BEATLE PAUL TO MARRY

March 12, 1969

Paul McCartney, aged 26, is to marry Miss Linda Eastman today at Marylebone Register Office W1. They first met two years ago when Eastman, a professional photographer, took photographs of the Beatles in America.

Mr. McCartney is the only unmarried member of the Beatles group. Miss Eastman, who is 27, is a member of the Eastman Kodak family. She has a daughter, Heather, by her first marriage.

Last night a group of teenage girls waited outside Mr. McCartney's home in Cavendish Avenue NW. When he arrived in his car three police cars accompanied him. A policeman said they had been asked to clear the pavement but there was no trouble.

—*Times*

MIAMI AUDIO EXPERT FINDS THREE PAULS

1969

At the urging of a Miami disc jockey, Dr. Henry M. Truby, director of the university's language and linguistics research laboratory, put the Mc-Cartney riddle to a "sound fingerprint" test.

After 20 hours of running experiments on dozens of Beatles records dating from the early 1960's, the professor said there is "reasonable doubt" that three voices popularly attributed to McCartney are produced by the same set of vocal chords.

"I hear three different McCartneys," Truby said.

Speculation that McCartney died in an automobile accident in November 1966 has touched off a world wide controversy in pop music circles.

The furor prompted Apple Corp Ltd, the Beatles London office to issue a brief statement from Paul: "I am alive and well and unconcerned about the rumors of my death. But if I were dead, I would be the last to know."

But Truby, an audio expert, insists, "I heard three different McCartneys."

Truby said experiments on a sound spectrograph machine indicated there were six different voices on the records he tested. Three were clearly identified as those of Beatles John Lennon, George Harrison, and Ringo Starr. The three others sound "roughly" like the same person, the professor said, but the spectograph—which makes sound "fingerprints"—show a different authorship.

"I cannot conclude that the same voice appears in these early and late passages," said Truby, who has spent 20 years in scientific audio studies.

—United Press International

JOHN LENNON AND YOKO ONO

Amsterdam, 1969

QUESTION: People are equal, but some are *more* equal than others, as you know.

JOHN: Yes. But they all have equal possibility.

QUESTION: You are to talk without philosophy because I'm not much of a philosopher.

JOHN: Me either.

QUESTION: Your attempt to think sensibly has gone out of it all, isn't it?

JOHN: No.

QUESTION: You see this whole roomful of reporters, photographers, and filmers . . .

JOHN: I think there's something beautiful about it because on all the Beatles tours there's always people who had laughs! The field reporters had a good time when they got the right photograph or the right interview. We always had a laugh because some photographer fell over, got the wrong picture, or something. It's a happening.

YOKO ONO: And there's plenty people in the world who are sensitive enough. When you report, they will see what we're doing and it's good.

JOHN: But it means this is a madhouse. Everything's too serious.

QUESTION: But you're sitting here singing, "Those were the days, my friend," and you give some kind of impression that you are very sensible and have a grown-up approach . . .

JOHN: Well, I'm pretty old now and she's pretty old, but we have a sense of humor and that's what this is about, partly.

YOKO: The world needs a sense of humor, I think, more than anything because the world is getting more and more violent and tense.

QUESTION: This flabbergasts a Dutchman a bit. Is Holland a honeymoon country?

JOHN: It's a beautiful place. Amsterdam's a place where a lot of things are happening with the youth. It's an important place.

YOKO: A romantic place.

JOHN: *Everywhere* is important, but Amsterdam is one of them. There's a few centers in the world and Amsterdam is one of them for youth.

YOKO: Many vitally alive youth, with high ideals and everything for the world.

JOHN: The Provos with their white bicycles.

QUESTION: Are those ideas that appeal to you, by the way?

JOHN: Yes, the peaceful ideas that the youth have. If we have any influence on youth at all, we'd like to influence them in a peaceful way.

YOKO: Communicate with them and each other.

JOHN: Say hello to them. We're here to say hello to people in Amsterdam or Holland.

QUESTION: What do you see in a conformist institution such as marriage?

JOHN: Intellectually, we know marriage is nowhere. That a man should just say, "Here, you're married," when we've been living together a year before it. Romantically and emotionally, it's something else. When our divorce papers came through, it was a great relief. We didn't realize how much of a relief it was going to be until Peter* [Brown] came up and said, "It's over." It was only a bit of paper. We'd made the marriage over by living together when we were still married to the other two people. Just the fact that somebody said it was a relief and the fact that we got married was another kind of joy. It was very emotional, the actual marriage ceremony. We both got very emotional about it and we're both quite cynical, hard people, but very soft as well. Everyone's a bit both ways. And it was very romantic.

---

*Peter Brown acted as the Beatles' personal assistant throughout their entire time together.

QUESTION: I should like to have your reactions on this, Mrs. Lennon.

YOKO: I got this ring and, of course, to many people in the contemporary world that's old-fashioned. I sort of broke down. I felt so good about it. When I think about it, it's an old ritual, but very functional. It has a lot to do with sex [slipping the ring on and off her finger] . . .

JOHN: Stop it, stop it!

YOKO: Ahh . . .

JOHN: I'm joking, I'm joking.

QUESTION: It's kind of loose, though.

JOHN: Pardon? Yes, we're having it fitted here.

QUESTION: You were talking about marriage as an institution, now the $64,000 question, what about the kiddies?

JOHN: We're thinking it might be nice if we conceive one in Amsterdam. We might call it "Amsterdam" or "Peace" or "Hair" or "Bed-In" or something. It would be beautiful.

QUESTION: How do you feel about English linen?

YOKO: Yes, it would be nice to conceive a child in this bed actually, wouldn't it?

CANADA PUTS WET BLANKET ON LENNON "BED-IN"

May 26, 1969

TORONTO—Beatle John Lennon and his wife Yoko arrived here Sunday from the Bahamas, reporting it was too hot there for their "bed-in for peace." But immigration officials made it hot for them here, too.

Lennon, Yoko and her five-year-old daughter, Kyoko, were detained for 2 1/2 hours at Toronto International Airport when they arrived on their way to Montreal.

Lennon and Yoko first planned to bed down in the United States, but he says the U.S. government barred him because of the marijuana conviction. U.S. immigration officials say he withdrew his visa application.

Paying $1200 in excess baggage charges, the affluent peace crusader arrived in the Bahamas Saturday with his wife, her daughter and four sound technicians. They planned to settle down in a $180-a-day suite, receiving admirers and photographs in-bed from 10 a.m. to 10 p.m. for a week, and broadcasting to the U.S. on the theme: "If everyone stayed in bed for a week, there'd be no killing."

After one night, Lennon said it was too hot and the Bahamas were "farther from the United States than I thought. They'll hear me better from Canada."

—Associated Press

JOHN LENNON

Montreal, 1969

QUESTION: Do you condemn civil rights demonstrations?

JOHN: I don't condemn them; I'm *with* them. I'm just saying: Isn't it about time they thought of something else? There have been marches for sixty years. It's ineffective. Someone asked us what would you suggest we do? I said you've got women, use sex. Every day in the popular papers, they have bikini-clad girls. Use sex for peace!

QUESTION: Do you condemn campus violence and building takeovers?

JOHN: Sit-ins are okay. I don't see why they have to destroy the building to take it over, though. Either sit in and take it over or leave. Take no notice of it. You don't need the building.

QUESTION: The Americans are very interested in what happens in Harvard, Berkeley, and City College. Are you condemning them and the methods used?

JOHN: If you're successful, we congratulate you. If not, think of something else. Be like the Indians and retreat. I know they lost and that, but the philosophy was right. Violence begets violence. The successful revolutions were in Russia, France, and England. They were successful and the new people took over power and built up all the buildings they brought down, had more babies, and became the Establishment. So we see where violence gets us.

QUESTION: Some of the people seem to think you're kind of revolutionary and the Establishment seems to fear they won't let you in and give you visas and everything. You're standing right in the middle now between two factions of two opposing philosophies. Have you found this kind of antagonism among your previous friends?

JOHN: It's not antagonism, it's just about Yoko and me. We're in two different bags. She was avant-garde and I was pop. We met, fell in love, but that didn't solve the problems of our personalities and our previous work and all that. We had to destroy each other's games and preconceived concepts about what avant-garde was. We had to find out what we really were. That's all we're doing with these people and that's what they're doing to us. They're saying, "What do you think you're doing?" That's the only way to communicate. If two lovers deeply in love still have to destroy each other's games to get through to each other, then we must do it with the world as well.

Ascot, Berkshire, September 11, 1969

SRILA PRABHUPADA (TO LENNON): You are anxious to bring about peace in the world. I've read some of your statements, and they show me you're anxious to do something. Actually, every saintly person should try and bring peace, but we must know the process. What kind of philosophy are you following? May I ask?

YOKO ONO: We don't follow anything. We are just living.

GEORGE: We've done meditation. Or I do my meditation, mantra meditation.

PRABHUPADA: Hare Krishna is also a mantra.

JOHN: Ours is not a song, though. We heard it from Maharishi. A mantra each.

PRABHUPADA: His mantras are not public?

JOHN: No, it's a secret.

YOKO: If Hare Krishna is such a strong, powerful mantra, is there any reason to chant anything else?

PRABHUPADA: There are other mantras, but Hare Krishna is especially recommended for this age [Kali Yuga, the Iron Age].

His Divine Grace A. C. Bhaktivedanta Swami Prabhupada, a lifelong proponent of the yoga of devotion (Bhakti) was sometime spiritual advisor to the Fab Four. He passed away in India in 1977.

JOHN: If all mantras are just the name of God, then whether it's a secret mantra or an open mantra, it doesn't really make much difference, does it, which one you sing?

PRABHUPADA: It *does* make a difference. For instance, in a drug shop they sell many types of medicines for curing different diseases. But still you have to get a doctor's prescription in order to get a particular type of medicine. Otherwise, the druggist won't supply you. You might go to the drug shop and say, "I'm diseased. Please give me any medicine you have." But the druggist will ask you, "Where is your prescription?" Similarly, in this age, the Hare Krishna mantra is prescribed in the scriptures. And the great teacher Sri Chaitanya Mahaprabhu, whom we consider to be an incarnation of God, also prescribed it. Therefore, our principle is that everyone should follow the prescription of the great authorities.

YOKO: If the mantra itself has such power, does it matter where you receive it?

PRABHUPADA: Yes, it does matter. For instance, milk is nutritious. That's a fact everyone knows. But if milk is touched by the lips of a serpent, it is no longer nutritious. It becomes poisonous. If you don't receive the mantra through the proper channel, it may not really be spiritual.

JOHN: But what if one of these masters who's not in the line says exactly the same thing as one who is? What if he says his mantra is coming from the Vedas and seems to speak with as much authority as you?

PRABHUPADA: If the mantra is actually coming through a bona fide disciplic succession, then it will have the potency.

JOHN: But the Hare Krishna mantra is the best one?

PRABHUPADA: Yes. We say that the Hare Krishna mantra is sufficient for one's perfection, for liberation.

GEORGE: Isn't it like flowers? Somebody may prefer roses, and somebody may like carnations better. Isn't it really a matter for the individual devotee to decide? One person may find that Hare Krishna is more beneficial to his spiritual progress, and yet another person may find that some other mantra may be more beneficial for him.

PRABHUPADA: But still there is a distinction. A fragrant rose is considered better than a flower without any scent. You may be attracted by one flower, and I may be attracted by another, but among the flowers a distinction can be made. There are many flowers that have no fragrance and many that do. Therefore, your attraction for a particular flower is not the solution to the question of which is actually better. In the same way, personal attraction is not the solution to choosing the best spiritual process. You've been speaking of the Maharishi. Hasn't he written some book on *Bhagavad-gita* [A sacred Vedic text]?

JOHN: Yes, that's the one we've read.

PRABHUPADA: So, why is he using Krishna's book to put forward his own philosophy? *Bhagavad-gita* is Krishna's book. Why is he taking Krishna's book?

GEORGE: Well, he didn't. He just translated it.

PRABHUPADA: Why? Because Krishna's book is very well respected.

JOHN: I've also read part of another translation by Paramahansa Yogananda.

PRABHUPADA: Yes, all these men take advantage of Krishna's book to lend an air of authority to their own speculations. Vivekananda has done it, Sri Aurobindo has done it, Dr. Radhakrishan has done it, Mahatma Gandhi has done it. Thousands of them have done it. But why do they use *Bhagavad-gita* as the vehicle for their own ideas?

GEORGE: In the versions I've read, the authors all claim theirs is the best. And sometimes I get something from one which I didn't get from another.

JOHN: I found that the best thing for myself is to take a little bit from here and a little bit from there.

YOKO: I mean, we're not just saying that. We want to ask your advice. In other words, what is your answer to this question of authority?

PRABHUPADA: If we don't take the *Gita* from the authorized disciplic succession, it won't help us. In our introduction to *Bhagavad-gita* we have carefully explained that aside from Krishna there is no authority. Krishna is the authority, because *Bhagavad-gita* was spoken by Krishna. Can you deny that?

JOHN: What about Yogananda, Maharishi, and all these other people who have translated the *Gita*? How are we to tell that their version isn't also Krishna's word?

PRABHUPADA: If you seriously want to understand this, you should study the original Sanskrit text.

JOHN: Study Sanskrit. Oh, now you're talking!

GEORGE: But Vivekananda said that books, rituals, dogmas, and temples are secondary details anyway. He said they're not the most important thing. You don't have to read the book in order to have the perception.

PRABHUPADA: Then why did Vivekananda write so many books?

JOHN: Who says who's actually in the line of descent? I mean, it's just like royalty, Yogananda also claims to be in a line, he talks about his guru's guru's guru's guru, like that. Maharishi claimed that all his gurus went way back. I mean, how are we to know?

PRABHUPADA: Whatever Maharishi may be, his knowledge does not extend up to Krishna, not up to His personal feature.

JOHN: That's what he used to say in exactly the same way about everybody else.

PRABHUPADA: But factually he cannot be an authority, because he does not speak anything about Krishna. If a postman comes and does not know anything about the post office, what kind of postman is he?

YOKO: But he does talk about *his* post office.

PRABHUPADA: No, you cannot create your own post office. There is only one post office, the government post office. If a postman comes and says, "I belong to another post office," then at once you can know he is unauthorized.

JOHN: In the Bible or any other holy book, they talk about one God. So it's just the one Being everywhere, in all the books. So why isn't Hare Krishna or something similar in the Bible?

DEVOTEE: It is in the Bible. In Psalms it says, "Praise the Lord with every breath. Praise the Lord with drum and flute."

JOHN: But they haven't got very good tunes. They haven't been passing on any good chants, have they? I mean, would it be effective to chant, "Lord Jesus, Lord Jesus, Hail Lord Jesus?"

PRABHUPADA: Lord Jesus says that he is the Son of God. He's not *God*, but the *Son* of God. In that sense, there is no difference between Krishna Consciousness and Christianity. There is no quarrel between God and God's Son. Jesus says to love God, and Krishna, the Supreme Personality of Godhead, says, "Love me." It's the same thing. All right?

MESSAGE FROM
GEORGE HARRISON

Everybody is looking for Krishna.

Some don't realize that they are, but they are.

Krishna is GOD, the Source of all that exists, the Cause of all that is, was or ever will be.

As God is unlimited, HE has many Names.

Allah—Buddah—Jehova—Rama: All are Krishna, all are ONE.

God is not abstract, he has both the impersonal and the personal aspects to his personality which is SUPREME, ETERNAL, BLISSFUL, and full of knowledge.

As a single drop of water has the same qualities as an ocean of water, so has our consciousness the qualities of GOD'S consciousness . . . but through our identification and attachment with material energy (physical body, sense pleasures, material possessions, ego, etc.) our true TRANSCENDENTAL CONSCIOUSNESS has been polluted, and like a dirty mirror it is unable to reflect a pure image. With many lives our association with the temporary has grown. This impermanent body, a bag of bones and flesh, is mistaken for our true self, and we have accepted this temporary condition to be final.

Through all ages, great saints have remained as living proof that this nontemporary, permanent state of GOD CONSCIOUSNESS can be revived in all living souls. Each soul is potentially Divine.

Krishna says in BHAGAVAD-GITA "Steady in the Self, being freed from all material contamination, the yogi achieves the highest perfectional stage of happiness in touch with the Supreme Consciousness." YOGA (a scientific method of GOD (SELF) realization) is the process by which we purify our consciousness, stop further pollution and arrive at the state of Perfection, full KNOWLEDGE full BLISS.

If there is a God, I want to see him. It's pointless to believe in something without proof, and Krishna Consciousness and meditation are methods where you can actually obtain GOD perception. You can actually see GOD, and hear him, play with HIM. It might sound crazy but HE is actually there, actually with you.

There are many yogic paths Raja, Jnana, Hatha, Kriya, Karma, Bhakti which are all acclaimed by the MASTERS of each method.

SWAMI BHAKTIVEDANTA is as his title says a BHAKTI yogi following the path of DEVOTION. By serving GOD through each thought, word, and deed and by chanting of his holy names, the devotee quickly develops God-Consciousness. By chanting:
HARE KRISHNA, HARE KRISHNA
KRISHNA KRISHNA, HARE HARE
HARE RAMA, HARE RAMA
RAMA RAMA, HARE HARE
One inevitably arrives at KRISHNA Consciousness. (The proof of the pudding is in the eating!)
GIVE PEACE A CHANCE.

ALL YOU NEED IS LOVE (KRISHNA) HARI BOL
GEORGE HARRISON 31/3/70

Apple Corps. Ltd   Radha Krishna Temple
3 Savile Row   7 Bury Place
London, W.1.   London, W.C.1.
Tel: 01-734 8232   Tel: 01-242 0394

JOHN LENNON

Denmark, 1970

JOHN: All right, you rumormongers, let's get going!

QUESTION: We've all heard a lot of rumors about you.

JOHN: So have I.

QUESTION: Can we get some truth about your visit here in Denmark?

JOHN: Well, I've just heard a new one in the *Daily Express* that I've bought seventy acres of land here. Every paper seems to think I'm going to buy seventy acres of land. I've been to Greece recently and they thought I was going to buy land there and Canada, wherever. I've got no other land except some in England and Ireland. We came to see Kyoko. And Tony and Melinda, of course, but Kyoko was the access point and we've had a nice seven days of peace.

QUESTION: What kind of man are you really?

JOHN: I'm a nervous guy, you know.

QUESTION: Do you and Yoko believe in peace in our time?

JOHN: Yeah. The thing is we have this poster that says War Is Over If You Want It. We all sit round pointing fingers at Nixon and the leaders of the countries saying, "He gave us peace" or "They gave us war." But it's *our* responsibility what happens around the world in every other country as well as our own. It's our responsibility for Vietnam and Biafra and the Israel war and all the other wars we don't quite hear about. It's *all* our responsibility and when we all want peace we'll get it. I support humanity, I don't belong to any left wing, right wing, middle wing, Black Panthers, white Christians, Protestants, Catholics, or nothing. People have said we're naive for trying to sell peace like a bar of soap. But I want to ask you, is Mr. Ford naive? Or is the soap powder factory naive? They're selling the same old soap that's been around for two thousand years, but suddenly it's *new blue soap*. So we're selling *new blue peace* and we hope some of you buy it. The war is here now and there's two ways of looking at it. Some people say, "Why did you spend your money on posters or peace campaigns? Why didn't you give it to the Biafran children, or something like that?" And we say, "We're trying to prevent cancer, not cure it."

QUESTION: Did you spend all your money?

JOHN: No. The people around us made more money than the Beatles ever did, I'll tell you that. None of the Beatles are millionaires. But there's a lot of millionaires who became millionaires around the Beatles, however. You know the story.

QUESTION: Where are you going from here?

JOHN: I don't know. We play everything by ear. We try not to make plans. I don't really like knowing what I'm going to do for the next eight months and we'll just stay until it's time to go back and work.

QUESTION: Are you feeling comfortable out here?

JOHN: Oh, it's beautiful. All the snow. We go walking in the garden and all that. It's beautiful, all the colors in the sky and the mist. It's just a fantastic place with good vibes, as they say in this generation. Very good vibes around and just the people we've met. We've met very few, but they're straight. They're not as paranoid as in the big cities or other countries. People are less paranoid in Denmark.

FINAL BEATLES PRESS RELEASE

April 10, 1970

Spring is here and Leeds play Chelsea tomorrow and Ringo and John and George and Paul are alive and well and full of hope. The world is still spinning and so are we and so are you. When the spinning stops— that'll be the time to worry, not before. Until then, the Beatles are alive and well and the beat goes on, the beat goes on.

APPLE BOTTOMS OUT

August 4, 1970

Earlier this week the Apple Press Office was closed down and the two remaining employees dismissed. Since the breakup of The Beatles their Apple empire has diminished to little more than a center for collecting their royalties and dealing with their private affairs.

—*Evening Standard*

GODS OF THE APPLE

Music and Myth

YOKO ONO SAID REASON FOR BEATLES BREAKUP

1970

LONDON—The official biographer of the Beatles said yesterday the major cause of the breakup of that top quartet appeared to be John Lennon's marriage to Japanese artist Yoko Ono.

"If there was one single element in the split, I'd say it was the arrival of Yoko," said Hunter Davies, author of *The Beatles, An Official Biography.*

Writing in the Sunday *Times,* Davies said that after Lennon and Yoko got together "The rest of the Beatles didn't matter anymore." Lennon and Yoko were married in Gibraltar in March last year.

Davies said that since the Beatles hadn't performed together in person since 1966, McCartney's statement "was pretty pointless."

McCartney himself, in an interview with Raymond Palmer in the *News of the World,* said: "No matter how much we split, we're still very linked. We're the only four people who've seen the whole Beatlemania bit from the inside out, so we're tied forever, whatever happens."

McCartney did not clarify in detail his reasons for breaking away from the group.

But Davies maintained that under Yoko's influence, Lennon began taking charge at Apple, the Beatles' business headquarters, and this "was a blow to Paul's pride ... Paul fell by the wayside and ... they were no longer bosom buddies ... George Harrison and Ringo Starr (the other two Beatles) are not exactly dotty over (endeared to) Yoko either."

With Yoko, Lennon has mounted campaigns for world peace, held zany art exhibitions, made radical movies, formed a wild rock and roll band and issued non-Beatle records. None of these activities included the other Beatles.

So far Lennon, Harrison and Ringo had kept silent about McCartney's breakaway. McCartney himself didn't make his reasons much clearer than his original vague announcement.

Asked by Palmer what sort of things he might try on his own, McCartney replied: "Anything and everything. There's no point in restricting yourself ...

"The only danger is that once you get into this kind of machine where you make a lot of money—where you can get a nice house, a car and stuff—the danger is in believing that is what life is all about.

Despite the breakup, another Beatles record is to be issued next month, and Davies said Apple had another 12 hours of recorded material to be released.

—United Press International

JOHN BLAMES PAUL FOR THE BUST UP

January 7, 1971

Beatle John Lennon, in a frank interview in the U.S. pop music journal *Rolling Stone*, blames Paul McCartney's attempts to dominate the group for leading to its breakup and claims the other Beatles insulted his Japanese-born wife, Yoko Ono.

Lennon also had some outspoken things to say about the solo albums recently issued by his former colleagues—Ringo: "Good, but I wouldn't buy any of it." McCartney: "Rubbish." George Harrison: "Personally, at home, I wouldn't play that kind of music."

Lennon, who has just issued his own solo album, said: "I prefer myself, I have to be honest, you know."

"Ringo was all right, so was Maureen [Ringo's wife], but the other two really gave it to us. I'll never forgive them."

Lennon said all the Beatles got "fed up of being sidemen for Paul."

Lennon listed his experiences with drugs and said he stopped LSD because he just could not stand the bad trips.

He said he started taking LSD in 1964 and made about a thousand trips.

Lennon said he started on pills at 17 and was on pills when he made his first film *A Hard Day's Night* and had turned to marijuana when he made the second film, *Help!*

Paul McCartney yesterday started High Court proceedings to end the Beatles partnership.

—Associated Press

JOHN LENNON

New York, 1975

QUESTION: What were you thinking and feeling when you were fifteen?
JOHN: I was thinking if only I could get out of Liverpool, I might get a break. I wanted to be a famous artist. Possibly I would have to marry a rich old lady, or man, you know, to look after me while I did my art. But then, rock'n'roll came along, and so I didn't have to marry anybody.
QUESTION: How do you feel now about your music with the Beatles?
JOHN: Beatle records stand up in any period unless the music really changes. We were all used to groups like the Grateful Airplane. We were always ourselves. You could pick any Beatle record and a few of them are obviously of an era. But most of them still sound pretty current, like "Hey Jude," or songs like "Eleanor Rigby." It doesn't matter what period or what era, they would go down well.
QUESTION: What were the Beatles really trying to do? And why all the hostility when you broke up?
JOHN: When it gets down to the nitty-gritty, it's the song, you know. And, if anything, the Beatles were figureheads. I could speak [about them] more succinctly later on when I thought about it. I call it a divorce, right? But when I thought about it, obviously, I could change my mind.
QUESTION: What did the Beatles actually contribute to their generation?
JOHN: I have a picture of it now. There was a ship sailing to the new

world. I saw this group on the ship, maybe the Stones were up there too, but I just said, "Land ho!" So we were all part of it. We were in the crow's nest. We contributed whatever we could. I can't designate what we did or didn't do, how each individual was impressed by the Beatles physically, or whatever. And we were all on this ship together, our generation. What we did was wake up the avant-garde in music and film. I mean, not just the Beatles, but rock'n'roll itself, you know. And this so-called avant-garde was asleep, and we were going around in circles.

QUESTION: What is your goal these days?

JOHN: I'm now thirty-four and a lot of things one *knew* before but you couldn't live them. So now I'm trying to live out all the things I've learned in thirty-four years, to apply everyday. All those things from the psychedelic era to Maharishi or Janov, or anybody like that.

QUESTION: Do you like people?

JOHN: I do like people, but I become whoever I'm with and so if I am with a madman, I become mad. If I'm with somebody I love, I become lovely. Right? So really, I'm like a cloud in the wind.

QUESTION: Do you want to clear up the idea that the Beatles were responsible for the drug scene?

JOHN: Hey! Actually that's a dumb question. Who gave the drugs to the Beatles? I didn't invent those things, I just bought them. We never invented the stuff. The big story about the Beatles and LSD started in the British press after they interviewed Paul on TV. They asked him if he felt any responsibility announcing that he had taken LSD. So he said, "Okay, well, just don't put the film out then." How dare they say that we propagated it.

GEORGE HARRISON

Brazil, 1979

QUESTION: The sixties—do they still mean anything?
GEORGE: Well, they are past, aren't they? What is left is in the history books and from what we've learned, if we learned anything, it means *something*. If we haven't, it is best to forget them. There were quite happy and turbulent times, a lot of wars, a lot of changes.
QUESTION: Is anything left of these changes?
GEORGE: Yes, I think so. For a start it made some young people, and older people as well, more conscious of the fact that you don't have to be particularly limited in your ideas. It opened up ideas, like everybody is asking me about Indian music and philosophy now. Fifteen years ago, at the beginning of the sixties, people would think you were a freak if you did yoga exercises. But now a huge percentage of the world does yoga. I think the sixties did help to broaden understanding. You know, when someone liked long hair or didn't wear a tie people used to think they were from a zoo, but now a lot of barriers have been broken. One thing, though, was a disappointment. At the end of the sixties, the concept of "All you need is love," which was a good idea, disappeared and it all went back to disco and music for idiots. People started fighting again and all that. So I hope maybe the eighties may bring back "start planting flowers" again and having a bit more love, really.

QUESTION: Do you think there ever will be any group which will rival the Beatles?

GEORGE: Well, there may be groups that can sell as many records. But the Beatles were unique because of the four particular personalities. The Beatles were bigger than the four people separately. There is always someone like Sinatra, Elvis, or the Beatles and maybe somewhere down the line there will be something bigger, but certainly not now. Not like the Bee Gees—they make good records, but they don't have whatever it was the Beatles had.

QUESTION: Are there any unreleased tracks by the Beatles?

GEORGE: "Not Guilty" is on my new album, actually. I wrote that for the White Album in 1967 and forgot all about it. I remembered it last year and we rerecorded it and it's really nice, sort of jazzy.

QUESTION: Which one of your songs do you like best?

GEORGE: I don't know, whichever *you* like best is best for me. "Something" was very good for me, because it had about 150 cover versions. It is nice if other people make recordings of your songs. But there are other songs that are better. There is one on the last album [*Thirty Three and a Third*] I think was as good as "Something," "Learning How to Love You." And there is a song on the new LP [entitled *George Harrison*] "Your Love Is Forever," which, I think is as good as "Something." But it might not be as popular because it was the Beatles who made "Something."

QUESTION: We heard your latest record is dedicated to motor racing?

GEORGE: Only one song out of ten. One is about my wife, one about the moon. All the tunes are about different things and, yes, there is one about racing. When I went to the races everybody kept asking me, "Are you going to write a song about it?" And so in the end I thought I'd better do one. It took me six months thinking "how do I start" because I just didn't want to write about engines, wheels, and noise. So I had to think of a way of approaching it which had some meaning. It's called "Faster" and I think the words are quite good, because it is abstract and not just one person. It could be about anybody and not just about cars and engines. It is about the circus around it and the feelings people have and the jealousy, all that sort of thing. The song was really inspired by Jacky Stewart and Nikki Lauda. I got the title from a book Jacky had written back in 1973.

QUESTION: What is your opinion of Brazilian music?

GEORGE: You know, I like the more wild music. I don't mean noise, or discotheque. More original music. If Warner Brothers have any good Brazilian music in their catalog, I'll take them home with me and study them. You know, in Europe, for a hundred years it was very popular to do the rumba, samba, and that sort of thing, so in broad contents everybody is aware of Brazilian music. But I must say I'm very ignorant when it comes to more specific things.

QUESTION: Do you think disco has any relation to Brazilian music?

GEORGE: No, no. Disco music is a result of people who are determined to make a lot of money. It's like a recipe. If you want to make a disco hit, just follow the instructions. You have the bass drum, the cymbal, the violin going, and that's disco. Rubbish!

QUESTION: What about punk music?

GEORGE: Rubbish, *total* rubbish. Listen to the early Beatles records. They were simple too, but they still had much more depth and meaning. It was innocent or even trivial, but it still had more meaning than punk, which is deliberately destructive and aggressive.

QUESTION: Have you had any more problems with "My Sweet Lord" lately?*

GEORGE: Well, in America it's all become a complete joke, because the man who wrote the song "He's So Fine" died years ago and the company was taken over by his accountants, who were suing me for all this money. When we were going to court the judge said there was no way that I copied that song, but, "because of the similarity we must talk about compensation." Then the mother of the songwriter started suing her own company, who was suing me! Then Allen Klein, who used to be the Beatles' manager—Klein had been suing us for years and then we made a settlement—was unhappy having no lawsuits against the Beatles. So when the composer died, he bought the case. So now it's Klein against me. But Klein was the one who was promoting "My Sweet Lord," so it is a very funny position and the judge doesn't like it. Ten years ago Klein did interviews saying "My Sweet Lord" had nothing to

---

*A suit was filed by the copyright holders of the song "He's So Fine," against George Harrison claiming that "My Sweet Lord" plagiarized their composition. The case was settled several years later finding George Harrison guilty of "unconscious plagiarism."

do with this other song. And now it's the other way round just to get some money off me. So it's just a joke, but for a few years it made me depressed. Having to go to court and do these things, it's terrible, it's a pain in the ass.

GEORGE HARRISON

Hambilden, 1983

GEOFFREY: How do you remember your guru, Srila Prabhupada?

GEORGE: Prabhupada always used to say that he was "the servant of the servant of the servant of Krishna." He was very humble. The thing about Prabhupada, he was more like a dear friend than anything else. We used to sit in this room in my house and talk for hours.

GEOFFREY: I understand that on his deathbed he called you "his archangel," took a ring from his finger, and instructed his disciples to make sure you got it. Did you?

GEORGE: Yes, I got it. I have it.

GEOFFREY: Were you his disciple?

GEORGE: As far as being a full-fledged devotee, no. I was never really into it that far. I liked him and his philosophy, though. I never followed all the rules and regulations that strictly, however. Except for maybe a few months.

GEOFFREY: Anything else to say about the Hare Krishna movement?

GEORGE: Well, I love the food. When I visited the place in India [Mayapur] last year I got up with them at four in the morning and after *mangal arti* [morning prayers] they brought me a forty-course breakfast. All on silver and everything. I was the honored guest. Which, of course, is better than being the unhonored guest!

GEOFFREY: What is your attitude towards spiritual life these days?

GEORGE: I was at the airport in Honolulu and I met a guy dressed in these old saffron corduroys. He approached me with a book and said, "My guru wants you to have this." I didn't make out if he recognized me or not. I said, "What do you mean, your guru wants me to have this book? Does he know I'm here?" The book said, "Something Something Guru, the World's Spiritual Leader." Now, I read the book and this guy doesn't like anybody. He ran down Sai Baba, Yogananda, Guru Maharaji, and everybody. Although he did quote Prabhupada's books (and everyone else's for that matter). It seemed very dogmatic. I'm just not into that. It's the organization of religion that turns me off a bit. I try to go into myself. Like Donovan said, "You've got to go into your own temple once a day." It's a very personal thing, spiritual life.

GEOFFREY: Tell me a bit about the new book [*The Love You Make*] on the Beatles by your former Apple attaché Peter Brown.

GEORGE: Peter Brown came by with this guy [co-author S. Gaines] for about ten minutes to Friar Park, had a cup of coffee, and they left.

GEOFFREY: What did he ask you?

GEORGE: Nothing. There was no interview, nothing. They just had a coffee and split. Then he goes away and acts like the three of us sat him down and said, "Right, Peter, you're the one. You should be writing this. You tell the story." The guy made millions, you know.

GEOFFREY: Millions, really?

GEORGE: Yeah. It's one of the best-selling books in the world. Well, a million anyway. But it's crazy.

GEOFFREY: What do you mean?

GEORGE: We took this guy from Liverpool. Made him. Gave him a job. Helped him establish himself. After all those years, then he comes out with this rubbish.

GEOFFREY: I've heard that Mal Evans's diaries were stolen and are soon to be published by an American magazine.

GEORGE: Well, Mal certainly kept diaries for years. He always wrote down everything that happened. The problem is the legal ownership of those diaries.

GEOFFREY: I've heard that the woman he was living with at the time of his death had them.

GEORGE: Yeah, but the rights are so unclear. They'll probably never be published.

GEOFFREY: How do you feel about the Beatles' myth today?

GEORGE: All this stuff about the Beatles being able to save the world was rubbish. I can't even save myself. It was just people trying to put the responsibility on our shoulders. The thing about the Beatles is that they saved the world from boredom. I mean, even when we got to America the first time, everybody was running around with Bermuda shorts on, brush cuts, and braces on their teeth. But we didn't really create any great change, we just . . .

GEOFFREY: Heralded it?

GEORGE: Heralded that change of consciousness that happened in the sixties. We went along with it, that's all.

GEOFFREY: Gave it a voice, maybe?

GEORGE: Yeah, I guess.

GEOFFREY: I met Yoko recently. She seems fine, you know. She seems to be trying to carry on with life, her and Sean, who, by the way, is a very bright kid.

GEORGE: Yeah. I'd love to meet Sean. I bet he is. I don't know, the whole Beatles thing is like a horror story, a nightmare. I don't even like to talk about it. I just hate it.

GEOFFREY: Sorry. What about gardening? I know you love that. Don't you have all kinds of exotic plants and trees from around the world up at Friar Park?

GEORGE: No, not really. I get all my stuff from a local nursery here in Henley. I've got a few gardeners working the place. Trying to spruce it up a bit. It was let go for years, but it's coming along, little by little. Getting better all the time, you might say.

GEORGE HARRISON

Henley-on-Thames, 1984

QUESTION: Oftentimes you speak of yourself as a plainclothes devotee, or closet Krishna. How did you first come in contact with Krishna?

GEORGE: Through my visits to India. So by the time the movement first came to England in 1969, John and I had already gotten ahold of Prabhupada's album, *Krishna Consciousness*. We played it a lot and liked it. That was the first time I'd ever heard the chanting of the "maha-mantra."

QUESTION: Even though you and John played Srila Prabhupada's record a lot and chanted quite a bit on your own, you'd never really met any of the devotees. Yet when [the devotees] came to England you cosigned the lease on their first temple in central London, bought them Bhaktivedanta Manor, which has provided a place for thousands of people to learn about Krishna Consciousness, and financed the first printing of the book *Krishna*. Wasn't this a sudden change for you?

GEORGE: Not really, I always felt at home with Krishna. You see, it was already a part of me. I think it's something that's been with me from my previous birth. Your coming to England and all that was just another piece of a jigsaw puzzle that was coming together to make a complete picture. Let's face it. If you're going to have to stand up and be counted, I figured, "I would rather be with these guys than with those other guys over there." I mean I'd rather be one of the devotees of God than one of the straight, so-called sane or normal people who just don't understand that man is a spiritual being, that he has a soul. And I felt comfortable with them, too, kind of like we'd known each other before. It was a pretty natural thing, really.

QUESTION: You were a member of the Beatles, a group that influenced not only music, but a whole generation of young people as well. After the dissolution of the group, you went on to emerge as a solo superstar with albums like *All Things Must Pass*. That was followed by *Living in the Material World*, number one on *Billboard* for five weeks and a million-selling LP. One song on that album, "Give Me Love," was a smash hit for six straight weeks. The Concert for Bangladesh with Ringo Starr, Eric Clapton, Bob Dylan, Leon Russell, and Billy Preston was a phenomenal success and would become the single most successful rock benefit project ever. So you had material success. You'd been everywhere, done everything, yet at the same time you were on a spiritual quest. What was it that really got you started on your spiritual journey?

GEORGE: It wasn't until the experience of the sixties really hit. You know, having been successful and meeting everybody we thought worth meeting and finding out they weren't worth meeting and having had more hit records than everybody else and having done it bigger than everybody else—it was like reaching the top of a wall and then looking over and seeing there's so much more on the other side. So I felt it was part of my duty to say, "Oh, okay, maybe you are thinking this is all you need—to be rich and famous—but actually it isn't."

QUESTION: George, in your recent autobiography, *I, Me, Mine*, you said your song "Awaiting on You All" is about chanting mantras on beads. You explained that a mantra is "mystical energy encased in a sound structure" and that "each mantra contains within its vibrations a certain power." But of all the mantras, you stated that "the Hare Krishna mantra has been prescribed as the surest way for attaining God realization in this present age." What realizations have you experienced from chanting?

GEORGE: Prabhupada told me once that we should just keep chanting all the time, or as much as possible. Once you do that, you realize the benefit. The response that comes from chanting is in the form of bliss, or spiritual happiness, which is a much higher taste than any happiness found here in the material world. That's why I say that the more you do it, the more you don't want to stop, because it feels so nice and peaceful.

QUESTION: Is it an instantaneous process, or gradual?

GEORGE: You don't get it in five minutes. It's something that takes time, but it works because it's a direct process of attaining God and will help us to have pure consciousness and good perception that is above the normal, everyday state of consciousness.

QUESTION: How do you feel after chanting for a long time?

GEORGE: In the life I lead, I find that I sometimes have opportunities when I can really get going at it, and the more I do it, I find the harder it is to stop. For example, once I chanted all the way from France to Portugal, nonstop. I drove for about twenty-three hours and chanted all the way. It gets you feeling a bit invincible. The funny thing was that I didn't even know where I was going. I mean I had bought a map and I knew basically which way I was aiming, but I couldn't speak French, Spanish, or Portuguese. But none of that seemed to matter. You know, once you get chanting, then things start to happen transcendentally.

QUESTION: Can you think of any incident where you felt God's presence very strongly through chanting?

GEORGE: I was on an airplane once that was in an electric storm. It was hit by lightning three times and a Boeing 707 went over the top of us, missing only by inches. I thought the back end of the plane had blown off. I was on my way from Los Angeles to New York to organize the Bangladesh concert. As soon as the plane began bouncing around, I started chanting. The whole thing went on for about an hour and a half or two hours, the plane dropping hundreds of feet and bouncing all over in the storm, all the lights were out and all these explosions and everybody terrified. I ended up with my feet pressed against the seat in front, my seat belt as tight as it could be, gripping on the thing and yelling "Hare Krishna" at the top of my voice. I know for me, the difference between making it and not making it was actually the chanting. Peter Sellers also swore that chanting saved him from a plane crash once.

QUESTION: Did any of the other Beatles chant?

GEORGE: John and I, with ukulele banjos, went sailing through the Greek islands chanting Hare Krishna. Like six hours we sang, because we couldn't stop once we got going. As soon as we stopped, it was like the lights went out. It went on to the point where our jaws were aching, singing the mantra over and over and over and over. We felt exalted; it was a very happy time for us.

QUESTION: In 1969 you produced a single called "The Hare Krishna Mantra," which eventually became a hit in many countries. That tune later became a cut on the *Radha-Krishna Temple* album, which was also produced by Apple. A lot of people in the business were surprised by this. Why did you do it?

GEORGE: Well, it's just all a part of my service, isn't it? Spiritual service, in order to try to spread the mantra all over the world.

QUESTION: How did the success of this record of Hare Krishna devotees chanting compare with some of the rock musicians you were producing at the time like Jackie Lomax, Splinter, and Billy Preston?

GEORGE: It was a different thing. There was less commercial potential in it, but it was much more satisfying to do, knowing the possibilities that it was going to create, the connotations it would have just by doing a three-and-a-half-minute mantra. That was more fun really than trying to make a pop hit record. It was the feeling of utilizing your skills to do some spiritual service for Krishna. One of the greatest thrills of my life, actually, was seeing [the devotees] on the BBC's *Top of the Pops*. I couldn't believe it. It's pretty hard to get on that program, because they only put you on if you're in the Top Twenty. It was just like a breath of fresh air. My strategy was to keep it to a three-and-a-half-minute version of the mantra so they'd play it on the radio, and it worked. I did the harmonium and guitar track for that record at Abbey Road Studios before one of the Beatles' sessions and then overdubbed the bass part. I remember Paul and Linda arrived at the studio and enjoyed the mantra.

QUESTION: Shortly after its release John told me they played it at the intermission right before Bob Dylan did the Isle of Wight concert with Jimi Hendrix, the Moody Blues, and Joe Cocker in the summer of 1969.

GEORGE: They played it while they were getting the stage set up for Bob. It was great. Besides, it was a catchy tune and people didn't have to know what it meant in order to enjoy it. I felt very good when I first heard it was doing well.

QUESTION: In the lyrics to the song "Awaiting on You All" you tell people they can be free from living in the material world by chanting the names of God. What kind of feedback did you get?

GEORGE: At that time, nobody was committed to that type of music in the pop world. There was, I felt, a real need for that, so rather than sitting and waiting for somebody else, I decided to do it myself. A lot of times we think, "Well, I agree with you, but I'm not going to actually stand up and be counted. Too risky." Everybody is always trying to keep themselves covered, stay commercial, so I thought, just do it. Nobody else is and I'm sick of all these young people just boogying around, wasting their lives, you know. Also, I felt there were a lot of people out there who would be reached. I still get letters from people saying, "I have been in the Krishna temple for three years and I would have never known about Krishna unless you recorded the *All Things Must Pass* album." So I know, by the Lord's grace, I am a small part in the cosmic play.

QUESTION: What about the other Beatles? What did they think about your Krishna Consciousness? You'd all been to India by then and were pretty much searching for something spiritual.

GEORGE: Oh yeah, well if the Fab Four didn't get it, that is, if they couldn't deal with shaven-headed Hare Krishnas, then there would have been no hope! The devotees just came to be associated with me, so people stopped thinking, "Hey, what's this?" you know, if somebody in orange with a shaved head would appear. They'd say, "Oh yeah, they're with George."

QUESTION: You and John met Srila Prabhupada together when he stayed at John's home, in September of 1969.

GEORGE: Yes, but when I met him at first, I underestimated him. I didn't realize it then, but I see now that because of him, the mantra has spread so far in the last sixteen years, more than it had in the last five centuries. Now, that's pretty amazing, because he was getting older and older, yet he was writing his books all the time. I realized later that he was much more incredible than you could see on the surface.

QUESTION: You write in your autobiography that "no matter how good you are, you still need grace to get out of the material world. You can be a yogi, a monk or a nun, but without God's grace you still can't make it." And at the end of the song "Living in the Material World" the lyrics say, "Hope to get out of this place by the Lord Sri Krishna's grace/my salvation from the material world." If we're dependent on the grace of God, what does the expression "God help those who help themselves" mean?

GEORGE: It's flexible, I think. In one way I'm never going to get out of here unless it's by His grace, but then again, His grace is relative to the amount of desire I manifest in myself. The amount of grace I would expect from God should be equal to the amount of grace I can gather or earn. I get out what I put in.

QUESTION: What do you think is the goal of human life?

GEORGE: Each individual has to burn out his own karma and escape from the chains of *maya* [illusion], reincarnation, and all that. The best thing anyone can give to humanity is God consciousness. But first you have to concentrate on your own spiritual advancement; so in a sense we have to become selfish to become selfless.

QUESTION: In *I, Me, Mine* you speak about karma and reincarnation and how the only way to get out of the cycle is to take up a bona fide spiritual process. You said at one point, "Everybody is worried about dying, but the cause of death is birth, so if you don't want to die, you don't get born!" Did any of the other Beatles believe in reincarnation?

GEORGE: I'm sure John does! And I wouldn't want to underestimate Paul and Ringo. I wouldn't be surprised if they're hoping it's true, you know what I mean? For all I know, Ringo might be a yogi disguised as a drummer!

QUESTION: Where do you think John's soul is now?

GEORGE: I should hope that he's in a good place. He had the understanding, though, that each soul reincarnates until it becomes completely pure and that each soul finds its own level, designated by reactions to its actions in this and previous lives.

QUESTION: Bob Dylan did a lot of chanting at one time. In fact, he drove across the United States with two devotees once and wrote several songs about Krishna. They spent a lot of time chanting.

GEORGE: That's right. He said he enjoyed being with them. Also Stevie Wonder had the devotees on one of his records, you know. And it was great, the song he put the chanting in, "Pastimes Paradise."

QUESTION: You wrote in your book: "Most of the world is fooling about, especially the people who think they control the world and the community. The presidents, the politicians, the military, etc., are all jerking about, acting as if they are Lord over their own domains. That's basically Problem One on the planet."

GEORGE: That's right. Unless you're doing some kind of God-conscious thing and you know that He's the one who's really in charge, you're just building up a lot of karma and not really helping yourself or anybody else. There's a point in me where it's beyond sad, seeing the state of the world today. It's so screwed up. It's terrible and it will be getting worse and worse. More concrete everywhere, more pollution, more radioactivity. There's no wilderness left, no pure air. They're chopping the forests down and they're polluting all the oceans. In one sense, I'm pessimistic about the future of the planet. These big guys don't realize for everything they do, there's a reaction. You have to pay. That's karma.

QUESTION: Do you think there's any hope?

GEORGE: Yes. One by one, everybody's got to escape *maya*. Everybody has to burn out his karma, escape reincarnation, and all that. Stop thinking that if Britain, America, Russia, or the West becomes superior, then we'll beat them and then we'll all have a rest and live happily ever after. That doesn't work. The best thing you can give is God consciousness. Manifest your own divinity first. The truth is there. It's right within us all. Understand what you are. If people would just wake up to what's real, there would be no misery in the world. I guess chanting's a pretty good place to start.

GEORGE HARRISON and DEREK TAYLOR

New Zealand, 1984

QUESTION: With the publication of *Fifty Years Adrift**, is there any more to be said about the Beatles?

DEREK TAYLOR: I'll answer that. I wanted to do it and did it and that should really be it. It was nice to do it, but we should draw the line there and publish some fiction.

GEORGE: One reason I liked him writing it was there have been so many [Beatle] books—and no doubt they'll be many more—written by people who are so-called experts and ninety-nine percent is lies or just written from other sources. So it's good to have a book that's from an inside point of view, but also isn't particularly nasty. Because there's a tendency of people to always take a negative approach. I think this book is more interesting, more revealing and at the same time it's not just stabbing you in the back like a lot of people because they think it means making more money.

QUESTION: Do you still have a present hold in the movie industry?

GEORGE: The movie business? Yeah, at the moment I'm negotiating to buy the rights to *Fifty Years Adrift* and make it into a movie with Robert De Niro playing Derek Taylor.

QUESTION: Who would play George Harrison?

---

*In 1984, Derek Taylor penned this deluxe autobiography of his life with the Beatles.

GEORGE: Oh, he'd just be a minor part. We'd get one of the Rutles or something like that.

QUESTION: George, what about music, where's that in your life these days?

GEORGE: Well, I don't *have* to make records any longer, which is a relief because I'm not really of the competitive nature. I don't want to have to go out there doing all this stuff which is necessary now. Let's face it, it's a cutthroat business and I'm not really into that, so I no longer have to make records. Since I don't have a commitment to the music industry, I've been writing much more music than in the past. For instance, the last couple of months I've written about twenty-eight songs and I make demos which are better because they can be of good quality. When you get to making a record, though, it's something serious.

QUESTION: Will you perform live again?

GEORGE: What do you think this is? This is a day's work. You mean musically, I don't know. I doubt it, it's too much trouble. Besides, I'm not sure anybody wants to see me.

QUESTION: Could you tell us the story from the book about how the Beatles got their name?

GEORGE: There's always been stories about who invented the name and about how we wanted it like the Crickets, but Stu Sutcliff was very much into Marlon Brando, particularly his movie *The Wild One*. Then in the years following it was always taken that John thought of the name. Recently, I came across a video of *The Wild One* and I couldn't believe it when I saw Lee Marvin saying to Brando, "We think you're a schmuck, Johnnie, and the Beatles think you're a schmuck." Wait a minute, back that up. Did I hear that, "the Beatles?" And so that's how it happened and I mentioned it and they went and found the script, so based on that I would say Stu had a lot to do with it.

QUESTION: Derek, how did you get the job as press officer to the Beatles?

TAYLOR: I slipped into it having been appointed personal assistant to Brian Epstein. I got the job because old colleagues on the press started to ring me up saying, "Come on, we know you're in there." And I'd say, "I'm not the press officer, he's in the other room." So they'd say, "You can't give us that . . ."

GEORGE: Also the press officer we had was useless. I think we all benefited when Derek got that position because he knew their needs having been a press man. We trusted his ability not to sacrifice us to them. I think it worked quite well.

TAYLOR: If there wasn't such a volume of press, it would have been a comfortable job. I felt not only a duty but a compassion for the individuals in this mass that were coming at us. They all had separate and competitive needs which I understood and tried to meet which was very difficult. But it was a pleasure because it was a good gang, wasn't it?

GEORGE: Yeah, I had fun.

QUESTION: How did your interest in the Hare Krishna movement come about?

GEORGE: I bought a record of the Hare Krishna mantra and I was familiar with it from my trips to India. It's not exactly a new thing, it was in the West. It's the Vedic culture of India. I met A.C. Bhaktivedanta Swami, who's the spiritual master, a few years after he came to the West and he was a great, great old man. He was wonderful and I was friendly with him. I knew a few of the guys and they were all trying to get temples here and there and I got them a temple in London once. I appreciate it, but I'm not as closely associated as people think. For instance, I wasn't here receiving sanctified food [prasadam] last night like it said in the Daily Herald. I mean, I like them, but in some ways the Krishnas are like groupies because they think, well, George is into it, so they all come. One of the things their master taught was the first problem in the world is that we all encroach upon each other and so what do they do? They do it to me, out of love maybe. Nevertheless, there's a limit to how many Krishnas you can meet in one day or one lifetime. The philosophy is great, however, and I wish them all the best.

QUESTION: George, what is it like for you to come out in public? It must be difficult even to walk down the street.

GEORGE: It's sort of strange. I don't do this very often and so I've forgotten how to act and I'm not sure quite how you do it.

QUESTION: What do you think of the music industry in 1984?

GEORGE: I think it's sort of picking up and getting a bit better. There are some things I genuinely like whereas a few years ago there was absolutely nothing. I don't know what's in your top twenty, but it tends to be the same in every country. It will get a bit better as soon as we have program planners and disc jockeys that don't have to bow to the sponsors, because that's the problem. Ten years ago when I was more actively involved you'd get a playlist and the DJs were allowed to play maybe three new records a week. Now you have each record company maybe putting out twenty or thirty and there's like fifty record companies. It's usually the program planner, for his own personal motives or whatever he's getting, backhanders, or how much you go and bow and scrape to them, they're the records that will get played. I'm not really into that anymore. We [the Beatles] genuinely got popular by people just playing our records because they liked them. I don't see the business settling down. It's going to get more and more about money, greed, and selfishness and on that basis people have tin ears as far as I'm concerned. I hear some stuff that's happening now and people are just tone-deaf but with fifteen million selling albums. It takes all kinds.

QUESTION: Everyone's avoided discussing John Lennon's death, but what about Paul McCartney's life since the Beatles? Do you still listen to Paul and keep in touch? What is your relationship with the other Beatles?

GEORGE: I recently have been very much in touch with Paul and musically I think "No More Lonely Nights" is a lovely song. I haven't seen his movie [Give My Regards to Broadstreet], so I can't comment.

QUESTION: What do you think of his new treatments of the old Beatles numbers?

GEORGE: Well, I've not really heard it all. I've heard "Eleanor Rigby" and "For No One," I think. I can't understand why he did it. It makes me think he got the publishing or something back off Sir Lew Greed.*

QUESTION: Do you think it's sacrilegious?

GEORGE: No. He wrote the songs. If I wanted to sing "Here Comes the Sun," is that sacrilegious? I mean, I wrote it. Paul wrote those songs and he can do them. I think he shouldn't have done so many of them. He's not doing so bad.

QUESTION: Have you come across Julian Lennon and what do you think his future might be?

GEORGE: I haven't seen him over the last two years, but before that I spent a lot of time with him. I try to give him a bit of help and direction. He went through a couple of years of going to clubs and being

---

*For the film Give My Regards to Broadstreet, Paul saw fit to record some of the old Beatles classics. Ringo, however (who was playing with Paul at the time), refused to participate. "Once was enough," he told reporters.

sucked into situations he should have avoided. I think now, having done that, he's a much wiser person. I've seen him on TV doing interviews and singing his songs. I think he's got a great future as a musician and a songwriter. And as a human, he's real charming. He's got the smartness of John, but he's got a softer edge. He's a sweetheart.

QUESTION: How do you feel about the death of John Lennon?

GEORGE: Everybody in this room has had friends who've died or parents, relatives or something. It's a particularly unhappy affair at the best of times. Let alone when some loony does it. It affects you the same as Gandhi, Mrs. Gandhi or Kennedy, except it's a bit closer to home. That's all.

QUESTION: Do you take extra precautions these days?

GEORGE: Well, I've been taking extra precautions before he was killed in as much as I try not to let people know where I am except today, unless any one of you are thinking of shooting me . . .

QUESTION: What about your family's security? Do you take special precautions? Is that an ongoing worry for your family?

GEORGE: The only ongoing worry is the way people take something, whether it's real or false and for the sake of filling a bit of print they hype some mad story. That doesn't help. I think that contributed to John's downfall in a way. If you noticed, before he got shot there was an upsurge in publicity saying, "He's got three apartments and a cow that cost $2,000 or something." We can all be positive or negative, but like we said earlier regarding people writing books about the Beatles, there does seem to be a tendency for people to be nasty rather than nice. And I think the press must accept responsibility for a lot of the attitudes prevalent in society. They have direct responsibility for educating, or at least not retarding man's consciousness. As you sow so shall you reap.

TAYLOR: And on that we'll see you all again. Thank you.

PAUL McCARTNEY

Broadstreet Press Conference

QUESTION: Did you have a hard time picking the old songs to rerecord?
PAUL: I pulled out about fifty songs that I fancied singing and I gave a list of those to the director and said, "Let's just choose." So some of them got chosen for pure story reasons. Like "Yesterday" was included on the director's request because he wanted to set up the thing that happens toward the end of the movie where I become a busker. But something like "For No One," that was just because I love that song and I realized I hadn't sung it since the twenty years ago we're talking about. I never ever did it in public. I did it only once on the record. And I thought, "Well, it's a pity that songs can just come and go that quickly." I wanted that one in just for my own pleasure. And then "Ballroom Dancing," for instance, was put in because it's a very visual number. So it was a mismash of reasons . . .

Why shouldn't I sing 'em? Just because I once recorded them with the Beatles? They're not sacred, not to me anyway. I wouldn't say I do a *better* version of those. Maybe those are the definitive versions, maybe not. You know, I think "Long and Winding Road" in this is better than the original version. Just that particular song. So that was it, really. I fancied singing them and didn't see why not.

John and I once tried to write a play when we were just starting out, even before we wrote any songs. We got two pages and just couldn't go any further; we just dried up. It would have been great, actually, because it was like a precursor to *Jesus Christ Superstar*. It was about this guy called Pilchard who you never actually saw. He was always upstairs in a room, praying. And the whole play was about the family saying, "Oh God, is he prayin' again?" It was quite a nice idea, but we could never get him out of that room and downstairs.

QUESTION: There are so many books out on the Beatles. Do you have any plans to write an autobiography?

PAUL: The only thing that would make me do it is that round about this age, you do start to forget, you know. After twenty years, you don't remember it so well. And that would be the motivating factor, to actually get it down. But I haven't actually thought of doing it, really. But it's beginning to sneak into my mind that maybe I ought to get it down even if it isn't going to be like Mick's. It's more a publicity stunt rather than a book.

QUESTION: You did the foreword for the Little Richard book. What did you think of it?

PAUL: It's a little bit gossipy . . .

QUESTION: It's pretty wild. He talks about John's penchant for farting.

PAUL: I thought that was good, actually, I remember that.

QUESTION: In the early press accounts, you were the good guy. But in later biographies, you're cast as the bad guy. Do you feel a need to give your side?

PAUL: Well, like anyone I wouldn't mind being understood rather than misunderstood. It's very tempting when someone like John was slagging me off in the press. There was a period there when he was really going for me. It's very tempting to answer back, but I'm glad I didn't. I just thought the hell with it, he's going over the top like he does. He was a great fella, but he had that about him. He'd suddenly throw the table over and on to a new thing. And I was the table. But, I mean, a lot of it was talk and I think John loved the group. I think, though, he had to clear the decks for his new life. That was my feeling at the time. And there's nothing really you could say. But I don't think I was the bad guy or the good guy. I think originally what happened is that I'm from a very close, warm family in Liverpool, and I was very lucky to come from that kind of family. John wasn't. John was an only child. His father left home at three. His mother was killed when he was sixteen. My mum died when I was fourteen, so we had that in common. But when it came to meet the press and I saw a guy in the outer office shaking, I'd go in and say, "Want a cup of tea?" because I just didn't like to be around that tension, that nervousness. So it fell to me to go and chat to the guy and put him at ease. Which then looked like PR. So I became known as the sort of PR man in the group. I probably was. The others would say, "I'm not bloody doing that interview, you do it." So I tended to look a bit the good guy in the media's eyes, because that's who I was being nice to. And I suppose the others may have resented that a little. But eventually, I've got this wild, ruthless ambition kind of image. If you do well, you get a bit of that. I don't really think it's that true. I think everyone was just as ruthless and ambitious as I was.

QUESTION: What do you think of the exploitation of Lennon's death?

PAUL: I think it's inevitable. You're talking about the West and capitalism. Exploitation's part of the game, really. I prefer to remember him how I knew him. I was in Nashville and saw a John Lennon whiskey decanter. *Argh!* He didn't even drink it. So, yeah, it's a bit yucky. But you can't do anything about it. This is America, folks.

QUESTION: What would you say to arguments that rock'n'roll was supposed to be a reaction against wigs, sets, and makeup (such as are used in the film)? And the whole thing is supposed to be not so heavily produced and a lot more intuitive?

PAUL: Maybe. I don't think it was really a reaction against that. I think it was a reaction against the current popular music of the time. We liked Chuck Berry, Little Richard, Carl Perkins, Elvis, all the American stuff. And all the black American stuff, Motown. You know, at that age, you tend to get cliquey. You like B-sides that people have never heard of. And our act was based on that kind of stuff. All our early Beatle albums are B-sides of black artists, most of the stuff. So I think really we just wanted a ballsier sound because some of the people, for us, were getting too sloppy. So we wanted to react against that, I suppose, in the same way punks reacted against stuff we were doing later.

QUESTION: You mentioned talking to MTV yesterday, which brings to mind that you were making promo films, as they were known then, when very few people were. What caused you to be a pioneer?

PAUL: I think when we started off, the first thing we did was appear on TV shows like *Hullabaloo!* In England it was *Ready Steady Go* and before that it was *Thank Your Lucky Stars*. That was what you did. You'd go on TV and do your song. And they made a little live video. And later on, if you couldn't be at the thing, people started to suggest, "Well, maybe you'll make a little thing and send it to us." So once that became available to us we started to get a bit imaginative. I remember one night meeting this Swedish director [Peter Goldmann] in a nightclub and he started saying, "Well, we could really be far out, you know? Yeah, wow, really heavy, psychedelic, up a tree." That turned out to be the "Strawberry Fields" promo, which was pretty far out for its time. And from there, we just continued. We got hooked, we just liked the idea of putting on strange clothes and riding white horses through rooms.

QUESTION: Is there any likelihood of compiling those films and putting them out on home video?

PAUL: Hmmmm. I suppose so. I hadn't actually thought about it. The old stuff tends to be a little bit sticky.

QUESTION: There've been reports you might bid upwards of $60 million for Northern Songs. How important is it to you to regain control of your old material?

PAUL: I'd really like to do it. Just because it seems natural that I should be allowed to own my own songs eventually. And I figure whoever's been publishing them has made a lot of money on me. But if you sign 'em away, you sign 'em away. That's the law of the land. And I signed 'em away, so I can't really blame the fella who bought them. But I'd like to get them back just because they're my babies, John's and my babies. Like "Yesterday." I think if you tell the man in the street that Paul doesn't own "Yesterday," it would surprise him. And the trouble is having to ask permission to sing it in the movie. That gets you. But actually, the publishers were quite fair. I think they only charged me a pound. I think they saw the irony too.

QUESTION: Would you tour again?

PAUL: Yeah, I think I might. I wouldn't rule it out. I think implicit in that question is, "Since John would you tour again?" Yeah, I think I would. I certainly wouldn't rule it out, because I don't think you can do that. You start to just live in fear of everything.

QUESTION: How have you kept from losing your hunger and drive? Why do you keep pushing so hard?

PAUL: Because I think to do the other would be really boring. I couldn't think what I'd do the other way. I'd sit at home, but then the kids go to school. While the kids are there, fine, but then the children are going to school and they've got their lives. I'm not the kind of person that can sit at home easily and just twiddle his thumbs. I can take a good few weeks' holiday, but I actually do like getting out there and talking to people and developing things. I've always had a kind of mania for that kind of stuff. Every so often I'll get an idea for something and think that might be good to talk to someone about, and I'm off again. And sometimes I bite off more than I can chew. It's just a little idea and it turns into three years' work. I don't know why I'm still so hungry. I think it's just because I enjoy it. I'm lucky enough to be in a profession where what you do is actually fun rather than banging rivets in a car on a conveyor belt. It's actually very creative. Other people do what I do for a living for a hobby.

QUESTION: Your current work will always be compared to your past work with the tendency to devalue the current. Is that difficult to live with? Do you ever just want to get rid of the Beatles?

PAUL: Not really. I know what you mean, though. I have to admit that looking at all the songs I've written that probably there's a little period in there that was my hottest period. "Yesterday," "Here, There and Everywhere," a little bunch of stuff that just came all in a few years. I suppose it was because we were at our height and the novelty became a very important factor. What's happened with me over the past ten years is I've tended to assume that the critics were right. Yeah, you're right. I'm not as good as I used to be. But in actual fact, recently I've started to think, "Wait a minute, let's check this out. Is this really true?" And I don't think it actually is. For instance, a song called "Mull of Kintrye," which sold more records than any other record in England, is from my "bad period." The song "Band on the Run," that's also from my bad period. I think what happens after such a success as the Beatles, everyone, *including me*, thinks there's no way we can follow that, so you just tend to assume it's not as good. I think as a body of work, my ten years with the Beatles, I would say, is probably better than this stuff. I do tend to be a bit gullible and go along with whoever's criticizing me and say yeah, you're right, I'm a jerk.

QUESTION: Do you feel as if you're competing with your past work?

PAUL: Yeah, a little bit. I think this new song, "No More Lonely Nights,"

I felt good about that. There are, I think, some decent things in there. It's not *all* rubbish. But I think it's a natural thing after the Beatles to assume he must be on a losing streak now. And I tend to go along with it. But I don't think it's really true.

QUESTION: Do you just sit and wait for the songs to come to you?

PAUL: No, I just tend to sit down and try and write a song. I think the best ones come of their own volition. "Yesterday," I just fell out of bed and that was there. I had a piano by the side of my bed. I mean, that particular song I woke up and there was a tune in my head. And I thought, "Well, I must have heard it last night or something." And I spent about three weeks asking all the music people I knew, "What is this song? Where have you heard this song before?" I just couldn't believe I had written it.

QUESTION: Is there anyone contemporary or historic you would ever dream of collaborating with?

PAUL: Yeah, Cole Porter. Or Gershwin. Someone like that. Those are my greats.

QUESTION: What about a Sting or an Elvis Costello? Have you ever thought of the chemistry that might develop there?

PAUL: I've thought of what if might be like to work with people like that. It'd probably be nice. But I haven't actually thought about it enough to do anything about it.

QUESTION: What do you think of Julian Lennon's album?

PAUL: I think it's great. What surprised me is he's got a very good voice. I'd heard that he sounds like his dad and I guessed that Phil [Ramone] was doing a sort of Lennon soundalike record. But I found it very surprising. His voice goes to some very pleasant places. Okay, it's a little like his dad, but that's on purpose, I think. He shows a musicality I didn't know he had. Mind you, I haven't met him for about ten years.

QUESTION: Are any of your kids involved in music?

PAUL: We just do little bits and pieces, never very formal. It's normally screaming. I'm not pushing them because I wasn't pushed. It just developed out of my love for it. That's probably why I still like it. I used to do piano lessons, but I hated them, it was like homework. And I had enough homework for school. So to have another batch was a definite loser. So I couldn't handle piano lessons ever. I still can't write music.

QUESTION: Do you worry about your public image?

PAUL: I try not to. I spent so long worrying about everything, never mind the image . . . just getting up in the morning. There's always something to worry about. So I'm really trying now with this film and everything. You can imagine the amount of worry when you've got a film riding on you. But I really do try to take the approach, "Now, look, I've given it my best shot. I've done all I can do, I'm not going to worry." It doesn't completely take all your worries away. But these interviews, for instance, I've just pretended I'm going on a holiday. It's silly in a way to do it, but it kind of works for me. I'm coming to meet a bunch of people rather than a threat. And I can get by that way.

QUESTION: But in doing all this, you expose yourself to a lot of ghosts, Lennon, the Beatles . . .

PAUL: You do. But that's the risk you run just going out in the morning. It'd be easier to just stay at home and just send out videos. But that's not what I'm here for. This is life, the main event. I'd rather just get out and run the risk than stay at home and rest on my laurels. But it is a risk, and once or twice in this movie I did have the horrors, thinking, "God, I've really exposed myself here." And one of my fears, actually, is that I've written this movie. And the people who're going to criticize me are all writers. Probably every single one of them figures they could do it better. And, in fact, may well be able to. But I think I'm going to pretend I'm just a fella in a film. It's either good or bad. That's all there is to it.

QUESTION: You used the phrase, "That's not what I'm here for." Do you have a feeling of what you're here for?

PAUL: I'm not sort of living a legend. I'm not doing the thing that's written about me. That's the sort of alter ego, all of that. I'm really just bringing up a bunch of kids, going from dawn to dusk. I'm here to just have a good life if possible, please.

QUESTION: But do you feel that any responsibility comes with your gift?

PAUL: I don't see it like that. Maybe there is one, but I'm just thankful for it and really feel lucky. It sounds a bit corny. But I make my money very cleanly. I don't have to exploit anyone. Which is pretty rare, you know, to make a lot of money cleanly.

GEORGE HARRISON AND MADONNA

London, March 6, 1986

GEORGE: Good afternoon. On behalf of us both and HandMade Films, welcome. I'd like to ask for maybe a bit of order. Whoever wants to ask a question, maybe you could say your name, what newspaper you're from, and also your intentions at the next general election.

QUESTION: Madonna, what kind of boss is George Harrison and were you a Beatlemaniac?*

MADONNA: I wasn't a Beatlemaniac. I don't think I really appreciated their songs until I was much older. I was too young to really get caught up in the craze. But he's a great boss, very understanding and sympathetic.

QUESTION: What sort of advice has he given you?

MADONNA: I think he's given me more advice on how to deal with the press than how to work in the movie.

QUESTION: Is it fun working with your husband, Sean Penn?

MADONNA: Of course it is. He's a pro. He's worked on several films and his experience has helped me.

QUESTION: Has it caused any personal problems off set? Do you argue at all?

---

*The film in question was the artistically and commercially disastrous *Shanghai Surprise*.

GEORGE: Do you row with your wife?

QUESTION: George, is it true you are playing a cameo role in the film?

GEORGE: Well, yes and no, really. There is one scene in a nightclub with a band playing in the background, and because I'm writing the music to the film I decided it would be easier if I was the singer in the band.

QUESTION: Mr. Harrison, are you confident that this film is going to be as successful?

GEORGE: I think so, yeah.

QUESTION: It seems as though it's a more ambitious film than A Private Function.

GEORGE: Well, it is certainly a larger-budget film than A Private Function, but it's totally different to any of the previous films we've made. It's a sort of adventure film, slightly humorous. I think it's actually a very good-looking film. This will be the thing in the end because there has been so much written in the papers that has absolutely nothing to do with what the film is about, and these two people have spent the last couple of months working on this thing.

QUESTION: George, when you hired Mr. Penn, did you think that there would be ... let's face it, this film is surrounded by a lot of hype ...

GEORGE: Well, you're the people who create the hype, let's not get that wrong.

QUESTION: What I'm saying is, did you expect the sort of coverage you're getting?

GEORGE: I did expect a certain amount of commotion from the press, but I must admit I overestimated your intelligence.

QUESTION: George, there's been a lot of reports that you've had to personally separate the warring factions on the set. Do you think this will affect the film adversely, and would you work with Sean Penn again?

GEORGE: Sure. I happen to like Sean very much because I don't see him like you. I see him as an actor who we hired and the role that he plays, and has played in the past—which is one of the reasons we chose him—is of a feisty young guy. That said, he's actually a human being who's very nice, and he's a talented actor. You just have to separate the two things, his job and his ability to do it and the sensationalism because he happened to marry Madonna.

QUESTION: Why isn't Mr. Penn here at this conference?

GEORGE: Because he's busy working.

MADONNA: He's in more scenes than I am.

QUESTION: Would some of the commotion have been cut down a bit if the original press conference hadn't been canceled? Isn't this just one of the old Hollywood ways of getting publicity?

GEORGE: The press conference was postponed because after we returned from Hong Kong the schedule had to be reorganized and, let's face it, we're here to make a film, not hold press conferences.

QUESTION: One of the people from HandMade told me that the reason they canceled it was that after the scene at the airport they didn't feel like giving the press an even break. Is that true?

GEORGE: Well, maybe that's true as well. I can't speak for whoever said that. You'll have to ask them. The purpose of this is to try and clarify some situation. I can see the attitude written all over your face. There's no actual point in you asking anything because you've already predetermined what it is you're going to say. I'd like to ask if there's anybody who is actually honest? That's what we want, a bit of honesty. Because if you want the truth, you'll get it. But I don't suppose that some people here are actually capable of recognizing it when they see it.

QUESTION: George, what do you think of the so-called British film revival? Did you see *Letter to Brezhnev* and do you have any plans to film in Liverpool?

GEORGE: Well, actually, *Letter to Brezhnev* resurrected my original belief in the character of the Liverpool people. It's a fantastic example of how someone with no money and no hope can actually get through that. I think it's fabulous. I've not spent a great deal of time in Liverpool over the years, but I'm happy to say the film has revitalized my image of Liverpool people. I think the British Film Year was a good idea, just to try and stimulate more interest from the public. I think to a degree it helped a lot.

QUESTION: Madonna, will you be singing on the sound track at all?

MADONNA: I'm not really thinking about the musical aspects of the movie. I'm just trying to concentrate on the acting.

GEORGE: At this point I'm doing the music. If she wants to, she's welcome, but she wasn't hired as a musician.

QUESTION: Madonna, I wonder if either you or your husband would like to apologize for incidents which have involved bad behavior on your behalf?

MADONNA: I have nothing to apologize for.

GEORGE: I would add to that. Everything that's been written in the papers has been started by someone in the press, either the photographer that sat on the hood of the car or the woman from the radio station who broke in and also the appalling behavior of the journalist who actually stole photographs from the continuity woman. So there's nothing to apologize for. I think certain elements of the press should apologize and at the same time I hope that all of them who do have intelligence will recognize that they're not the ones who have made us angry.

QUESTION: Do you think that situation has been antagonized by the enormous amount of security that's being used?

MADONNA: We don't have an enormous amount of security.

QUESTION: There is today.

GEORGE: Yes, today. If you had been with us in the car trying to get in here, you'd realize it's like a bunch of animals. Absolute animals. Do you just want us to get torn apart and beaten up? Because that's really what those people are like.

QUESTION: You must have realized what the British press are like. Do you regret shooting the last few weeks here rather than in the States?

GEORGE: It's a British film. You know, if you like, we'll all go to Australia and make our movies there in the future. We'd like to make them in England. We'd like to be reasonable and we'd like you to be reasonable because it doesn't do anyone . . . I think in a way certain of the press have actually got in the way. You would have achieved more if you had a different attitude.

QUESTION: But big stars come over here and make films perfectly well.

GEORGE: You know it's *you*, the press, who decide how big you want the stars to be. Let's face it, stars are actually people, human beings who have become famous for one thing or another and that is usually encouraged by the press to the point where the only thing left to do is to knock them. It's a historical fact and it's unfortunate that she happens to be going through that at this time.

QUESTION: Surely it was worse in the sixties?

GEORGE: It was worse because it was a new experience to me. But now I don't give a damn what you say about me, because I know who I am and I know what I feel and I know you can't get me anymore. The press can't get me. You can write your snide little things about me, but ultimately I'm all right. I know I'm all right. I don't care about those kind of snide remarks. I care about the truth.

QUESTION: You depend on the media for publicity. Without the publicity no one would go to your films. So what are you standing there saying we're wrong to be here for?

GEORGE: I didn't say you were wrong to be here. I was just making a point. He asked, "Is it any different from the sixties," and I said, "Well, in the sixties it was a new experience for me, but now I've been through so much I've learnt how to deal with it." I didn't say anything about what you said.

QUESTION: We have had loads of film stars over here, but have never had these sort of fights.

MADONNA: When Robert De Niro comes to the airport, are there twenty photographers that sit on his limousine and don't allow him to leave the airport?

GEORGE: Those people, let's face it, are big stars, but they're not news.

QUESTION: But I've never seen scenes like this.

GEORGE: Yes, but it's been created by the press. All those photographers are out there to get as many pictures as they can because they sell them to everybody. They make money out of it and because she's hot they're trying to make as much money as they can.

QUESTION: But that's why you hired her.

GEORGE: Yes, but we expected nonanimals. You're all quite nice now, aren't you?

QUESTION: Talking of animals, is it true that Sean Penn has been on the set giving orders . . .

GEORGE: What kind of introduction is that? That doesn't even deserve an answer.

QUESTION: What about the incident at the airport?

GEORGE: That was the press jumping all over the car.

QUESTION: It wasn't the press that were at fault. There were two other people who got involved who were plainclothes detectives and they shouldn't have been involved.

GEORGE: But nevertheless he was trying to jump on the front of the car as it drove away. What do you expect? Whatever the facts, it is still something which doesn't really justify the amount of attention it's been given.

QUESTION: How do the naked scenes fit into the film?

GEORGE: It's not that kind of movie.

MADONNA: There are no naked women in the movie.

GEORGE: Lots of naked men, though!

QUESTION: Madonna, do you care what's said about you in the press?

MADONNA: I think what George meant was he doesn't feel it anymore when bad things are written about him.

GEORGE: I don't particularly want you to say more nasty things, but I've learnt not to read them. It's just water off a duck's back. Otherwise we would all be ulcerated, wouldn't we? The sad thing is that people have got brains in their heads and maybe we should just try and use some of the other cells in our brains rather than the ones that are just to do with all this sensational stuff.

QUESTION: What's your favorite scene in the movie?

GEORGE: I like it when she kills the monster from outer space!

QUESTION: What state of production are the other current HandMade titles in?

GEORGE: We've got a number of films in the making, because we've been able to break even, or have been able to come up with the funding for certain films. Some of them are scripts that are being worked on. Others are in the casting stage. For instance, there's a film called *Travelling Men*, which has been in preproduction for a number of years. That's to say that the script is being improved, we've had certain actors we've wanted in the film and then we've had to wait because one of them would already be making a different film.

QUESTION: When did you first become aware of Madonna?

GEORGE: I don't know. A couple of years ago . . .

MADONNA: When he wrote "Lady Madonna"!

QUESTION: Were you aware of her records?

GEORGE: Sure, I was aware of her with all the TV, videos, and stuff. The first time I heard her was on the radio when I heard her singing something about living in the material world!

QUESTION: Madonna, I hear your management contract is up for sale. And, George, would you like to buy it?

MADONNA: You're a little troublemaker, aren't you!

QUESTION: Was this film written for Madonna and Sean Penn?

GEORGE: It wasn't. It was taken from a book called *Farraday's Flowers* and the producer wrote the screenplay. We talked about various possibilities for casting and someone suggested Madonna. Apart from the fact that everyone knew she was a famous singer, if you say *Desperately Seeking Susan*, you know even Barry Norman agrees that there was some potential there. She got the screenplay, and Sean Penn, who had also worked with John Combs, the producer, on a couple of other films, read the screenplay and said that he would do it too. It was quite a coincidental thing. It wasn't any sort of huge plot to get these newlywed people; I don't think they had even got married then. In a commercial sense, it was obviously good to have her in it because it's better than having someone nobody has ever heard of. But the rest of it was just luck. But I mean, lots of our films do have people no one's ever heard of. It's not any policy.

QUESTION: How many actresses had you seen for the part?

GEORGE: I'm not too sure of that. I wasn't in the country at the time. There were obviously other considerations, I know there were for Sean's part. But there's no point in me giving you a list of people who I thought would play the part well.

QUESTION: What are your responsibilities as executive producer?

GEORGE: Well, really the part I've played in the past was to provide the film unit with the money—and apart from that, if there's any comment I would like to make on the screenplay or the casting. It varies from film to film. Some films I have very little to do with and others, like this one, I have a lot to do with. But there's no other way around it on this one because originally I was just going to do the music, but I got dragged in much more than I would have normally. Usually I tend to like a low-profile existence and it's been years since I got involved in the newspapers like this.

QUESTION: George, are you happy with the progress of the film despite any difficulties you've had?

GEORGE: Whatever difficulties there have been are all behind us. I hope this press conference will help us to calm things down a little. I'm very pleased with what I'm seeing on the screen, which is the main thing. That's all I want, to get them to be able to complete shooting with the least problems.

QUESTION: Is it true that there have been problems between Jim Godard and Sean Penn?

MADONNA: No, it's not true.

GEORGE: No more than in any other film, you know. Every film has discussions and debates as to how it should proceed.

QUESTION: Do you tell the director to change camera angles?

MADONNA: I don't tell anyone anything and neither does Sean.

GEORGE: I think most people look through the camera, because when you're on the other side it's handy to know what is actually in and out of shot.

QUESTION: Did you say it's been a great many years since you held a press conference?

GEORGE: Me personally, yeah. I think 1974 was the last time I did anything like this. I just do gardening, you know. I like a nice quiet life!

QUESTION: Despite it all, Madonna, are you happy?

MADONNA: I am.

GEORGE: That's about it, thank you.

MADONNA: We're not such a bad bunch of people, are we? Bye.

PAUL McCARTNEY

Auburn Hills, Michigan, February 2, 1990

QUESTION: You made a comment last night about how you took a lot of your musical roots from this city. Were you referring to Motown or were there other things?

PAUL: I mainly meant Motown, yeah. We were major fans of black American music, a lot of which came from this city, so . . .

QUESTION: You've met a lot of the Motown people over the years. Any particular favorites?

PAUL: Oh, I love them all, you know. They kind of happened alongside us happening. The English people and the black Motown boom was great. So we were good mates, like Diana Ross and the Supremes. We were kind of contemporaries happening together.

QUESTION: Did you think of having any Motown artists do a guest shot with you last night?

PAUL: It's kind of difficult to work in guests. We've sort of got the show set now. Really the only person who's guested so far is Stevie [Wonder] in LA, who is very much Motown, as you know. But that was easy because we do "Ebony and Ivory" in the set. It's not too easy to open up the set when you get to this stage with the production.

QUESTION: What made you decide to tour after thirteen years?

PAUL: Maybe the fact that I got a good band. You know, I've been recording and doing solo stuff and little guest spots like Live Aid and shows like that but during the recording of the *Flowers in the Dirt* album the band felt really good. We've got a sense of humor in common and they're good musicians, too. So it was either a question of saying good-bye, see you next album or, like, should we stay together and if we stay together, what should we do—Let's go on tour.

QUESTION: A lot of critics are quick to judge anything that you or any of the other Beatles do. How did you go into this LP mentally? Do you ever get to the point where you thought to heck with them? "I'm going to shove one down your throat?"

PAUL: Yeah, I get to that point. I was not pleased with the album before it, which is *Press to Play*. So I wanted to make this one better and shove it down a few people's throats. I'm quite happy with the album itself. It has some of my best songs on it.

QUESTION: Has coming out on the road reinspired you to go back in the studio a little earlier than you have in the past?

PAUL: Not really, but it's good for you, getting on the road. It's a stimulating thing, actually seeing your fans instead of just getting letters from them. It really lifts you.

QUESTION: In your program last night I noticed you said the best thing about touring is the audience. Was the audience last night as good as you expected?

PAUL: It was a serious audience last night, really, because we've always been playing . . .

QUESTION: What do you mean by that?

PAUL: Seriously good, seriously fab. Seriously doody. We've just come from England and Wembley, which was a great series of concerts. We did eleven on the trot, I think, but the English are a little bit more reserved, you know. They get going, but it takes them like half an hour. This audience, it didn't take them but a second and then screams.

QUESTION: Paul, a lot of people said your show was an emotional experience. Why did it take twenty years for you to come back out and finally play the classic Beatles songs?

PAUL: When the Beatles broke up, it was a little difficult. It was a bit like a divorce and you didn't really want to do anything associated with the ex-wife. You didn't want to do *her* material. So all of us took that view independently and John stopped doing Beatles stuff, George, Ringo, we all did. Because it was just too painful for a while. But enough time's gone by now. On the last tour I did in 1976 with Wings we avoided a lot of Beatles stuff because of that. So now it feels really kind of a natural to now do those songs. It's a question of either getting back to those songs or ignoring them for the rest of my life. And as I say, some of them I haven't actually done before and I didn't realize that until we were rehearsing with the band and I said, "This feels great, 'Sgt. Pepper.' I mean, why is this so great?" And someone reminded me, they said, "You've never done it." It's like a new song to me. It's just the right time to come back with that stuff.

QUESTION: Will there be a time when you get together with George and Ringo? Not really a reunion without John but kind of a jam maybe?

PAUL: I don't know. That's always on the cards, but a reunion as such is out of the question because John's not with us. The only reunion would have been with John. But, like you say, we might easily get together. There's a couple of projects that are possible now that we've solved our business differences. I don't know, I haven't actually seen them. I've been living this whole thing through the press. People say to me, "George said he won't do it." I haven't even spoken to him yet.

QUESTION: Why did it take so long to resolve your business differences?

PAUL: Have you even been in a lawsuit? I was in one for the last twenty years. It just took forever. What happens is you get your advisers and they get theirs and then lawyers, I think, are trained to keep things like that going. The first rule in law school, you know: keep it going.

QUESTION: Do you regret that the four ex-Beatles never got together again before John died?

PAUL: Well, I regret it, you know, but, I mean, this is life. It just didn't happen for a number of reasons. It would have been great, but John not dying would have been even better.

QUESTION: What's going on in Eastern Europe?

PAUL: I think it's very exciting. To me it seems like the sixties kicking in again. That's my point of view. It's all the stuff that was said in the sixties: peace, love, democracy, freedom, a better world, and all that stuff. It's finally kicked in. The way I look at it, people like Gorbachev grew up with the sixties and I don't think you can be unaffected by it and I think it's all kicking in now. Look at those people who are coming across the border and a lot of them are wearing denim. It's us coming across that border. I think it's very exciting. I think China's next.

QUESTION: Are you going to play any dates in Eastern Europe now that the Iron Curtain is history?

PAUL: I'd like to, but we've got so many dates on this tour and they don't include Eastern Europe. I'd like to go to Russia, but the promoters say it's too cold, so we went to Italy.

QUESTION: What are your plans after the tour?

PAUL: I'll be writing after the tour. I've got a lot of writing I want to do. I'm doing a very interesting thing. It's a classical thing for an orchestra which is due to be performed by the Liverpool Philharmonic Orchestra in the Liverpool Cathedral in 1991* and that's like a serious work, so I've got a lot of writing to do.

QUESTION: Why don't you write your memoirs?

PAUL: I don't know, really. I always thought that you had to be like about seventy before you did.

QUESTION: What new things are you listening to right now?

PAUL: Um, I listen to everything. I listen to all sorts of things.

QUESTION: James and Stella are traveling with you right now. Would you ever invite either of them on the stage?

PAUL: Not really. It's too sort of show-bizzy, that kind of thing. I know a lot of people do that. If they really desperately wanted to do it, then I'd help them, but it's got to come from them. I'm not going to push them onstage because it's a tough game.

QUESTION: How do you compare the thrill of performing in the sixties with performing today?

PAUL: It's very similar actually. That crowd last night was strangely sixties. It's very good, you know.

QUESTION: But now you can hear yourself.

PAUL: With the new technology, yeah. I mean, you compare all this equipment here and you've got like Cape Canaveral. But when we started out it was like two guitars and a bass in one amp.

QUESTION: What was your inspiration for the film presentation before the concert? How did you go about putting the film footage together?

PAUL: I talked to Richard Lester, who made *A Hard Day's Night* and

---

*Here McCartney refers to his first full-fledged classical exercise known officially as the *Liverpool Oratorio*. Although the album sold briskly, critics were generally less enthused about the musically predictable work.

Help!, and we were thinking of having a support act before our act, but the promoters told me that was going to get difficult. So I suggested, "Well, how about if we do a film?" So I rang Dick Lester and said to him, "Could you do a film that says, 'First there was the Beatles, then there was Wings, and then there was *now?*' He said, "Let me think about it," and he came back with the film, which I like—it's kind of uncompromising; it's a very grown-up film, gives people something to think about.

QUESTION: Are you going to change the show when it comes to stadiums?

PAUL: Yeah, we will magnify it a little bit. This style of show is fine in an arena like this, but when you get into a forty-thousand [seat] arena it starts to look a little small, so we'll just make it bigger. But basically keep the same show.

QUESTION: There's been a flood of unreleased Beatles recordings, very high quality like the *Ultra Rare Trax* you probably heard about. What are your feelings on the release of those things and would you like to see EMI release them officially?

PAUL: That's kind of a difficult question. It's like as far as the Beatles were concerned, we released all our good material, except for maybe one or two little things that at the time we didn't like. And there are one or two tracks I think are worth looking at. "Leave My Kitten Alone," John sings, which I think is very good. But in the main we released all our best material, so now you know, it's like memorabilia. People just like to hear the tracks that were the takes we didn't use or something. If people are interested, it's fair enough. I mean, I don't get uptight about bootlegs. What are you going to do?

QUESTION: I just wondered if you plan to tour again after this.

PAUL: Yeah. It's funky because I think a lot of people come to the show and think, "Well, it's the last time you'll see him." I don't know why they think that, but, yes, the Stones and I, well, we're getting up there kind of thing, but as far as I'm concerned I feel twenty-seven, not forty-seven.

QUESTION: Will you rock-and-roll after you're fifty, do you think?

PAUL: I think there probably is life after fifty, yeah.

QUESTION: Paul, of all the songs you've written, what would be your favorite if you still have one?

PAUL: That's a very difficult question. I mean, musically, I might say "Here, There and Everywhere," but as far as success is concerned, it has to be "Yesterday," because it's just done more than I could have ever hoped for.

QUESTION: Does "Yesterday" mean something different to you now that you're forty-seven?

PAUL: Yes, it sure does. When I wrote it, I was a twenty-year-old singing, "I'm not half the man I used to be." It's like, it's very presumptuous for a twenty-year-old. At forty-seven, however, it *means* something.

QUESTION: At that time did you ever think you'd be rocking now?

PAUL: I didn't think we'd be still rocking now. The great thing, as I say, is you look at what a lot of us have done recently and you look at people like Muddy Waters and you think, It didn't matter that he was seventy, he's still singing the blues. Instead of a youth-oriented thing, it's become a music-oriented thing, so I think as long as you can still deliver, I mean, you look at the age of these audiences, I'm very surprised, the sort of young people, I thought it just would be my age group mainly, but there's a lot of young kids and they know this material.

QUESTION: Are they simply looking for nostalgia?

PAUL: I don't know, I'm always talking to my kids about that. You tell me. What songs are going to be remembered? It's going to be, I don't know, some rap song . . .

QUESTION: Are you enjoying all of this, Paul?

PAUL: Yes, it's great. I really am.

QUESTION: How do you like your music today?

PAUL: My music? I still like it.

QUESTION: How do you feel when you look out into the crowds and you see parents holding their children to see you?

PAUL: It's really beautiful because I've got four kids and the great thing about me and my kids is that there isn't this generation gap that I thought would be there.

QUESTION: Do they listen to any music that bothers you?

PAUL: No. But I know what you mean. I thought that they'd get into some odd punk music and I'd be saying, "Well, the sixties was better," but they're not. My son loves the Beach Boys. His big new turn-on album that I turned him on to is *Pet Sounds*. And he loves James Brown, Otis Redding, the Commodores, he's got some good taste.

QUESTION: Are you surprised how many young people on this tour are responding to your music?

PAUL: Well, kind of. But a couple of years ago I started to notice how kids like my nephews, who are eighteen now, but who I've known since they were two or whatever, started getting into the Grateful Dead. Now they're all Deadheads, it's incredible. I think maybe it is because modern music is a little bit synthetic and shallow that they're looking back to the sixties. And the great thing about a lot of that sixties stuff is that it does stand up still.

QUESTION: Are your children musically inclined?

PAUL: Yeah, they are, but Linda and I have always said that we'd never push them because it's a tough game and unless they're really keen . . . But they're all very good, they're all very interested in music and they can all carry a tune and stuff.

QUESTION: When you get away from this for a while, is there anything that strikes you that you would like to effect, being a father and with your stature in the world?

PAUL: The thing we're doing on this tour is hooking up with the Friends of the Earth and mentioning the environmental issues a lot. I mean, I'm no expert, but I've got four kids and I see this Exxon spill and how well they cleaned up . . . joke. I don't think anyone wants that to happen. I don't think anyone wants the hole in the ozone layer to get any bigger. But I was like anyone else, I thought "Well, the government will fix it for us," but last year it became apparent that no one was going to fix it and we've got to address the problem ourselves. So that's what I'm doing on this tour, I'm mentioning it just to give the issues publicity because I really think we have got to get serious on all that stuff.

QUESTION: What are you trying to do with Friends of the Earth?

PAUL: Friends of the Earth are basically just trying to clean up the planet; instead of putting your toxic waste in your water, instead of blowing a hole in the sky, instead of having acid rain . . . If someone had told me when I was a kid that when I grew up the land would have poisons in it, the rain would have acid in it, the sky would have a hole in it, I would not have believed them. But here we are, we're at that point now and my hope is that going into the next century we really address that problem and get the planet straight. My point is that we are definitely the species that's won. Man has definitely beaten all other animals hands down, and what I'd like to see is us be cool dudes about that. But instead we're still blasting the hell out of everything. It's time we realized we're the only ones on Earth that fouls its own nest. Everything else, all the birds and stuff, go over someplace else to take a dump, but we don't. We do it right here, right where we live. We put all our toxic waste in our lakes and we put all these poisons in cans and dump it under the sea, saying "It'll be all right for a hundred years." But what about a hundred and one years, when it blows up?

Tokyo, November 29, 1991

GEORGE: Short message: hello! Very nice to be here after such a long time.

ERIC CLAPTON: Yes, it's nice to be back in Japan, this time with a friend. I love to come to this country. I come as often as I can and will continue to do so. I hope this will be a success and hope you will enjoy it.

QUESTION: What attracts you to each other?

GEORGE: Well, it's very difficult; it's simple, but difficult, because something mutual that you like, you can say it's the way he bends the strings or the way he says hello. It's difficult to say. It's just an attraction we have, an attraction in our lives and it's also the way he bends the notes. Was that good enough?

CLAPTON: Well, George is senior to me by, what, I don't know, a year?

GEORGE: I'm about thirty. How old are you?

CLAPTON: Seventy-nine. But I've always thought that he's a great songwriter, a great musician, a very unique man, and he gave up smoking. I have to respect him for that. I think he's very brave to come here because he hasn't worked on the stage for a long time and it can be a very frightening experience, but I think it will be rewarding. But I always thought of George as being a little like the elder brother I never had, so I respect his judgment and his values and I think he's a wonderful man. I like the way he bends the strings, too. He's a great slide player; most of all he's a fantastic slide player.

QUESTION: What do you think about Prime Minister Major?

CLAPTON: Very anonymous. He seems to be okay, but he just seems to be rather blank.

GEORGE: I've not met him. I've only seen him a couple of times on TV, because I also gave up watching television as well as smoking and I also gave up reading newspapers. So I don't really know much about him, but I still think he's better than Mrs. Thatcher.

QUESTION: How did the idea of a tour come about and why did you come to Japan?

GEORGE: Well, the reason that I came to Japan was because Eric suggested to me that this time of year would be good if I wanted to do a concert tour. He was not working and he and his band were available to become my band. That was one reason why I thought about working, because Eric asked me. And the reason we came to Japan was, he likes Japan and he suggested that we come here. That was the first question. To convey to the fans, really, just whatever the meaning of the songs are, if they have some meaning for the fans of Japan. I've had a lot of mail over twenty-five years from Japan. Very nice letters from the Japanese people and they seem to like—or the ones who write anyway— seem to like my records. So I just hope they like the live music as much as they like the records.

QUESTION: How were the songs chosen?

GEORGE: They were chosen by either the fact that they were hit singles or that it had a feeling for me that it would be good to put on—like the song, "Taxman"—it's a song that goes regardless if it's the sixties, seventies, eighties, nineties. There's always a taxman, so if the song seems to fit. Just what I felt would be reminiscent like, "If I Needed Someone" I sang at the Budokan twenty-six years ago, maybe, so might as well sing it at the Dome twenty-six years later. The rest were mainly singles or a selection from different albums going right from 1965 until last year.

QUESTION: Will you play "Roll Over Beethoven"?

GEORGE: Yes. It's very popular in Japan.

QUESTION: What would you like to do in Japan?

GEORGE: Well, I'd like to see all the bits I didn't see last time. That's maybe from the hotel to the Tokyo Dome and back. I'd like to go to Kyoto and see some temples and some gardens although it's not the best time of the year to see the gardens. But still, I may not come back for another twenty-six years so I better go now. And maybe go to the electric shop and buy an electric toothbrush or something.

QUESTION: Why is your song "Tears of the World" not included in your book *Songs by George Harrison?*

GEORGE: It fell out on the way to Japan. I don't know, really. You should write to the publisher and ask him. Or you'll have to buy volume two. The publisher of the book is coming to the Tokyo Dome, so I'll tell him.

QUESTION: Will the Beatles reunite?

GEORGE: No. It can't be possible because the Beatles don't exist especially now that John Lennon is not alive. It just happens, every time Paul needs some publicity he announces to the press we're getting back together again. I wouldn't pay much attention to that.

QUESTION: Eric, what are your plans?

CLAPTON: When this is finished, I go back for Christmas and then I'll start a world tour next year. I don't know what George will do. Maybe he will start a world tour on his own, I don't know.

GEORGE: Who knows, we'll have to wait and see.

QUESTION: December ninth, the anniversary of John's death, takes place during your tour. Do you plan to do anything special on that day?

GEORGE: I'd have to look at the itinerary. We'd have to be doing a concert or if not we'll be traveling to a concert. But we won't be doing anything other than singing songs. We won't be doing anything special. No, the day doesn't have any special meaning to me.

CLAPTON: I think the fact that George will be playing is tribute enough.

GEORGE: It's not that I don't respect the day John Lennon got killed or anything, I'm just not into days. I don't remember my own birthday, I don't remember anniversaries or anything. I'm just not into remembering days.

QUESTION: What changes have you experienced since you were last in Japan?

GEORGE: Everything has changed over twenty-five years. First of all, I'm much younger now than I used to be. I think I can sing better, I can play better, and I can be a happier person. Everything's changed.

QUESTION: Are you planning to play "Layla"?

CLAPTON: I don't think so, unless there's some kind of riot or public out-cry and we have to play it. I've played it at nearly every show for the past twenty years, so it doesn't bother me not to play it now and then. And George has only given me a very limited space [laughter], so I'm going to try and do a couple of new songs. But it's all negotiable, don't worry.

GEORGE: I don't mind if he does it.

CLAPTON: We'll see, we'll see.

GEORGE: Thank you all very much, it's nice to be here.

Los Angeles, 1990

QUESTION: "Time Takes Time" has a seventies feel to it. I especially like the tracks you did with Jeff Lynne.

RINGO: Oh, that's interesting, because two of them I wrote. So that's a double-plus.

QUESTION: I really like the fact that Jeff Lynne was playing everything and you were just playing drums and singing.

RINGO: Yeah, well I think that "Don't Go Where the Road Don't Go" is a really strong record, too.

QUESTION: Obviously you've worked with Jeff before on Tom Petty's video and George's last album.

RINGO: Well, that's how it started. I started with Jeff because I'd known him. I worked with Jeff on George's album and I'd done some other stuff with him. So when it came to starting the album, I called him to see if he'd like to do a couple of tracks and he said yeah.

QUESTION: And what was the thinking on doing the tracks with different producers?

RINGO: Well, it was because I hadn't made an album in several years that we thought we'd do it this way. It's not new for me. I've done it before and used other producers. I just felt this was the way to do it right now.

QUESTION: Is it different producers for different types of songs or different feels?

RINGO: Well, that's how it started. It started also that I didn't want to get into a project with one producer and maybe it wasn't going to work all the way down. You can have a lot of fun on three or four tracks and just come into a job then. And then you move on and it's all fresh again for the next guy, you know. Fresh for me and for them.

QUESTION: Were these all people that you wanted to work with?

RINGO: Yeah, sure. Look at their credits. I feel I got lucky, you know. Throughout the year, everyone had some free time for me, it took a year because I worked with Jeff and then I went to Europe for two months. Then I came back to work with Don Was. I mean, everyone was setting it up. And it was Peter Asher and this year we came back just to do those two more tracks that we always wanted to do and did it with Don. So it worked out really well.

QUESTION: Yes, and "Don't Go Where the Road Don't Go," definitely has that ELO feel as well.

RINGO: It certainly has that Jeff Lynne stamp on it. I mean the separation and the clarity is because everything was recorded separate. That's how he gets that sound.

QUESTION: I talked to him when he did his solo album, which was a neat album. But I also talked to Dave Edmunds a few years ago about being produced by Jeff Lynne after being a producer himself and he said he likes Jeff because he just makes great-sounding records.

RINGO: He does, he does. And he's a lovely man.

QUESTION: Of course, bringing people together on one album is a trademark of yours, too.

RINGO: Sure, also with the band for the tour. That's how I do it. But on the album, mainly the bands were brought together by the producers. It was okay by me because each producer brought along some really good players.

QUESTION: It must have been fun making the record.

RINGO: It was. It was a lot of fun. It was interesting just being the drummer on the tracks. We didn't have anyone else around this time, which meant a change. I'm really just focusing musically. Just getting back into my craft as a musician and an entertainer.

QUESTION: I remember when you did the last tour, you were saying it was really good to just get back there and actually play live.

RINGO: Sure, it's what we do. That was the fantasy, the dream of a young boy of thirteen, and it came true and then he forgot it. And now he's getting back into it.

QUESTION: How about writing? Like you say, there's four songs that you cowrote. Is that something that you didn't do for a while?

RINGO: I didn't do *anything* for a while, never mind writing. Now I'm doing that as well and that's also a thrill.

QUESTION: A whole new beginning of sorts?

RINGO: Yeah, it's like starting again. But starting over from a place that I'd already been. It's like the battery went dead on the car. And we just changed.

QUESTION: Is rock'n'roll—I mean, you were always pretty much of a rock'n'roll guy. That's you.

RINGO: I'm the best rock'n'roll drummer on the planet.

THE INNER CIRCLE

Friends and Family

Bournemouth, 1970

QUESTION: What do you really think of the Beatles?

MIMI SMITH: The boys had talent, yes, but they also had a lot of luck as well. When they first played me "Love Me Do," I didn't think much of it.

QUESTION: How do you view the many troubles the Beatles have been going through these last few years?

SMITH: I don't know what all this business between John and Paul is about and I don't dare ask John. I did ring Paul about it, and he told me things would straighten up. The boys have been friends so long. I remember them coming home from school together on their bikes, begging biscuits. I'm sure they'll get back together again. This is just a phase they're passing through.

QUESTION: These days your nephew is very involved in a variety of social, political, and avant-garde causes. How do you feel about all that?

SMITH: I've just quit reading the papers these days. Apple sends me his records, but I won't play them. And I've asked my friends not to tell me about them. That shameful album cover* and that [erotic] *art* show of

---

Mary "Aunt Mimi" Smith was John Lennon's maternal aunt who raised him as a boy. She passed away at home in December of 1992.

*Here, Mimi refers to controversial *Two Virgins/Unfinished Music #1*, on which John and Yoko appeared nude.

his. He's been naughty and the public doesn't like it, and he's sorry for it. Now he wants sympathy. That's why he's come out with all these fantastic stories about an unhappy childhood. It's true that his mother wasn't there and there was no father around, but my husband and I gave him a wonderful home. John didn't buy me these furnishings, my husband did. John, Paul, and George wrote many songs together sitting on the sofa you're sitting on now, long before you'd ever heard of the Beatles. Why, John even had a pony when he was a little boy! He certainly didn't come from a slum! None of the boys did. The Harrisons weren't as well off as the other families, perhaps, but George wasn't from a slum, either, the way the press had it. And that's why you never saw photographs of John's boyhood home. We certainly weren't impoverished, the way John's talking now!

QUESTION: What do you think changed John so much from his early days as a carefree kid?

SMITH: She's responsible for all this, *Yoko*. She changed him, and I'm sure she and Linda are behind this split with John and Paul. Cynthia was such a nice girl. When she and John were in art college, she'd come to my house and say, "Oh, Mimi, what am I going to do about John?" She'd sit there until he came home. Cynthia really pursued him. He'd walk up the road and back until she got tired of waiting and went home. I think he was afraid of her, actually.

QUESTION: You realize, of course, that to many people John is something of a political leader with such songs as "Power to the People," for example . . .

SMITH: Don't talk to me of such things! I know that boy. He doesn't know what he's saying! It's all an act. If there were a revolution, John would be first in the queue to run! Why, he's scared to death of things like that! That's Yoko talking, not John! Yoko is not exactly right in the head. Every time John does something bad and gets his picture in the papers he rings up to smooth me over. See that new color television? It was a Christmas present, but he had it delivered early. A big present arrives every time he's been naughty. I usually have a large photograph of John hanging in the lounge. When he's a good boy, it'll go back up again!

KEN BROWN

London, September 13, 1965

QUESTION: How does it feel to have left the Beatles just before they really made it big?

KEN BROWN: Sometimes I could kick myself—*hard!* I could still be one of the Beatles, earning thousands of pounds a week, instead of living in a caravan. I was with John, Paul, and George the first time they played together at the Casbah. I knew John's wife, Cynthia—in fact, I saw their romance blossom. I knew George's first girlfriend, Ruth Morrison. We shared everything—our music and the three pounds a night we used to earn in those far-off days of August 1958. Now my old ten-watt amplifier lies in a corner of my caravan. The Hofner guitar I played hangs on the wall, but I still play for my wife, Marcia. These are my only souvenirs, and I often think if it hadn't been for a row over a paltry fifteen bob, I might still be with them.

QUESTION: What do remember best about those days?

BROWN: The memories flood back ... I was with the Beatles the day they were formed—quite by accident. It was summer 1958 and Harrison and I were playing in the Les Stewart Quartet with a chap called Skinner. We spent hours practicing in the Lowlands Club, Heyman's Green. We would probably have gone on playing at clubs but for George's

---

Ken Brown played with the Quarrymen during their final days together.

girlfriend, Ruth. George had never been really too keen on girls. He was only sixteen and at the Liverpool Institute with Paul McCartney. Later, he suddenly seemed to go head over heels for Ruth, who eventually moved to Birmingham to become a nurse. One evening the three of us were sitting in the Lowlands drinking coffee, moaning about the fact that we had nowhere regular to play when Ruth suggested we see Mrs. Best at the Casbah. She promised that the Les Stewart Quartet would play at the club when it opened. On the Saturday we were due to open, so I went round to Stewart's house. George was sitting in the lounge, his Hofner across his lap, idly plucking at the strings. The atmosphere seemed a bit tense. "What's up?" I asked. George looked down at his guitar and said nothing. So I turned to Les. He looked daggers saying, "You've been missing practice," he said. "I know," I replied, "but only so's we can have somewhere to play; I've spent hours working at the club." "You've been getting paid for it," challenged Les. "No, I haven't." "Well, I'm not going to play there," said Stewart, as our argument got steadily more heated. I turned to George. "Look," I said, "the clubs opens tonight. We've spent months waiting for this, you're not backing out too?" George thought for a moment. Then he said he would go on with me, so we left Les at his house. As we were walking down the road, I turned to George and said: "We can't let Mrs. Best down now. Let's try and get a group together ourselves. Do you know anyone?" "There's two mates I sometimes play with out at Speke," ventured George. "Okay, let's ask them," I said, and George went off on the bus, joining me two hours later at the Casbah with his two mates— John Lennon and Paul McCartney.

QUESTION: Did you have any idea who his two mysterious mates were?
BROWN: No, not at all. This was the first time I'd ever met them. Paul was fifteen, still at school, and had a schoolboyish haircut. But John was already a bit of a beatnik, with his hair hanging over his collar, dressed in a check suit coat and old jeans. I told them we would each be paid fifteen bob a night. They seemed glad about that; in those days most groups played just for experience.

QUESTION: What were you called at this point?
BROWN: We talked over various names to call ourselves and finally settled on the Quarrymen, a name John had used once or twice before for skiffle groups he had formed since leaving Quarrybank Grammar

School. So, that night the Beatles were born and the Casbah opened after all. We went down great particularly when Paul sang "Long Tall Sally." Our most popular numbers were John and Paul's vocals—I was the rhythm guitarist. John's pet solo was "Three Cool Cats," which he used to growl into the mike.

QUESTION: What are your thoughts these days on John?

BROWN: John was always very quiet. He was a lonely youngster, seldom talking about his family, maybe because his father had deserted him in childhood, and then his mother had been killed. John seemed in need of affection and depended on Cynthia.

QUESTION: How did your days with the band finally end?

BROWN: One night, just as we were due to start a Saturday session, I felt a crippling pain in my leg. I could barely stand but insisted on doing something, so Mrs. Best asked me to take the money at the door and, for the first time, John, Paul, and George played without me. Just as everyone was going home, I was in the club when Paul came back down the steps. "Hey, Ken, what's all this?" he said. "What?" I asked him. "Mrs. Best says she's paying you, even though you didn't play with us tonight." "That's up to her," I replied as Paul bounded back up the stairs, still arguing with Mrs. Best. They all came downstairs to me. "We think your fifteen bob should be divided between us, as you didn't play tonight," said Paul. "All right, that's it, then!" shouted McCartney, and they stormed off down the drive towards West Derby village, shouting that they would never play the Casbah again. But that wasn't the last time I saw them—not the last time they played the Casbah—though we didn't play together again. The last time I saw the Beatles was on March 16, 1963. I had moved to London and married Marcia. The telephone rang and it was Neil Aspinall, their road manager. He told me the boys were in a bit of a jam; they had run out of money; the next night they were due to appear in Sheffield; unless someone helped them out they would have to sleep in the van. Neil wondered if I would lend them twenty quid. Eventually, I agreed, and they all turned up at our flat. Neil came to the door, then Marcia and I went down to the van to see the boys. I handed over the money, which they repaid six weeks later. I told them we were moving into a caravan. "Great," said Paul. "We'll all drop in to see you some time." And with that they drove off into the night.

PETE BEST

Liverpool, 1986

GEOFFREY: When did you first meet the boys?

PETE BEST: The first one I laid eyes on was George Harrison because he was playing in a group called the Les Stewart Quartet. They were a skiffle group, a kind of semi-rock band I suppose. They were supposed to open the Casbah. George said, "We'd like to open the place. The problem is the band's broken up. But I happen to know two guys, John Lennon and Paul McCartney. I'll ask them whether they'd be prepared to form a band." Anyway, they came down, had a look at the club and said, "Oh, yeah, great." So Mum said, "What are you gonna play as?" There was John, George, Paul, and Ken Brown. So they said, "Well, we'll play as the Quarrymen." That was the first time I met all of them together. Stu Sutcliff wasn't with them at the time, but he came down to watch the band because he was a friend of John's from art college. And, of course, John used to bring Cindy [Cynthia] down. I got to know Stu through the boys, so to speak. Then, of course, when I was asked to join them, Stu had already joined as the bass player.

GEOFFREY: You were quite close to John, I know. When Stu came in, was that somehow jeopardized?

BEST: No, I mean the relationship between John and Stu was always there. Stu had a lot of respect for John as a person and John had total respect for Stu because of his artistic ability. It was like two different dimensions meeting up and making one force. When I joined the band, it didn't sever the relationship between John and Stu, because that was ongoing. I mean, even after Stu left the band, in April 1961, he and John still got on. After we finished a gig, we'd all come back, go into the Casbah; raid the fridge, stock up on sweets, Coca-Colas, go upstairs, switch on the record player, and they'd spend the night. Bacon butties in the morning. Maybe if we had a lunchtime session to play, we'd be off to the Cavern. We were like that.

GEOFFREY: They intimated in the television docudrama *Birth of the Beatles* (for which you were the creative consultant through Dick Clark) that Stuart's death may have been a result of a beating you guys took on the way home from a gig by some jealous boyfriends. Can you tell me about that?

BEST: It's hard to say, to be quite honest. A lot of people have said that. It could have been because of what happened.

GEOFFREY: He was kicked in the head, wasn't he?

BEST: What happened was that Stu had come out and these so-called hard knocks picked on him. They were giving him a good working over, and John and I stepped in and broke up the situation. But to say directly that the brain hemorrhage, which Stu consequently died of, had anything to do with it, I just don't know. It may just as easily have been the fact that Stu was overworking himself in Hamburg. Because when he finished with the group, he put all of himself back into the Hamburg College of Art. So I don't really know the answer to that.

GEOFFREY: What was it like being in Hamburg with the boys?

BEST: Fantastic.

GEOFFREY: Living conditions were rather spartan, I hear.

BEST: When we first went there, we were supposed to play the Kaiserkeller. Derry and the Seniors were already there, which was another Liverpool band. Anyway, we went down into the Kaiserkeller and the place was jumping. It was Neon City, Sin City, you name it. Bruno Koshmider [the club's owner] said, "Oh no, lads, you're not playing here. You're playing at the Indra, which is just at the bottom of the street." It was a different club altogether with a very different atmosphere, so that took us down a peg or two. We asked him, "Well, where are we staying?" We expected a hotel or maybe rooms in the club. But actually we were staying at the Bambikino [cinema]. Paul and I nicknamed it the Black Hole of Calcutta. Before Stu linked up with his girl Astrid we spent a lot of time there. John, Stu, and George got the best room in the house, so to speak. The middle room, which had one old neon light in it, two camp beds and a couch. Paul and I were too late running up the alley to claim our space. You went in through to the back of the cinema. So we said, "There's only three beds here. Where are we going to stay?" John pointed us down the corridor and we found this black hole with no lights, just an old bed with enough room for us to climb in on top and go to sleep. That was our accommodations.

GEOFFREY: Roy Young [from Cliff Bennett and the Rebel Rousers] told me that more than once he had to come up there and give you guys hell because, apparently, there was a little German woman that would come in and clean and she refused to go up there because it was so bad. People were pissing on the floor.

BEST: That wasn't in the Bambi, because the first time we went out, we spent as little time in there as we could.

GEOFFREY: Did you take many girls back there with you?

BEST: That goes without saying. Sometimes we didn't even have to take them back. They knew where we were staying. They'd come in through the movie house. The time Roy's talking about is when we were playing the Star Club. We had moved into proper accommodations facing the club, which was great. We had a self-contained flat with proper wash basins and all that. This particular occasion was when George threw up by the side of the bed and didn't bother cleaning it up. The cleaning lady came in the next morning, and said, "Oh, I'm not cleaning that up." It was like the beginning of a Mexican standoff, and he said "Well, I'm certainly not cleaning it up." Anyway, this thing just grew, started heaving and smelling and all the rest of it, so she just refused, point blank, to clean our living quarters. In the end she told Horst (who was the manager of the Star Club), thinking, "If anyone can get the guys to clean it up, it'll be Horst." So, of course, Horst comes over, and he says, "Come on, lads, just clean it up." "No." And it went on and on like that.

GEOFFREY: For how long?

BEST: Days, weeks. This thing was growing. It was fungusing, it even grew hair. It became a pet. We were feeding it beer, throwing ciggie stumps into it. We nicknamed it the Big Thingy. People were even coming in to see it, because it was growing. In the end Horst just came in one day with a shovel, and scooped it into the bin.

GEOFFREY: I've seen pictures of John standing in the street in his underwear. They also say he pissed on a nun's head. Is that true?

BEST: Yeah, [singing] "Raindrops keep falling on my head." It's true. But it's just one of the many mad things he did. That particular day, he wanted to go for a pee and the balcony was the nearest place. He just unloaded his water over the side and nuns happened to be passing underneath.

GEOFFREY: Was he more outrageous than any of the others?

BEST: Yeah. I had a lot of respect for him that way. I mean, simply because he didn't give a damn. John had bought a pair of long johns, great big woolly things. We'd gone back to the Bambikino, and said, "Hey, John, we dare you to go and stand in the middle of the street in your long johns with your sunglasses and read a paper. He was getting ready for bed and without saying a word stormed outside and kicked the bucket doors open. People were going up and down the street, and John's there in his long johns reading an English newspaper. We used to do leapfrogging and rolling about on the pavements, but John was by far the most outrageous. He also used to do it with a very deadpan face.

GEOFFREY: On the other hand, people say he was actually a very gentle, sensitive guy.

BEST: Very much so. There were two definite sides to John, which I was fortunate to see. One was the outrageous guy onstage who loses his temper, takes the mick, and genuinely acts the goat. But the other John, which the public didn't see, was a very loving, tender person. That came out with his initial love and tenderness for Cindy.

GEOFFREY: Still, there was great anger inside of him. He used to hit her and things like that.

BEST: That may have happened. I'm only talking about my experience, and from what I could see, you never saw that.

GEOFFREY: Was John very much in love with Cyn?

BEST: Yeah, we used to talk. For all the screwing about with the girls, there would be moments we'd be relaxing. John and I would go and have a couple of quiet beers, just to sit down and chew the fat. And he'd talk about Cynthia and how much he missed her.

GEOFFREY: Tell me about when Epstein came on to the scene for the first time to have a look at you guys.

BEST: That was as a result of the many inquiries going into NEMS for the record, "My Bonnie." He found out we were playing the Cavern, which was only about a hundred yards from his door, basically. He came down and must have been very impressed with what he saw because he left a message that he wanted to see us. Talking to him afterwards, he was just captivated by the charisma, the sensuality, the force which was coming out from the Beatles as a unit.

GEOFFREY: It is well known he was very gay. Do you think he fancied you guys?

BEST: He may have done. The thing with Brian, he made it quite clear when we went up to see him. He said, "I have no musical knowledge nor do I know very much about show business or the record business." He laid it on the line, so at least he was genuine. At that time we needed someone who could pull strings a little for us. He had a reputation as a good businessman. He was always very honest with us. He didn't say, "I promise to make you all stars." He simply said, "I'll be prepared to do what I can." And we accepted him for that.

GEOFFREY: I have yet to hear anyone say anything bad about the guy. The bottom line, I guess, was that he was a real gentleman.

BEST: He was. His personal life had nothing to do with anything, as far as we were concerned. What amazed us was he was trying to get as close to us as possible. He wanted to be a part of it. He could see we were a very tight unit. He even wanted to dress the same as us. He even started wearing leather jackets.

GEOFFREY: You guys—John and Paul in particular—could sometimes be very cruel to him. Is that true?

BEST: Yeah. He took a lot of verbal abuse, which I think really hurt him. You could see the expression on his face sometimes like, "Why pick on me?" or, "What have I done to deserve this?" But he didn't ever hold a grudge. Whether he ever mentioned it to them personally, I don't know. But as a group, no, never.

GEOFFREY: What do you remember about John's life with Aunt Mimi?

BEST: I only went up there a couple of times, actually.

GEOFFREY: She wasn't too encouraging as regards the band, was she?

BEST: No. The first time I went up there to see Mimi, John turned around and said, "Oh, you're gonna meet Mimi." I said, "Fine." He said, "Look, let me just warn you she's a little bit, I won't say straightlaced, but she's a little severe in her approach to what I'm doing, and the way I go around. So, if she says anything, don't pay any attention to her." Actually, she was fine. She just sort of laughed and joked.

GEOFFREY: Do you feel there was a competition between you and Paul as regards the group?

BEST: Not unless Paul took it upon himself that there was going to be a rivalry. Lots of people have said it was the jealousy factor. My answer to that is if he was jealous, then it was a bloody stupid thing to be. I mean I was never vying to be number one.

GEOFFREY: Did you ever sing lead on anything?

BEST: On a couple of songs, yes. "Matchbox," "Peppermint Twist," "Roses Are Red." A few of times I got up and sang.

GEOFFREY: Pete, do you know why you were sacked from the group?

BEST: No. I wish I did. I think as time goes on, there's more and more information coming out. It's becoming a bit more open now. Suspicions which we've had in the past are now beginning to come to light. But to actually say, *I know the reason.* No. A lot of it tended to be the fact that they didn't want me the focal point of the band, being the drummer. I was taking too much attention away from them. As I've said before, if that was the reason, they're damn stupid.

GEOFFREY: I put this to Mike McCartney, and he said, "They would have had had a better chance of success if they had a really good-looking drummer who was a combination of Tony Curtis and James Dean, moody and magnificent, and these two crazy, lively guys doing the vocals. It would have been that much bigger."

BEST: This was the ironic thing about it.

GEOFFREY: You were a complement to their wildness and aggressiveness, being so laid-back and cool.

BEST: Look, we were a unit. If the birds screamed and paid more attention to me, as far as I was concerned, it didn't make any difference. They were simply contributing to what the Beatles were. If they came to see the Beatles or they came to see me, it didn't make any difference because they were screaming and shouting and it added to the overall atmosphere. If that was the reason, then as I keep stressing, they were bloody stupid!

GEOFFREY: Well, personally, I'm convinced it certainly wasn't because you weren't a good enough drummer, as legend sometimes has it. That was a convenient, accessible, tidy little reason to give people to skirt around the real question. As a matter of fact, Bob Gallo [Best's former producer] told me in no uncertain terms that you're actually a bit better than Ringo. Anyway, you were certainly *as good*, if not better than, Ringo Starr, as a drummer.

BEST: I've always advocated it. There's drummers in Liverpool who swear that I was top dog as drummers go.

GEOFFREY: Obviously, it's been hell for you. You're world famous now as the bloke who wasn't quite good enough, and that must feel really terrible.

BEST: But there's always two sides to it. That's the way I look at it. Sure, by a Kiffey trick, I was ousted. I didn't become part of the acclaim, which we worked for. So, okay, there was some heartache. But now I have a great family and good friends. I can do basically what I want to do without fear or trepidation. I'm still a happy guy. As long as I'm happy and healthy, that counts for an awful lot.

GEOFFREY: Did it take a long time to come to terms with it?

BEST: Many years of heartache and resentment.

GEOFFREY: Did you ever ask the Beatles personally what happened?

BEST: No, I never saw them, it was a funny thing.

GEOFFREY: Not only did the band end that day, but the friendships ended as well, didn't they, in Brian's office?

BEST: Basically, yeah. But I actually played on the same bill as them later on two occasions. I joined another group and we were runners-up to them in the Mersey Beat poll.

GEOFFREY: Did you ever speak to them?

BEST: There was nothing mentioned. There was just a stone-cold silence from that day to this.

GEOFFREY: Mona said they came to the Casbah afterwards.

BEST: I wasn't here. It was still an open house.

GEOFFREY: You were good friends with Neil Aspinall,* weren't you?

---

*Neil Aspinall is the Beatles' longest-surviving employee, having been with the Beatles from the early days in Liverpool right up to the present day. He has, I might add, suffered several near-fatal heart attacks.

BEST: Oh yeah. We always got along very nicely.

GEOFFREY: Did that friendship go that day as well?

BEST: The funny thing was, Neil was with me that day I was sacked. We'd gone down in the van when I met Brian. When I came out of NEMS he looked at me, and said, "Peter, what's happened? You went in happy as Larry and you've come out as though you've got your crotch kicked." I said, "Basically, that's what happened. They've kicked me out." Neil turned round and said, "That's it, if you're out, I'm out." Later, we went for a couple of pints just to appease the situation and talked. I said, "Look, Neil, they're going places. You can feel it." We had the recording contract by then and it was an inner belief. We *knew* it was going to happen. So I said, "What's the use in cutting your nose to spite your face? Stay with them." He said, "Well, okay," and he stayed with them.

GEOFFREY: And he's still with them to this day.

BEST: Well, he's director of Apple. Whatever he does, he's the guy. He put in a lot of hard work. He progressed, he became their road manager. What he's got now, he worked pretty hard for.

GEOFFREY: What would you say if you met Paul McCartney and had a chance to sit down and chat with him? And what do you think he would say?

BEST: As for me, the animosity's gone.

GEOFFREY: You wouldn't want to sock him, would you?

BEST: No. That would defeat the whole object. It might just be embarrassing. I don't know how he'd feel about it. I should imagine, knowing Paul it would be a case of, "Hi! How ya doing?" Where the conversation would go from there, I don't know. You couldn't rehearse it.

GEOFFREY: When the Beatles went out and started doing *Sgt. Pepper*, *Magical Mystery Tour*, the White Album, *Abbey Road* and *Let It Be*, did you enjoy the Beatles' *new* music?

BEST: When they got into the psychedelic era, as far as I was concerned, that wasn't my cup of fish. That wasn't the Beatles for me. I admire them for what they were doing because it was something different. They were leading the world in the sounds. But my memories of the Beatles was of their early stuff. That was really the Beatles to me.

GEOFFREY: Did you follow their careers?

BEST: Not avidly. I never made a point of it because you didn't have to.

You'd switch the radio on. The papers were full of it. The concert in Tokyo. It was in the shops. It was all around you.

GEOFFREY: Was it the same thing with their solo albums after the Beatles finally broke up?

BEST: Yeah, in my opinion Paul has more or less dominated the scene as the solo artist. He is a great songwriter. You can't take that away from him. A very talented guy. But it would have been interesting to see how John would have challenged him as solo artist had he lived. George went completely out of music and into Handmade Films. Ringo did a few things but really didn't have much of a solo career. But the two the eyes of the world were on was John and Paul, and that would have been very interesting.

GEOFFREY: Tell me about the moment you heard John had died. Was that very tough for you?

BEST: Yeah. A lot of people said, "What difference does it make to you? You hadn't seen the guy for twenty years." I said, "What you fail to remember is that I have very fond memories of the guy." I knew him for three, four years. I spent a lot of time with him, we battled for one another, we fought for one another. We swapped beds with one another in Germany and all the rest of it. I had a lot of respect for him. It upset me deeply because I knew the guy and I had great respect for him, and I still have very, very fond memories of him. I always will.

GEOFFREY: Do you have any show business aspirations today?

BEST: I would be open to offers. I have had offers.

GEOFFREY: You mean you're just waiting for the right offer, is that it?

BEST: No, I've got an awful lot to consider.

GEOFFREY: You have a career, an established life here. You wouldn't want to jeopardize that on a lark.

BEST: No. There's other things . . . It would depend. It would have to be the merit of the offer. But I would give it serious consideration. A lot of thought would have to go into it.

GEOFFREY: I guess you realize in America right now, "Twist and Shout" is in the top ten, the Monkees, which is a shit group, has probably made a million or two in the last month alone.

BEST: A sixties comeback.

GEOFFREY: There's such an aura, mystique, and charisma about you. People want to know more about you.

BEST: It sounds great the way you make it sound so positive. But I'd have to see. If it's going to happen, it'll happen. Because my cards are planned, that's the way I look at life, okay? I wasn't meant to be part of the phenomenon, even though the miniphenomenon had already started. Who's holding the deck for me? It's got to be fate.

GEOFFREY: The other thing was, in all, there were probably only about six Beatles. There were other guys who bounced in and out, but there were really only John, Paul, George, Ringo, you, and Stu. That is a very select group of six human beings. Sadly, two of them are now dead. There are now only four Beatles left alive in the world, and you're one of them. George Harrison said that the best music the Beatles ever made was in Hamburg, when you were their drummer. You were the tightest group no matter what anyone says. You weren't with them for a number of years, but you were with them for about half the time they existed, their acknowledged peak as performers, and today you're still around. The Beatles, as it turns out, may be remembered as the Beethovens of their day. How does that make you feel?

BEST: When you meet people like yourself it sets the adrenaline flowing and it's nice. I've always been willing to talk about it. I didn't pull shutters down and close myself off. It's great to see people feeling the way they do, the admiration, the loyalty and the remarkable tenderness. It gives me a very good feeling.

GEOFFREY: Bob Gallo once told me recently that the album you did with him [Best of the Beatles] didn't really work because there was still a bad taste in the mouth of some of the fans. "If the Beatles kicked him out, he must be no good," and "Stay away from him, he's poison." But now that has turned itself around. Everyone has grown up, and those feelings have been transformed into a deep respect, admiration, and even love.

BEST: Look, I don't go climbing the walls and say that I *must* get back into show business because I feel that if I'm meant to go back into it and the breaks are going to be there . . .

GEOFFREY: We will close the interview now, but first let me ask you just a few more quick questions. I'll shoot you the name of some people, and you give me an impression or remembrance. Mal Evans.

BEST: A gentle giant. A great guy who started as a Beatle fan and became the Beatles' road manager.

GEOFFREY: Brian Epstein.

BEST: Polite, reserved, he knew people credited him with losing millions for the Beatles, but the way I look at it, he also made millions for them as well.

GEOFFREY: Cynthia Lennon.

BEST: A very nice, deep, tender person.

GEOFFREY: George Harrison.

BEST: Still very much into his music. Always was, and it's great to see. Although he stepped out of the limelight for a few years and stayed away from the music, he is now coming back into it again.

GEOFFREY: Allan Williams.

BEST: What can you say about Allan? A Welshman with a great sense of humor.

GEOFFREY: John Lennon.

BEST: John was the closest to me as far, as I'm concerned. As they say, there are two sides to John, but I was fortunate to know both and he was one hell of a person.

GEOFFREY: Thanks, Pete.

GERRY MARSDEN

Liverpool, 1986

GEOFFREY: Tell me about your first meeting with the Beatles.

GERRY MARSDEN: They were called the Quarrymen and I was with the Gerry Marsden Skiffle Group. We played a show together—I think I was fourteen or fifteen. The nice thing was, we got on well then and we're still basically getting on well together.

GEOFFREY: You used to gig with them?

MARSDEN: Yes, in fact, one time at the Liverpool Town Hall we formed a big band. It was the Beatles and ourselves. It was good fun.

GEOFFREY: When you met the Quarrymen was Paul with them yet?

MARSDEN: Yes, sure. There was Paul, John, George, and Pete Best.

GEOFFREY: What about when Pete Best was replaced by Ringo? Tell me about that.

MARSDEN: I think the reason was that George Martin, their recording manager, didn't like Pete. But he was a good drummer, he had a lovely rock'n'roll feel. He was tremendous, so I don't know really why the split occurred. It was sad because Pete was a good lad. Ringo was playing with a band called Rory Storm and the Hurricanes.

Gerry Marsden, the congenial lead singer of Gerry and the Pacemakers, has been friends with the Beatles from the very beginning.

GEOFFREY: Do you think Ringo's personality fit in better with the group than Pete's? Best being more laid-back, the James Dean type.

MARSDEN: I don't think so. Pete was a good-looking guy, for Christ's sakes, and lots of girls, fans of the Beatles, liked him. As I say, I think it might be George Martin saying Ringo was better. I don't know.

GEOFFREY: Give me a John Lennon anecdote we haven't heard before.

MARSDEN: There's a million I *could* tell you, but I *can't* tell them, really. John was a great friend of mine. We spent many years together. John was not as aggressive as people say. That's what I always notice when I read these books about John being a tough teddy. John wasn't a teddy boy. I mean, John was always the last guy in a fight and that's the truth.

GEOFFREY: But he had a big mouth, right?

MARSDEN: Yeah, but that's different than fighting. If a fight occurred, John wouldn't be first in line. The saddest thing was, when John was killed, I think he was reaching his peak. He was a great guy, not at all an aggressive person.

GEOFFREY: Let me toss off a few names and you give me just a few one-liners, okay? Brian Epstein.

MARSDEN: Brian had more charisma than our good queen.

GEOFFREY: No pun intended, right?

MARSDEN: Not at all, no. Brian had great charisma, and he could see what the Beatles had. Eppie also had the connections to meet people who were out of our level. A great, great man.

GEOFFREY: Mal Evans.

MARSDEN: Big Mal, God bless him, was great. He was typically rowdy. Basically he and Neil worked hard. They did their jobs correctly.

GEOFFREY: George Harrison.

MARSDEN: George, God bless him, yeah.

GEOFFREY: Do you see George anymore?

MARSDEN: No, I haven't spoken to him for many years.

GEOFFREY: Let me interrupt you a second. George lives just down the road in Henley. How come you don't go and see him?

MARSDEN: We'd love to see each other. There's no animosities. We're all good friends. Paul McCartney is still a great friend. I see Paul in obscure places like Perth, but it's not that we don't want to see each other. And George, okay, he's in Henley, but I live up here. George was an integral part of the Beatles. He wasn't a great genius like John or Paul, but

George, bless him, fitted in and played a nice guitar, as he's proved on his albums.

GEOFFREY: He was much younger than the others.

MARSDEN: Age never mattered in bands in those days. If you had the talent, you were in. It was just that John and Paul were so powerful in composing, that's the closest I've ever come to genius, seeing them as kids writing their music.

GEOFFREY: In those days bands did a lot of cover tunes. How was all this original material accepted by the audience?

MARSDEN: The good thing was there were lots of things to play onstage, of course, and this all goes back to Hamburg in 1959, before recording. We played seven hours a night with a fifteen-minute break every hour. So we played lots of music, Gary Lewis, Ray Charles, Arthur Alexander—great American stars. When we were actually writing songs the influence was chiefly the American writers, so when we played it onstage the audiences accepted it. The kids we played for in Liverpool knew what was happening and they loved the new songs. There was never any sort of, "Ugh, that's crap, writing your own gear."

GEOFFREY: Tell me a nasty Hamburg story.

MARSDEN: There are no nasty stories.

GEOFFREY: Come off it, you guys got up to some very heavy stuff over there.

MARSDEN: Heavy gear in those days was nothing. It's only heavy now because people have heard about it through third parties. The aggro was nothing. The whole situation in Hamburg, people make it up. What I would say is that Hamburg taught us musically to be better. It showed us life. But there was no incredible violence.

GEOFFREY: There were knifings, there were people getting bottled in the audience while you were playing, transvestites . . . Am I exaggerating?

MARSDEN: But that's *life*. That's no different than Liverpool, New York, Chicago, Detroit, or Glasgow. People just pick up on it and say it was a heavy scene, but it *wasn't* a heavy scene, we approved of that stuff. Knifings were always very, very rare, as were fights.

GEOFFREY: The bands, I'm told, were pretty well exempt from all that, right? You were protected.

MARSDEN: We had people like Horst Fauscher and his family living in

Hamburg—who became my second family—but we didn't need protection as there was really no violence against the bands.

GEOFFREY: Let me drop in a name we don't really know too much about, Stu Sutcliff.

MARSDEN: Yeah, Stuart, a brilliant bass player.

GEOFFREY: Wait a minute, he was a good bass player?

MARSDEN: In those days, yes.

GEOFFREY: Admittedly, he was *not* a very good bass player, from everything that's been said.

MARSDEN: It depends. Stuart fitted in with the band. Sadly he died at such a young age. I always liked him.

GEOFFREY: What was his relationship with John like?

MARSDEN: The same as mine. You see, John had this thing about relationships. If you and John jelled, then that was it. Period. John wasn't that aggressive or sarcastic.

GEOFFREY: So there wasn't a particular relationship between Stu and John which was any more intense than any others? Because there's this feeling that here was one of John's first intellectual relationships. Together they were getting into art, they were getting into photography, they were getting into leather clothes, they were getting into . . .

MARSDEN: No, that's crap.

GEOFFREY: Thank you.

MARSDEN: It is. Stu had a girlfriend called Astrid who was into photography. She took some lovely shots of the boys which I have at home. They were brilliant, Stu got into that. Stuart was just a nice guy, for Christ's sakes. People write too much bloody crap.

GEOFFREY: When the Beatles got very psychedelic, you didn't follow along, did you?

MARSDEN: No. Basically, I never liked the Beatles' psychedelic situation at all. Their ideas were correct, it just wasn't the Beatles to me.

GEOFFREY: When you think of the Fabs you think of "She Loves You," "Twist and Shout," "I Want to Hold Your Hand" . . .

MARSDEN: "Please, Please Me." Yeah, that to me is the Beatles. It's what John was doing before he was killed. John was going back to his roots. To me the psychedelic period and the Transcendental Meditation crap was a joke.

GEOFFREY: So did you see them during these days and ask them what they were doing?

MARSDEN: Sure, I did. Silly boys.

GEOFFREY: And what did they say?

MARSDEN: They said it was a new field, it's what's happening. I could see it was a fad, just crap.

GEOFFREY: Would you see them during the Apple days?

MARSDEN: Certainly, but that was a different thing. They became businessmen and they couldn't be businessmen.

GEOFFREY: Is that why they broke up? Did they lose their sense of humor?

MARSDEN: When bands have been together for twelve or fifteen years there's no having conversations together. You know everything about everybody else and it just gets very boring. The breakup was inevitable. They would have broken up at some time in their career. I don't think it was because of Apple. They were only a band. They were only kids playing and it got very heavy.

GEOFFREY: Why do you think the Beatles are so important today?

MARSDEN: Because they changed the whole concept of music. Basically, they were just four guys from no background, not a star school, not from the States, not too good-looking, and they proved you don't have to be all that. Their lyrics were nice, the music was pleasant. Very, very simple type of songs.

GEOFFREY: You did "How Do You Do It," didn't you? It was rejected by the Beatles.

MARSDEN: I'm so glad they rejected it, or I wouldn't have had my first number one record. That was written for a guy called Adam Faith. George didn't like it.

GEOFFREY: I've heard that George Martin once guaranteed that whoever recorded "How Do You Do It," would have a number one hit and the Beatles said, "Look, we're sorry, but we're doing 'Please, Please Me.' " Isn't that how it went?

MARSDEN: George Martin was an A&R man and "How Do" was written by Rick Murry through Dick James Music. Adam Faith didn't like it. I liked it though because I thought, "God, now that's a record." I can make a record and that's why I did it. I don't think George, God bless him, could ever be that clever to say that whoever recorded "How Do" would have a hit. If the Beatles would have recorded it instead of "Love Me Do," they would have had their first number one record.

GEOFFREY: How do you remember George Martin?

MARSDEN: George was a very pleasant guy. He had been recording people like Matt Monroe, Shirley Bassey, and so on. He wasn't into the pop scene basically. Decca had turned down the Beatles, which was rather sad for them, and George got in with the boys through Paul McCartney, a great genius. John didn't have time at all to talk to A&R men, which Paul did. So George, to me, was a truly lucky man to get the Beatles. That's all I can say. Without the Beatles I don't think George would be as big a name as he is today.

GEOFFREY: He hasn't really done much since with any other groups.

MARSDEN: No, he does lots with Paul because Macca goes to his place in Montserrat. The Beatles really helped George.

GEOFFREY: Regarding Rory Storm and the Hurricanes, apparently Rory was intensely charismatic and good-looking. Everybody liked him. There were so many groups back then, why did the Beatles click so much more?

MARSDEN: They had talent and that's all it is. You're talking about three guys—forget Ringo—John, Paul, and George, and there's this great charisma and talent they shared. When I was a kid every street had a pub filled with music and it was the seamen home from the States and all over the world playing music. We *grew* music in the pubs, as did Glasgow, Newcastle, and Southhampton, but in Liverpool we stayed with rock. When I say rock I mean more rhythm and blues until we found Fats Domino, Chuck Berry, Ray Charles, the greatest rock in the world and the greatest jazz musicians in the world. We never did songs by Cliff, Bill Fury, or Adam Faith. We always stayed with rock.

GEOFFREY: That must have taken a lot of courage. The Shadows were doing these tight little dance steps in their silk suits, but you guys said, "We want to do rock'n'roll." That must have been very tough, going against the market.

MARSDEN: The point you're missing, we never thought of making records. We were playing to enjoy what we were doing. The only time we thought of records was when Brian Epstein came on the scene because Eppie would say, "Why are you asking for these obscure records?" We'd say, "Because we play this music." Then Brian came down to the Cavern one last time, Paul and I got him down, and I've never seen a man find his forte so quickly. He went, "Wow, this is where I should be." Here was a very gentle, lovable man whose father had been selling furniture who didn't know music and just fell in love with the whole idea and saw the potential. We didn't. We always wanted to play music wherever we were. Like I did on the railways. I worked for the woolies, just to get a new guitar. Brian said, "Hang on, you've got a thing here I can sell." We said, "Brian, what do you know about bleedin' records?" He said, "I'll go to London." And Brian went to London and it happened. Even when we had the first hit record we were still basically a nothing commodity. We'd done Hamburg, we played there for three years, seven hours a night playing all types of music. So when we did a live show we had so many numbers to play and out of that came this thing called the Mersey Beat. It was just American gear, not *our* gear, and through that the Mersey Beat evolved. Of course the Mersey Sound is a stupid phrase because nobody actually sounds like each other. But the Mersey Beat came from that.

GEOFFREY: It did to us.

MARSDEN: Sorry, I never sounded like Cilla Black, though I tried to.

GEOFFREY: I suppose you look a bit alike.

MARSDEN: It was basically Epstein who picked up on everything and said, "Right, we can utilize this." That's why Brian was the greatest manager ever.

GEOFFREY: I talked to a lot of people who were closely associated with the Beatles and they say that now that it's all over they find the story of the Beatles somehow very sad. How do you see it?

MARSDEN: I think it must be very sad when you think that they're all worth about £250,000,000. I think that's awfully sad. We never thought we'd make any money at all in music. Why is it sad, for Christ's sake? George is doing what he wants. Paul, God bless him, is into everything, he's a genius. John, sadly, gone so quickly, because John would have been great. Well, *is* great, but he could have been even better. Ringo is doing what Ringo will always do, nothing. Just mess around and have fun.

GEOFFREY: If he heard you say that, would he be angry?

MARSDEN: I don't think so. It doesn't matter. I'm telling you what I think. I've known Ringo since he was a kid—if he's mad, he's mad. If you sat down and talked to Paul or George, there's no sadness. We started playing for *nothing*. So anything we got was a bonus from J. C. God smiled on us. He said, "All right, Liverpool, you're going to happen in the sixties." And we did. We had the best football team in the world and we still have. *Everything was a bonus*. We were only kids playing. It's not sad at all. We were lucky and the Beatles were and Billy J. Kramer was. We never thought about making bread and when we did we invested. The sad thing is, people think, "Maybe I could have been just that much better," but they should be thinking, "I could be working on the railroad in Liverpool and I could be a train washer by now."

GEORGE MARTIN AND JOHN BURGESS

Los Angeles, 1988

QUESTION: The production values of your work with the Beatles were certainly very unusual for pop records. Did your early comedy records influence your later work?

GEORGE MARTIN: It was bound to, I suppose. You do what you do and you do it in the way you think is right. So you build up a technique over the years and I suppose a lot of that rubbed off in things like "Sgt. Pepper" and "Yellow Submarine." When I left EMI in 1965 I thought I might be leaving behind some young people who were pretty good. I felt it would be smart to take them with me. Ronny Richards and Peter Sullivan came and I asked my mate John [Burgess] to join our merry band. The four of us set up what is now AIR Studios in London.

JOHN BURGESS: I remember George saying to me, "The reason we're all getting together is that I am getting older and you guys will have all the success and keep me in the manner to which I am accustomed." As it happened, the Beatles turned out to keep everybody. We all had individual successes, but obviously the biggest earner was the Beatles.

Often called the Fifth Beatle, George Martin was the Beatles' record producer, adviser, and close personal friend.

John Burgess, who has worked with the Beatles, is now business partners with George Martin.

MARTIN: We put everything back into the company, that's how AIR Studios began.

QUESTION: How did you come up with the name?

MARTIN: AIR stands for Associated Independent Recording. We thought of "AIR" first and then figured out the words to fit it.

BURGESS: The studio opened in October 1969. We'll be twenty years old next year.

QUESTION: What about Montserrat?

MARTIN: That didn't happen until ten years later, 1979.

BURGESS: George is always coming up with crazy ideas. Previous to Montserrat, we spent a year and a half . . .

MARTIN: Two years.

BURGESS: Wandering around the world trying to find a boat big enough to put a studio on. We went to Malta . . .

MARTIN: Iceland, Yugoslavia, Poland . . .

BURGESS: Trying to find a boat so that George's dream studio would come to fruition.

MARTIN: And we did find a boat, marvelous, would have been fantastic. One hundred sixty feet long, twin screw . . .

BURGESS: A Yugoslavian ferry boat. A very good bargain, actually.

MARTIN: I wish we would have done it.

QUESTION: Doesn't the sea air present problems?

MARTIN: No, not humidity. In Montserrat we've got sulphur springs and that causes a problem, but very similar to a boat. You can overcome these things. The only problem with a boat is that it would never really be possible to make a recording while under way. You can isolate most sounds, but you cannot get rid of the low frequencies of a diesel engine in a steel structure. Virtually impossible. So you would always have to be at anchor for recording.

It would have been a marvelous ocean-going studio, but oil prices tripled in 1973 and it meant that the overhead of running a diesel-powered ship would increase enormously. I was persuaded to abandon the project and we built AIR Montserrat.

QUESTION: How's it working out?

MARTIN: It's a wonderful place . . .

QUESTION: Only one room?

MARTIN: Yes, only one room, but that's what we wanted. Basically, the whole point of going there is to have the place to yourself. Once you are there, you own the place. You don't have people running around.

On the other hand, we've found that in the London studios people like meeting up with other artists while recording.

BURGESS: Paul McCartney enjoys playing on other people's sessions and getting feedback from other musicians.

QUESTION: You started off as an oboe player, didn't you?

MARTIN: Well, I started off as a writer and then turned to the oboe, "the ill wind that nobody blows good."

QUESTION: Did the oboe influence your development as a musician?

MARTIN: It improved my diaphragm. Not really, no, I just chose the oboe because I liked it. It's a difficult instrument to play.

QUESTION: You were the first producer I ever met, Abbey Road was the first studio I saw, and my first session with the night Ringo was tuning in the BBC for a track on "I Am the Walrus." Later on in Scotland, I was studying King Lear and realized the song has lines from act 4 the play. I don't remember you well, we met, but I was so overwhelmed with the experience. That night, John seemed to be running the show . . .

MARTIN: I wonder if I was there?

QUESTION: Oh, you were there, but you seemed more like a father figure. Ringo was reading a comic book and tuning the radio and John had his hands on those big gearshift faders. The next year, 1968, I was invited back for "Revolution Number Nine" and I don't remember seeing you; George was raiding the EMI tape vaults, John was with Yoko by this time, I learned about splicing, and there was a flurry of activity with huge tape loops running across the room. Was there a period of change, of participation, as a producer?

MARTIN: Yes, the accent changed, but both occasions you mention were when John was experimenting. John liked playing around, but he was not a very good technician. He couldn't handle equipment all that well, but he was always trying to get new and different effects. Now the King Lear thing you're talking about, we used some of that on the record.

QUESTION: Yes, tuned right in off the radio and mixed in.

MARTIN: "I Am the Walrus" was at the mixing stage when you were there. It had already been recorded with cellos and horns and so on. "Revolution Number Nine" was a mélange of sounds. John was moving the faders around during "Walrus" because someone had to do something at random.

After the Beatles ended, John went on to do even wilder things. He didn't have the great toy shop at Abbey Road, but he used to bring me cassettes. "George, can we make a record out of this?" It would be Yoko screaming in a bag and, you know, that was the kind of thing you were seeing in those sessions. In fact, it was in its infancy there. I'm not surprised that you would think he was running the show, but he wasn't really running the show. He was being allowed to indulge himself.

Those sessions had grown out of something before that. The very first really successful bit of that type of work was "Tomorrow Never Knows," which started not with John but with Paul. Paul had a Grundig tape recorder, and he found that by removing the erase head and putting a loop of tape on he could saturate the tape with eternal sound by putting it into record. He could do just one lick on guitar and it would go round and round and round till it saturated itself and you'd have a loop. He would bring in a loop and make some weird sounds. The other boys—John, Ringo, and George—would go away and do the same thing out of it all.

We would assemble them on different machines all over the place, listen to them forwards, backwards, at different speeds, and select which ones we liked and then have them continually going. It was like a primitive synthesizer. You had a loop turning over and it was making a sound. If you opened up a fader, you would hear it. That's when the mix became a performance. While mixing, whatever you brought up at the time would be there. We wouldn't know what point of the loop would appear. It was a random thing. So "Tomorrow Never Knows" can never be remixed again, because all those things happened at that time in that particular way. It's one of the greatest things about that record. It is a page in history that happened there, can't happen again.

QUESTION: I like that.

MARTIN: So did John.

QUESTION: This brings to mind the CD reissue of the work ...

MARTIN: With "Tomorrow Never Knows" all we could do was take that existing master and clean it up a bit.

QUESTION: Have you done any other enhancements?

MARTIN: We actually remixed *Help!* because it wasn't very good originally and *Rubber Soul,* as well. Most of the latter ones were really quite well recorded, if I do say so myself, and just required a little bit of cleaning up for CD.

As for the earlier ones, you know there is still a controversy about mono versus stereo in the early records. We might well go back and make some stereo versions.

BURGESS: It's strange, you're talking twenty-five years ago, and people still want to hear those songs in stereo form. I don't think the stereo could be very sophisticated anyway, could it?

MARTIN: The problem is that a lot of people have heard the bad stereo and like it, they've been indoctrinated. People have said to me it's great to hear Paul and John coming out of one speaker and all the backing out of the other. I think it's terrible, myself. There's no way that I would have agreed to those records being issued as stereo in that form. But if they do want a stereo, we'll do one.

QUESTION: How did the mixup occur on the American releases?

MARTIN: Well, all the early records were done on twin-track for mono records. Never intended to be stereo. But they were issued in America by taking a twin-track tape and using it as a stereo master. The first albums came out over here by Capitol, without my jurisdiction. When I discovered what was happening, I protested against it. By this time, I had left EMI and the Beatles were at a distance from EMI. When I heard what happened, I was told that it was because no Beatle record must be changed and it must be put out exactly as it was. Some idiot had taken this to mean that those twin-track masters should be put out as stereo and, of course, it was never intended. They said they had strict instructions not to play about with the masters.

QUESTION: Getting back to those moments of spontaneity and fun in the studio, do you still . . .

MARTIN: We still have fun in the studio, sure.

BURGESS: Not as much . . .

MARTIN: No, not as much as we used to. There's no fun in taking three days to get a snare drum sound, which some people do . . .

QUESTION: Is the role of the producer changing?

MARTIN: The role of producer has already changed. There are more engineer/producers now. I'm the old-fashioned type, a producer who is a musician and likes to work with an engineer who's an engineer. I think that the two roles are very difficult to combine. I feel that the guy who concentrates on the art—the production and the music—shouldn't really be bothered with whether the microphone is on the blink or not, or whether the EQ switch is dirty or not. I like to say, that's your job.

Similarly, I think the engineer shouldn't be concentrating on his work and have to deal with the tantrums of a drummer who is feeling a pain in his back. There are distinct problems, but if you have these guys working in harmony, it's the best possible team you can get. Having said that, the majority of producers now are, in fact, engineer/producers. Some of them do it extraordinarily well.

As for the future, people are tending to do more things themselves. I'm afraid that maybe I've had something to do with that, but I think that the cachet, the role, the name of producer has become a bit too important. Because of that, people say, "I want to produce. I want to do this myself. Look at my album, I produced it myself!" It's a boast and I don't think it should be. I think they should say, "Let's get a good producer, a good one to help us." The star is still the writer and the singer is still the most important part of a record.

GEORGE MARTIN

London, 1987

QUESTION: Why is Ringo performing the vocals on "A Little Help from My Friends"?

GEORGE MARTIN: Well, that song was especially written for him. That was the standard practice, we would always have one Ringo vehicle on every album. And Paul had the idea of writing this song which fitted in well with the Sgt. Pepper idea. With creating the Billy Shears character, Ringo *became* Billy Shears, in the same way that all the Beatles became Sgt. Pepper. It was a jolly good song and suited his voice very well and was supported nicely by backing vocals from the group. So it was custom-built.

QUESTION: Why do you feel so strongly that "Penny Lane" and "Strawberry Fields" should have been on Sgt. Pepper?

MARTIN: It was actually designed that way. I mean, we went into the studios in December 1966 in order to start the new album. It wasn't a question of recording "Strawberry Fields" and "Penny Lane," it was a question of beginning work on a new album and those were the titles we started with. That and "When I'm 64." The only reason they didn't become part of the album was that Brian Epstein came to me and said we badly need a single because the Beatles were slipping a bit and he didn't want that to happen, quite rightly. So we rushed out a single which was the best coupling ever, I think. It was so good that it didn't make number one the first week for the first time. It was kept out of the English charts by Engelbert Humperdinck with "Release Me." So that's justice for you. And in those days we liked to give as much value for the money as we could to the public and, wrongly, we decided to keep our singles separate from our albums. Nowadays, of course, you must have a single off the album. If we weren't so high-minded then, "Strawberry Fields" and "Penny Lane" would have been part of *Sgt. Pepper*.

QUESTION: Would you have liked to have put them on the CD?

MARTIN: I was sorely tempted to. But then it would have unbalanced everything. I mean, even on the CD there is a little explanation which says we were dickering around with the order and if you wanted to hear the original running order you could program your CD player. So it would have been quite wrong to put on "Strawberry Fields" and "Penny Lane." It would have destroyed history, wouldn't it?

QUESTION: I think people feel that things were done in the making of *Sgt. Pepper* that had a profound effect on the way albums were produced and engineered from then on.

MARTIN: They may have affected other people, but it didn't affect me because I just went on making records the same way I had been doing for ages. As far as technology is concerned, there was no great revolution. *Sgt. Pepper* was done on a four-track, as was *Beatles for Sale*. *Abbey Road* was only the beginning of eight-track, so there wasn't a great deal of difference there. Technology didn't evolve that rapidly. As far as the techniques involved, the kind of musical collage, the use of orchestras and overdubbing was the beginning of something.

QUESTION: So, by the time *Sgt. Pepper* was made, using many overdubs even on as few as four tracks, was a technique with which you were well acquainted.

MARTIN: We overdubbed as much as we could with the techniques and the facilities available. We couldn't overdub too much on two-track, obviously, but we did. Sometimes we would just put down a backing on one side and add the vocals or replace them on the other. We generally did things live. It was quite interesting when I was listening to the tracks for "Yesterday"—it was a four-track, of course, and two tracks were used for the initial performance of Paul with his voice and guitar simultaneously. A third track was the string quartet overdubbed and the fourth track was a first attempt by me to get a better vocal performance.

In fact, it wasn't used except for one little part where you hear a double track voice, so that was obviously an overdubbing technique in the fairly early days of four-track. With *Pepper*, it was a question of going beyond one four-track and on to another because we did run out of tracks. Obviously, if we had had twenty-four tracks available, we would have used them, but we didn't. So I had to go from one four-track machine to another mixing four tracks down to maybe two over a stereo pair, and then filling up another two tracks.

QUESTION: So it was bouncing down rather than syncing two machines?

MARTIN: Absolutely. Syncing didn't exist, therefore we didn't have any sync unit which enabled two machines to run together. It was hit or miss. Even when we overdubbed the orchestra in Number 1 Studio for "A Day in the Life," we just ran the machines in sync by hand. In other words, they weren't in sync and you can hear that. If you listen, you can hear the ragged ensemble of the orchestra because there are several orchestras coming in slightly at a distance from each other.

QUESTION: Did your role as producer on *Pepper* change from the way it had been before? When you started with the Beatles on the early albums, they were quite rightly totally subordinate to yourself as the experienced person. They were new to their craft, certainly in a recording studio. By the time you got to *Pepper*, which is a great leap in inventiveness all around, how much greater part were they taking in the building of the album musically.

MARTIN: Oh, very much so. Obviously, Paul and John were the prime movers of *Sgt. Pepper*, Paul probably more so than John. But their inspiration, their creation of the original ideas, was absolutely paramount, it was fundamental to the whole thing. I was merely serving them in trying to get those ideas down. So my role had become that of an interpreter, particularly in John's case, who was not all that articulate. His ideas were not very concise, so I had to try and realize what he wanted and how to effect it. I would do it either by means of orchestras, sound effects, or a combination of both. The songs in the early days were very simple and straightforward, you couldn't play around with them too much. But here we were building sound pictures and my role was to interpret those and realize how to put them down on tape, which we eventually did.

QUESTION: It's been reported that since the band had stopped touring about six months before recording *Sgt. Pepper*, this was their most prolific period as recording artists and writers. In the case of John and Paul, did you notice any change in attitude or ability regarding songwriting and performance?

MARTIN: Well, yes, because the last track we recorded on *Revolver*, in fact, pointed the way to the future, and that was "Tomorrow Never Knows." Which was a very imaginative track, you could say almost psychedelic, because it was John's idea. The song was based on the *Book of the Dead* and it was very wordy material, pretty far-out stuff. John actually said that he wanted his voice to sound as if he were the Dali Lama singing from a hilltop, but what could we do to give him that effect? What I did was I chose to put his voice through a Leslie speaker for the first time, but then the rest of the track was also pretty far-out. There was a tamboura and Ringo's very insistent drumming. The thing that made it, of course, were all the little tape loops the Beatles themselves had prepared at home on their Grundig recorders. They were into experimenting and they always wanted to try different things. It was Paul who hit upon the idea of removing the erase head on his tape recorder. Then playing some stuff, maybe just a guitar phrase into the microphone, and if he made a loop of tape that would go around and around, the effect was of saturation so that the tape would absorb no more. He would then have a piece of concrete music. They would bring these tapes for me to listen to. In the case of "Tomorrow Never Knows," they brought over thirty tapes and I played them at different speeds, backwards and forwards. I selected some, and they became the input of that particular track. This kind of work, this building up of sounds and collages, was exciting. I enjoyed it and they thought it was great fun and part of discovering life for them. That really pointed the way to *Pepper*, which became an experiment in itself.

QUESTION: Is it true that there were three songs which were recorded but never included and indeed have never been released in any form? Harrison's "Pink Litmus Paper Shirt," Lennon's "Colliding Circles," and "Peace of Mind"—do any of those ring bells with you?

MARTIN: I haven't any recollection of them at all. Quite often they would do busking things and they would put down something, a little bit of nonsense. A lot of the songs didn't have titles when we recorded them, so it is quite possible that someone, at a later date, has found this and said, "Oh, that's 'Peace of Mind.'" But I have absolutely no recollection of anything like that. They couldn't have been very good.

QUESTION: Was the laughing at the end of "Within You, Without You" George Harrison's idea and if not, did he like it? Bearing in mind it was his only song on the album.

MARTIN: It was George's idea and I think he just wanted to relieve the tedium a bit. George was slightly embarrassed and defensive about his work. I was always conscious that, perhaps, I didn't devote as much attention to George as I had the other two. I actually think that "Within You, Without You" would have benefited a bit by being shorter, but it was a very interesting song. I find it more interesting now than I did then. I think it really stands up extremely well.

QUESTION: Going on to orchestration and arrangement: this was entirely your responsibility and, considering it was done on four-track, did that present a problem?

MARTIN: Well, no, because it was just a question of recording in stereo on whatever we did. So on "A Day in the Life," for example, I didn't use the whole four tracks or even the four-track machine. Incidentally, when we had the orchestra in the Number 1 Studio, we would be playing to a guide track, which was an existing rhythm track, of "A Day in the Life" on one four-track machine, but we were not recording on it. We were recording on another machine, which was wild. At a later stage I just laced the thing together, so that I used a four-track machine, but I wouldn't be recording the whole orchestra because I'd probably only be using two of them in a stereo effect.

QUESTION: So you were using a sort of matched pair of stereo microphones for the entire orchestra.

MARTIN: That was what I invariably did for most of the orchestras I recorded. Later on we started dividing up the orchestra into more segments, but if you get the balance right, you have to come down to stereo in the end, so you might as well do it then.

QUESTION: Is *Sgt. Pepper* your favorite album of all the Beatles' albums?

MARTIN: It's not really my favorite, but I do like it very much. I'm very happy I was involved in it, but I have a sneaking regard for *Abbey Road* as being a better album. Don't ask me why, except I think it's such a nice contrast between one side and another. And there's some great writing on it too.

QUESTION: What are some of the particular tricks you played on tape? Two things that constantly come up are the famous run-out groove, and the organ music "For the Benefit of Mr. Kite"?

MARTIN: The run-out groove was just a giggle, a silly schoolboy prank. I think it was probably Paul who said, "When you have an automatic record player, the record lifts before you reach the run-out groove on the end." But in the old days before you had an automatic, the needle would get stuck in that groove and go round and round forever. Paul said, "It's just a terrible hissing noise, why don't we put some music in that? So if people don't have the modern machines, they will hear something a lot less singsong." So we said, "All right, let's do it." They just went down into the studio and said, "Sing the first thing that comes into your head when I put the red light on." And they did that. They hadn't got any prior warning, all four of them sang something quite ridiculous, and I lopped off about two seconds of it at random and then stuck it round in a circle and laid that in the groove. We also put in a fifteen-kilohertz note for dogs. Again, a stupid prank, but it was fun. Later on, I believe the vinyl discs had that removed, so that now, quite a few discs don't have it. And, of course, the problem came when I put it over to CDs. CDs don't have run-out grooves. What we thought what would be nice was to go back and have that again, so we just gave the sound as though it were a run-out groove. We had several revolutions going on and it gradually fades at the end. Giving an idea to people what it was all about.

QUESTION: And the "Mr. Kite" thing was basically the same operation, but for a different reason.

MARTIN: Well yes, "Mr. Kite" was an attempt to create an atmosphere. John wanted a circus fairground atmosphere for this song. He said he wanted to *hear* the sawdust on the floor, so I had to provide that. And apart from providing this sort of organ sound, I wanted a backwash of sound, as tin on metal is a sound. You know when you go into a fairground and shut your eyes and listen, you hear everything; you hear rifle shots and hurdy-gurdy noises and people shouting, and so on. Well, that is what I wanted to convey, so I got a lot of old steam organ tapes, which played things like "Stars and Stripes Forever" and Sousa marches and chopped them up into one-foot sections. I then joined them together again, sometimes back to front. The whole thing was to create a sound that was unmistakably that of a steam organ which had no particular tune at all. By putting that in very quietly in the background it gave that sort of fairground, open-air effect.

QUESTION: Your studio equipment, very briefly, at the time of *Pepper* . . .

MARTIN: A Studer four-track, which used one-inch-wide tape. These were sort of standard machines made in Switzerland or Germany and mixed down on BTR twin-tracks. We had Fairchild compressors that we still use today, by the way. Which are the old valve-operated compressors, awfully good, Neumann microphones where it was possible, because they just were coming out then. And the old antiquated EMI disc cutter in Number 2, which was pretty primitive.

QUESTION: But obviously effective.

MARTIN: Oh yes, it was clean, that was the main thing.

QUESTION: Geoff Emerick worked with you as engineer. Was anybody else directly involved on a notable level in that recording?

MARTIN: We had lots of second engineers. The main second engineer was Richard Lush, who I believe is now working in Australia. Phil McDonald was second engineer—he's now quite a well-known bigwig—and lots of other people. We even had maintenance engineers working on sessions as engineers. Quite often the Beatles would come in on a session without any warning and by this time they'd gotten pretty important. They would ring me up in the morning and say, "Want to come in tonight at eight o'clock?" And if the guy wasn't around, we just used whoever was. In fact, Dave Harris who is our technical director of the AIR Group here, was maintenance engineer at Abbey Road in those days. And he reminded me that on the first recording of "Strawberry Fields," he did the engineering; Geoff Emerick and I weren't there because we were attending a Cliff Richard opening. And we arrived about eleven o'clock at night, after he had done the first track. So that was the kind of thing that happened.

QUESTION: Was Ken Townsend involved?

MARTIN: Yes, he was, because Ken, alongside Dave Harris, was maintenance engineer, in fact, senior to Dave. Ken was always involved in creating toys for us to play with. I don't think he actually did any direct recordings, if I remember, but he was always around in case something went wrong.

QUESTION: And for the record, of course, you would say that Ken is now general manager of Abbey Road and still there after all these many years.

MARTIN: Indeed he is.

QUESTION: Did the Beatles themselves ever become interested in studio technicalities?

MARTIN: Not in technical terms. They never wanted to know how a thing worked, they just wanted to know that it *did* work and what it did. George was the most technical one, he is the bloke who could mend a fuse. The others weren't, really. John, the least of all. John never bothered with the intricacies of things, he just wanted it down and was rather impatient.

QUESTION: On a slightly more delicate subject, EMI and maybe for the Beatles themselves: relationships at that time were possibly getting strained, certainly between the Beatles and EMI. Were you aware of any such tensions? Is tension part of the magic mix of *Sgt. Pepper?*

MARTIN: Well, they themselves, the Beatles, I don't think were very strained. I think the strain of fame and touring had taken its toll. I think they were going through a period when they secretly wanted not to be famous and go back to being ordinary people again. Which is maybe a psychological explanation of why *Sgt. Pepper* existed in the first place, because it was a band they could refer to, like the Beatles. They often refer to the Beatles as being somebody quite separate. In the same way that Paul, I, and George look back on those days as though it were other people doing it rather than ourselves. Between the Beatles and EMI, they were always antiestablishment. Even when I first met them in 1962, it was them against the world. And anybody who existed in any authority was someone they wanted to be contemptuous of. It was part of their makeup. Fortunately I didn't come into that category because I was already a maverick with EMI, so they kind of sided with me, in a way.

QUESTION: And after *Sgt. Pepper*, how many more albums were there?

MARTIN: After *Sgt. Pepper*, then the next one, of course, was the White Album, *Magical Mystery Tour, Let It Be,* and then *Abbey Road.* In between that were all the odd singles. The next immediate thing that I remember after *Sgt. Pepper* was "All You Need Is Love," which was the first live television broadcast to over two hundred million people.

QUESTION: You double-tracked a lot of vocals on the Beatle records, didn't you?

MARTIN: That all started in the early days with the Beatles when I was recording not only them, but Billy J. Kramer and Gerry and the Pacemakers, and so on. I started double-tracking voices way back in 1962. I thought it was a useful technique for getting different sounds. John, in particular, was always wanting his voice changed, so we did quite a lot of double-tracking. But I used it quite a bit with Billy J. Kramer as his voice sounded very good double-tracked. When it came to the Beatles, they had gotten a little bit fed up with having to double-track everything physically and they said to me, "Why can't we just tell you when we want our voice doubled?" It seemed so simple. I spoke to Ken Townsend about it, discussed the problem and said, "Couldn't we effect some kind of double image by playing about with tape speed or something?" And he went away and worked on it. He came back with a huge machine which was a valve-operated frequency controller. By taking the sound off a playback head, and putting it back again, delaying it, bringing it into line with the live recording, he was able to shift the image or create two images. If you think of it in photographic terms, and imagine two negatives, if you had them overlapping so they're completely identical, then it becomes one and you only hear one sound. If you move one away slightly, and we found that if we moved them away by as much as a ten milliseconds, you get a kind of echoey, what I call a telephone-box effect. Then widen them a bit and you get to about twenty milliseconds, and you get what we think of as ADT or two voices. Widen them still further to about eighty milliseconds or one hundred milliseconds and you get a kind of Elvis Presley echo. We found that out by experiment. The great thing about Ken's device was that his variation of the gap between the two images was done by speed control with this huge power-operated device, which got very hot and it was done manually. There was no automatic wiggling a little knob trying to keep it more less in space. And the very fact that you physically controlled it, that it varied the pitch slightly and gave you a better artificial double-tracking than we have ever heard since. All the devices you have which are digitally controlled now are not as good as those early days.

QUESTION: In fact, you pointed to a difference in what it's called, because you thought of it as "artificial double-tracking." Somewhere along the line, presumably when it became automatic.

MARTIN: There's another word like that which came into use called "flanging," because when John Lennon first heard about artificial double-tracking (and we used it a great deal) he thought it was a knockout. And he said, "How do you do it, George?" Joking, I said, "It's very simple, John. Listen carefully. What we do is take the original ridge and split it through the double-wire vacators flushing plan. Then we bring it back into double-negative feedback." All he could remember about that was double-wire vacators flushing plan. He said, "You're pulling my leg, aren't you? Well, let's flange it again." After that, whenever he wanted ADT, he would ask for his voice reflanged. So *flanged* is a word I've used a great deal. Many years later I was in America and a fellow said, "George, should we flange the vocals?" I said, "Where did you hear that word?" And he said it was a word that comes about from people putting their thumb on the flange of a tape machine. So that's it.

GEOFF EMERICK

Los Angeles, 1992

QUESTION: You took over as the Beatles' engineer from Norman Smith on Wednesday, April 6, 1966. You were twenty years old.

GEOFF EMERICK: You've been studying the Beatles *Sessions* book, yes, that would be correct. I'd started at EMI in 1962, the same month that the Beatles went in for their recording test. I was a second engineer, which meant that you just operated tape machines. I believe my first session as a second with Norman was for "She Loves You." And then I did a lot of Manfred Mann records with him.

The reason I was named as the Beatles' engineer was because Norman wanted to become a producer. I got along well with George Martin because I could keep my mouth shut. As a first engineer with the Beatles, I started with *Revolver*.

QUESTION: Do you feel that the limitations of the studio can sometimes be a challenge that enhances creativity?

EMERICK: You couldn't put forward a better question. I would go into the studio and sit on a chair while Ringo played, listening to the tonalities. You know the microphones that can enhance, or capture, the different

---

Geoff Emerick was the Beatles' longtime sound engineer working on many of their classic recordings.

tones you are hearing. It was a challenge and there were certain things I couldn't do. I had to find other ways to make it work.

QUESTION: With Ringo's drum sound, you were miking much closer than had ever been done before. And it's said you stuffed the famous four-headed sweater in the drum and sent the signal through a Fairchild six hundred sixty tube limiter?

EMERICK: Yes, that's true. To get that sound, I'd first go down and listen to Ringo's drums. Put my ear next to the skin, or to the bottom, looking for the resonance from the skins. We took the bottom skins off the tom-toms and put the mike up inside. This gave us the slap of the top with no resonance of the bottom skin, what a thought. In my opinion, *Revolver* was the album to change all sounds. Better than *Pepper* from a sound point of view.

Prior to that, you probably found one overhead mike, one bass mike, and one snare mike on the drums. Recording mixers only had eight inputs, so we didn't have enough feeds into the board to do much more. We built little premixers and had all sorts of stuff going on.

QUESTION: Was "Tomorrow Never Knows" the first song to use tape loops?

EMERICK: For the Beatles, yes, but I believe George Martin used tape loops before, probably on a *Goon Show* album or a Spike Milligan record. Basically, that was our first use of a primitive "synthesizer." Each of the Beatles had their own Brennell tape recorders at home to play around with and you could actually block off the erase head on those machines. The tape could pass the record head without it being wiped.

If Paul wanted to play a guitar through it, he could build up a strange new sound. He knew that if you recorded on the loop more than a few times, without the erase head connected, you would whack the original sound. You had to do it quite quickly to get the image you wanted. If you went on too long, you'd just get a mess.

That seagull sound on "Tomorrow Never Knows" was just a looped guitar strum, but when we put the loop backwards that's what it sounded like. You have to remember that our tape machines then were about three feet wide and four feet high and we had to put one loop on each machine. For that song, we must have used about eight machines. You had to lace up the machine and then hold the loop out with a pencil to keep it going around. We had the engineers from the maintenance department just holding the loops and then we put the feeds on faders. You just played the tune and because we knew which loops had which notes you could just blend them in.

QUESTION: Are we going to hear more recordings from that period?

EMERICK: My wife, Nicole, and I worked on the famous Beatles *Sessions* album, which has been bootlegged. It was going to be an issue from EMI, with lots of outtakes. We worked on that in Montserrat, but there was never final permission to release it. The album does exist, with a really good alternate version of "While My Guitar Gently Weeps." It was a good album and one day I'm sure it will be issued.

QUESTION: Have all the original Beatles tapes been archived on digital?

EMERICK: Yes. The original master tapes sit in tins, you know. But they have been transferred. The textures and tonal qualities on the CDs, though, are so different that they don't even resemble the original records.

QUESTION: One of your last Beatles sessions as engineer was "The Ballad of John and Yoko," which was also the first Beatles stereo single in Britain. It's interesting that it was only John and Paul playing, because Ringo was making a film and George was out of the country.

EMERICK: Yes, that session was put together in about two days. Malcolm Davies, the cutting engineer at Apple, phoned up and told me he couldn't believe that track. We were always into the sounds, the top on the snare, the bass. Malcolm used to work at EMI and Abbey Road and then at Apple, and when he got the tape he couldn't believe the sound on the snare for the first time, because it lent itself to the sound of that record. It was an AKG KM-56, a condenser, which I had never done before.

QUESTION: Since you worked mainly with four-track machines with the Beatles, did you have to do a lot of ping-ponging?

EMERICK: Some, but not a lot. I was talking with George Martin and he was recently listening to some of the old tapes. He couldn't believe what we were actually laying down on one track; bass, drums, guitar, voices with and without echo. It was just live recording with all the finished embellishments. That's the way we worked.

QUESTION: What about all the rumors that the Beatles were putting subliminal messages on their records?

EMERICK: Nonsense, not true.

QUESTION: It seems to me that it was *Revolver* where all the Beatles' weirdness began.

EMERICK: *Revolver* was the first album I engineered. It was, "Well, Geoff's the engineer. We don't want the piano to sound like a piano. We don't want the guitar to sound like a guitar and we don't want the drums to sound like drums." This was mainly coming from Lennon.

QUESTION: Was this irritating at all?

EMERICK: Not really—it was a challenge. That's when we started using the Leslie speaker. When we first put a voice and a guitar through those speakers it made the most amazing sound ever. It was so tuneful and melodic. "Wow, let's make a whole album of this!" We were creating all these sounds without magic boxes. All the plug-in boxers now are derived from what had to be done mechanically, or by stretching tapes, chopping tapes up, or slowing tapes down.

QUESTION: Is it true you actually had John suspended from the ceiling, swinging around for a vocal?

EMERICK: It was his idea, but it didn't really work out. He'd gone through a funny stage at that time. We'd put the voice through the Leslie and the speaker revolved around. I think he once asked George if he could just plug a voice feed from himself and swing around from the ceiling to get a similar effect. George explained that he would have to have an operation to put a voice box in his throat and have a jack plug attached to his neck.

QUESTION: You and George Martin must have spent a lot of time together on your side of the glass, observing the antics.

EMERICK: Yes, a lot, but the antics weren't too bad, really. Experimentation and playfulness went into the making of those records, which you don't find a lot of now.

QUESTION: Were you part of the raids on the tape libraries for "Revolution Number Nine"?

EMERICK: Oh yes.

QUESTION: Were you actually taking library tapes and cutting them up?

EMERICK: It wasn't as bad as that. We were just taking tapes from the EMI sound effects library. You were allowed to use the tapes and we did.

QUESTION: *Abbey Road* was your final album with the Beatles . . .

EMERICK: Yes, and that was the first time we used a transistorized recording console. EMI made it and at that point I could not re-create the bass drum or snare drum sounds, guitar sounds. Previously I had used tube consoles and tube tape machines. And then we got the new batch of Studer tape machines which were half tube and half transistor.

If you listen to "Paperback Writer," a good example, you really hear the kick of that bass drum. There was no way you could re-create that through a transistorized desk. There are many theories—unnatural harmonics, distortion, whatever—but we couldn't create those sounds anymore. The new desk was a lot smoother, a lot mellower, which gave *Abbey Road* its texture. It's still a great album.

QUESTION: Let's talk about some of your recent projects; the McCartney *Unplugged* project for MTV which was also released as an album. What technical tools did you employ?

EMERICK: Well, it was very simple. First of all, Paul phoned up and asked if I would like to work on this MTV acoustic project, mikes into desks and so forth. There is one particular mixing console I really like, the old API board. Record Plant's remote truck had one and we used it for the America albums here in Los Angeles. There's another in a mobile truck in England; it still sounds so clean and good. Paul wanted to rehearse at his studio for three days. I suggested that we do that with the mobile, get all the sounds and EQ and just go down to the television studio in London with the truck and away we go. That's what we did.

There were no overdubs. We took it down to multitrack and also to DAT. The actual issued album came from the DAT.

QUESTION: You were pleased with the results?

EMERICK: Sure I was, sounds superb. It meant, of course, doing all the echoes at the right time and taking them off. I wasn't under any great direction from Paul; just do it. What you hear on the album is exactly as he sang it. No overdubs on vocals or instruments.

QUESTION: Of all the sounds you came up with for the Beatles, is there any one that you are especially proud of?

EMERICK: I guess it would be "A Day in the Life." The gradual long fade, done manually, was monumental. To make that end crescendo loud, it wasn't written, the orchestra was told to go from A to E in thirty-seven bars and do the best they could. I was playing the faders as the song progressed and realizing that what I wanted was another six dB by the time I got to the end. I pulled the whole thing way up. I'm proud of doing that—how else could you have done it?

QUESTION: Because you were working with the Beatles, did you have the clout to do whatever you wanted?

EMERICK: Oh yes, we could get away with just about anything. With the recording of the drums, I wanted to move closer with the bass drum mike to get that impact. EMI's directive was to place the mike about three feet away. Whilst I was doing this, I was sent a letter from the technical division that said you couldn't do this because of the air pressure against the diaphragm in the microphone, but they would give us permission nonetheless to do it.

QUESTION: Just as Norman went on to producing, how did you make that transition?

EMERICK: Well, I had left EMI and was working with Apple. The record companies were relying so much on the engineer to carry the sessions. The few of us who had some sort of clout could say we wanted a piece of the action. We were not only engineering, we were actually making the record, with all the decisions necessary.

PETER ASHER

Los Angeles, 1993

QUESTION: Tell us about your job as head of A&R at Apple Records. How did this transition happen?

PETER ASHER: I remained friends with Paul throughout that period and he told me a lot about his plans for Apple, what the company was supposed to be, and what they were trying to accomplish. He was aware that I was interested in producing records. Indeed, I had produced a couple after I stopped recording.

The first record I produced was with Paul Jones, who used to be the lead singer with Manfred Mann—"Do-Wa-Diddy" and all those great tracks. I owe him a lot because he was the first person who said he liked my ideas and asked if I would produce his record. A bold step on his part, for which I am grateful. Actually, the first track I produced was a Bee Gees song called "And the Sun Will Shine." It's interesting in retrospect because the rhythm section was Paul Samwell-Smith from the Yardbirds playing bass, Jeff Beck on guitar, Nicky Hopkins piano, and Paul McCartney playing drums. It was a good record, actually, minor hit in England, but didn't do anything in America.

Based on that experience and from working with me on various

Peter Asher is the brother of Paul McCartney's former fiancée, Jane, and was head of A&R at Apple Records. Today, he is a successful record producer.

things, Paul initially asked if I would produce some records for Apple. He also asked if I would like to be the head of A&R to run that aspect of the label. They also hired a man named Ron Kass, who was a real record company executive, an American who used to run Liberty Records. Good man; now, sadly, dead. Ron was the boss and I was second in command to him, running the artistic aspect of the label, in conjunction with whatever quorum of Beatles was in the building at the time.

QUESTION: So you had given up the idea of being a recording artist yourself?

ASHER: I never had any interest in being a solo singer. I'd always liked singing, whether it was singing in the choir at school or doing four-part madrigals; I was more interested in harmony singing and never saw myself as a lead singer. I don't think I have the kind of voice or the style for that, but I still like singing harmonies. On some of the records I produce, I end up singing some of the parts.

QUESTION: What happened to Gordon and what was his last name?

ASHER: Wall. He pursued a solo career for a while and then got out of the music business altogether and went to Australia. He's back in England now and runs a gift shop in a seaside town, last I heard.

QUESTION: You were associated with James Taylor, of course, in the early Apple days. Did you discover him? Was he an American hanging out in London?

ASHER: Well, going back to the Peter and Gordon days, one of the bands we had backing us was called the Kingbees. The lead guitar of that band was Danny Kortchmar and we became great friends. Even when our tour was over, we remained in touch. I used to visit him when I was in LA. He's a wonderful guitar player and since then, as I'm sure you're aware, has become a very skilled record producer and made tons of hits of his own with Don Henley and others. anyway, Kootch was later in a band called the Flying Machine with James Taylor. He and James had known each other since they were about twelve years old and had a duo when they were kids.

When the Flying Machine broke up, James decided to go to London and seek his fortune. I apparently met him at a Flying Machine rehearsal in New York, which I don't remember. Kootch gave him my number and he called and asked if he could play me a tape of his. He

ABOVE: Harrison at the end of the Beatles' days together. (SQUARE CIRCLE ARCHIVES.) BELOW: Inside the Lennons'
"Bag" office at Apple with the parents of convicted mur-
derer James Hanratti. (SQUARE CIRCLE ARCHIVES.)

ABOVE: John and Yoko's extraordinary "Bed-In for Peace," Amsterdam, 1969. (SQUARE CIRCLE ARCHIVES.)   BELOW: Ballooning in the name of love and peace. (SQUARE CIRCLE ARCHIVES.)

ABOVE: Ringo on location during shooting for the amusing *Magic Christian,* costarring Peter Sellers. (COURTESY PINK SHOES CAFE.) BELOW: George answering questions from the media for the now legendary Concert for Bangladesh, 1970. (SQUARE CIRCLE ARCHIVES.)

ABOVE: Meeting with activist Dick Gregory on Ronnie Hawkin's Ontario farm, December 21, 1969. (MORNING GLORY ARCHIVES.) BELOW: Promoting the Lennons' twin Plastic Ono Band LPs with Apple promo man Pete Bennett. (COURTESY PETE BENNETT.)

ABOVE: A pensive George deep in conversation with musical guru Ravi Shankar in the early seventies. (SQUARE CIRCLE ARCHIVES.) BELOW: Krishna guru Srila Prabphupada on his way to visit George Harrison in London, 1972. (PHOTO BY GEOFFREY GIULIANO. COPYRIGHT INDIGO EDITIONS.)

ABOVE: A rare public appearance by John and Yoko at a peace rally in New York in the seventies. (GEOFFREY GIULIANO COLLECTION) BELOW: George Harrsion on tour, 1974. (THE PUBLISHER'S TRUST)

ABOVE: May Pang, Harry Nilsson, and John Lennon hanging out in Hollywood, 1974. (SQUARE CIRCLE ARCHIVES.) BELOW: Paul playing the drums at Denny Laine's birthday party in the mid-seventies. (SQUARE CIRCLE ARCHIVES.)

ABOVE: The McCartneys huddle with Jo Jo Laine and her father backstage at Boston Garden, 1976. (SQUARE CIRCLE ARCHIVES.)   BELOW: Mr. and Mrs. McCartney out for a rare night on the town, 1975. (SQUARE CIRCLE ARCHIVES.)

ABOVE: Denny Laine escorts the young daughter of one of the Fool on a pony ride outside his country home, 1976. (SOMA RASA SERVICES.) BELOW: Arriving at Jimmy Carter's inaugural ball with James Taylor in tow. (SQUARE CIRCLE ARCHIVES.)

ABOVE: Cavorting on London's rooftops during one of the Lennons' many public campaigns together. (SQUARE CIRCLE ARCHIVES.) BELOW: McCartney's magical revolving meditation room in the back garden of his posh London digs. (GEOFFREY GIULIANO COLLECTION.)

ABOVE: Heather and Linda McCartney at a Wings gathering in the late seventies. (SQUARE CIRCLE ARCHIVES.) BELOW: Sultry Jo Jo in repose. (PHOTO BY SESA GIULIANO. COPYRIGHT INDIGO EDITIONS.)

```
876G
   U R G E N T

        LENNON-SUB

   (NEW YORK)-- NEW YORK POLICE SAY FORMER BEATLE JOHN LENNON IS IN

   CRITICAL CONDITION AFTER BEING SHOT THREE TIMES AT HIS HOME ON

   MANHATTAN'S UPPER WEST SIDE. A POLICE SPOKESMAN SAID "A SUSPECT IS IN

   CUSTODY," BUT HE HAD NO OTHER DETAILS. A HOSPITAL WORKER SAID--

   QUOTE-- "THERE'S BLOOD ALL OVER THE PLACE. THEY'RE WORKING ON HIM

   LIKE CRAZY."

        UPI 12-08-80 11:35 PES
```

ABOVE: The tragic news of Lennon's shooting as it first hit the wire at 11:35 P.M., December 8, 1980. (GEOFFREY GIULIANO COLLECTION.) BELOW: Paul relaxing at Air Studios during sessions for his groundbreaking *Tug of War* LP. (SQUARE CIRCLE ARCHIVES.) OPPOSITE: Inside the Dakota, 1983. (GEOFFREY GIULIANO COLLECTION.)

CLOCKWISE, FROM UPPER LEFT: Rocking away on the 1988 *Blue Suede Shoes* special, starring veteran rocker Carl Perkins. (SQUARE CIRCLE ARCHIVES.) Laine following his financial fall from grace after leaving Wings, London, 1990. (PHOTO BY SESA GIULIANO. COPYRIGHT INDIGO EDITIONS.) Lennon's sister Julia Baird during a sentimental journey home to Liverpool, 1986. (PHOTO BY SESA GIULIANO. COPYRIGHT INDIGO EDITIONS.)

CLOCKWISE, FROM UPPER LEFT: Nature boy George communes with the dolphins, 1990. (SQUARE CIRCLE ARCHIVES.) Ringo, out on the road again in 1992, fronting his All Starr Band. (COURTESY CHARLES F. ROSENAY, GOOD DAY SUNSHINE.) Julian Lennon with his great-uncle Charlie in front of a Liverpool theater in 1990. (CHARLES LENNON COLLECTION.) OVERLEAF: Paul and Linda times four during their 1990 world tour. (COURTESY CHARLES F. ROSENAY, GOOD DAY SUNSHINE.)

came by my house that evening with a tape of "Something in the Way She Moves," "Something's Wrong," "Knocking Around the Zoo," and all sorts of fantastic songs. I was knocked out and said, "Listen, it so happens I've just started working for this new label. I'd like to sign you and produce your record." It all fell into place very easily.

James has since mentioned that it was all rather odd that within a couple of weeks of landing in London, he was in the studio with Paul McCartney and hanging out with the Beatles. Fairly startling, but I didn't realize it at the time because I was there anyway and they were my friends.

QUESTION: Proceeding from that tape of his, what did you do musically for James?

ASHER: Too much, probably. When we made that first album, I was very anxious that it really stand out and that each song stand out. I tried to make every song different and with that aim, we did a lot of arranging. One song has a string quartet, one song has horns; I think it may have been a little overdone. Some of the songs sound a bit better now when James does them with a lot less stuff. But on the other hand, the album did get people's attention and it's become some sort of a classic.

James is singing a hell of a lot better now than he was then. If you listen to that record, it's surprising—his voice has gained so much strength and maturity and his phrasing is more interesting since that time. For what it was then, the record is absolutely fine, but listening to it with today's ears, there are things that clearly we could have done better.

What I brought to it, I suppose, was a determination to get people to listen to him and take him seriously at a time when the singer/songwriter era had not yet dawned. Joni Mitchell, Eric Anderson, and people like that were just starting to make waves in America, but they were still pretty much folksingers in a sea of rock'n'roll. My intention was to get people to pay attention to James and realize how good he was, as it has remained to this day.

QUESTION: Why did you leave England in 1970 to start your management firm?

ASHER: Apple had started to get pretty weird. It was crumbling and there was a lot of dissension among the Beatles. Allen Klein had come in and was changing the character of Apple, John was all for him and Paul was against him. All this weird stuff was going on and it became clear that Apple was on its last legs. James wanted to go back to America anyway and I followed shortly after and became his manager. We agreed we didn't know who else should undertake this task, so it made sense for me to try. Based on advice from people I knew, I started managing James and set out to get him a record deal in America.

Henley-on-Thames, 1984

GEOFFREY: Tell me how you first got your big break.

MARY HOPKIN: I appeared on a national television show, which I was very embarrassed about. It was a competition which some agent in Wales had put my name down for. Twiggy was watching. She met Paul a couple of days later. He was telling her all about the Apple label. They were just starting up and wanted people to record for Apple. She said, "Oh, I saw this great girl on television a couple of days ago." So I had a telegram, which I completely ignored. It sat on the mantelpiece for a couple of days.

GEOFFREY: What did it say?

HOPKIN: It said, "From Peter Brown at Apple Records." I thought, "Oh, I'd heard of the Apple Boutique," but it didn't really strike a bell.

GEOFFREY: Do you still have the telegram?

HOPKIN: Yeah, I think my mom has it in a scrapbook somewhere, but I ignored it and she said, "You ought to ring these people back." I said, "Oh well, okay." So I rang this number and this chap with a very strong Liverpool accent said would I come to London and record? I said,

Apple artist Mary Hopkin, known for her folksy, acoustic singing style, was perhaps Apple's single greatest discovery. Her first big hit while at Apple was the lilting "Those Were the Days," followed by the plaintive McCartney-penned "Goodbye."

"Well, that depends on a lot of things." Eventually, he said, "Go and ask your mom if you can come to London tomorrow." That was unheard of in those days. You used to plan for six months for a trip to London from Wales. So my mom came on the phone and he said, "Hello, Mrs. Hopkin, this is Paul McCartney," and she went into shock and so did I because I adored the Beatles. They were my idols. So we went to London the next day and I met with Paul.

GEOFFREY: Did they put you up in a hotel and all that?

HOPKIN: Yeah, I'll say that for Paul. So anyway we went to Dick James's demo studios.

GEOFFREY: And you did "House of the Rising Sun"?

HOPKIN: "House of the Rising Sun" and a few old Donovan songs, it was all terrible. I broke a guitar string halfway through.

GEOFFREY: You must have been devastatingly nervous.

HOPKIN: No, I never really got nervous at that time. I was shy. Terribly shy of Paul, but he was very sweet.

GEOFFREY: So what happened at the end of the day? Did he say, yes, okay?

HOPKIN: I suppose it was just taken for granted that I was in, that I was going to be signed. They had more trouble with my father than anything else, because he was very cautious about the contracts and things. But they immediately signed me up. I think it was about three or four weeks after that Paul said, "I've got this lovely song I'd like you to do. See if you like it," and he strummed "Those Were the Days." I don't think it ever would have occurred to me to say, "No, I don't like it."

GEOFFREY: Where'd you record that?

HOPKIN: At EMI, Abbey Road.

GEOFFREY: Paul produced?

HOPKIN: Yes.

GEOFFREY: How much of an active hand does he actually take in producing?

HOPKIN: A great deal. He sat with Richard something . . . I can't remember his name now, the arranger. He sat with him and sang a lot of the parts. He would say, "I want the string parts to do this and the guitar to do this." Then he actually played guitar, just bits and pieces. He took a great interest in it.

GEOFFREY: Was that the first time you ever recorded?

HOPKIN: Me? No. I'd recorded in Wales. I was a recording artist in Wales from about sixteen, I think.

GEOFFREY: Were they in Welsh, these songs?

HOPKIN: In Welsh, yes, folk songs.

GEOFFREY: How did you first become interested in the guitar?

HOPKIN: At thirteen my grandmother bought me a guitar. I was longing for one. I was a Joan Baez fan. I started playing along with records and teaching myself fingerpicking.

GEOFFREY: So you recorded this song, "Those Were the Days," and it became a worldwide . . . What was it, number one around the world?

HOPKIN: Yes, in thirteen countries.

GEOFFREY: There's a big difference between recording something in a room in St. John's Wood and suddenly realizing that in thirteen countries simultaneously around the world you're the number one singer on the planet.

HOPKIN: It's funny, but I reacted quite calmly to everything. I was delighted and pleased, but it didn't throw me at all. I don't suppose I ever took it very seriously anyway. I was eighteen. I thought, "Oh well, it's all good fun? I'll enjoy it, and see how it goes." I didn't really expect anything from it.

GEOFFREY: What was life like as a singer on the Apple label on a day-to-day basis? Was it good fun?

HOPKIN: It was, yes. It was very interesting to see the whole setup at Apple. It really was like one big party. Like one big happy family, I suppose. But I didn't know the ins and outs, of course. I didn't know what was going on behind the scenes because the business side wasn't as it seemed to be.

GEOFFREY: Did they seem to know what they were doing at Apple?

HOPKIN: No. People like Derek always seemed to be in control, but there appeared to be a lot of hangers-on. The money that was spent was astounding. Booze coming in every day, and God knows what else.

GEOFFREY: Tell us about how your image was put together while you were at Apple.

HOPKIN: I don't think it needed much putting together at that point because I *was* very shy, sweet, and vulnerable. I don't think they had to try. In fact, they did try to exaggerate that, which seemed ridiculous because I was already sugary enough.

GEOFFREY: When you went out to discos for a bit of dancing what did they do?

HOPKIN: If I were sitting somewhere with glasses of wine or Scotch on the table, I'd be whisked away if a photographer came by. It's ridiculous. It didn't need any help, that image. It became a great embarrassment to me, and I think to them, to have me on the label because it was such a sugary image. I mean, they had James Taylor and Jackie Lomax, so it was quite a contrast. But it wasn't my doing. If they'd let me develop in my own way, I'd have come through that.

GEOFFREY: You think maybe if this whole Apple/Beatle thing had never happened to you, it might have been better?

HOPKIN: In some ways, yes. I don't mean to sound ungrateful because, obviously Paul, in particular, did a tremendous amount for me. But I think if I had been left to my own devices, I would have just grown and progressed musically in other ways. I also might have been able to re-tain a little bit more self-respect. I would have only worked at the music that pleased me and I wouldn't have really considered the com-mercial value of it so much.

GEOFFREY: You made four records altogether, didn't you?

HOPKIN: Did I? I only really recorded two albums. The others were com-pilations, I think.

GEOFFREY: You weren't pleased, then, with the music that was presented to you to record?

HOPKIN: Not exactly, no.

GEOFFREY: What was wrong with it?

HOPKIN: It was bubblegum music. It got more and more talky, silly, and shallow. I wanted to do something with more substance.

GEOFFREY: I know that at one point you worked with Donovan. It seems a good combination.

HOPKIN: Yes, I enjoyed it. It was a lovely experience sitting with Paul and Donovan on guitar. They sat on the side playing guitar and I just read straight from the book of Donovan's lyrics. It was lovely. I did "Lord of the Reedy River" and I can't remember the title of the other one, but it's on the *Post Card* album.

GEOFFREY: You came into the Beatles' lives at just about the time they were breaking up. What was that like?

HOPKIN: Well, I attended some of their sessions; but I didn't really pick up on that. I used to sit quietly in the corner taking it all in. It was lovely. I mean, I certainly remember when Allen Klein first came on the scene. It was instant hostility. Everyone hated him.

GEOFFREY: I'd be interested to know your first impressions of John Lennon?

HOPKIN: Oh, I hardly dared speak to John. I was painfully shy at the time. Can you imagine actually meeting your idol, somebody you idolized since you were thirteen?

GEOFFREY: Did the boys seem unapproachable personally?

HOPKIN: They weren't standoffish at all, it was just me at the time. I had the problem. They were very sweet. John was lovely. On various occasions he spoke to me. He was very kind.

GEOFFREY: Tell me about the tune "Goodbye." How did that come about?

HOPKIN: It was the year after "Those Were the Days." Promoting that kept me going for a whole year, playing all these dreadful cabarets, the whole thing. I went to South America as well, which was terrific from the traveling point of view, but the work was God-awful. So it was a year later before "Goodbye" came, and Paul thought, "Oh, I think it's about time Mary should record another song." So he wrote "Goodbye," in about ten minutes flat, I think.

GEOFFREY: Did you like "Goodbye" any better than . . .

HOPKIN: No. I liked "Those Were the Days." "Goodbye" was fun, but I thought it was obviously a step in the wrong direction because by then people had already put me in that little bag.

GEOFFREY: So what would have been the right direction then for you as far as you're concerned?

HOPKIN: Well, I think something more moody, deeper stuff. If I'd been encouraged to record . . . I suppose by the time I got to the end I was more in control. I was choosing more "meaningful" songs then. I hate using that word, but that's what it's about, really. If you're trying to express yourself, you might as well find the right vehicle. And you certainly don't do it through releasing such shallow, silly pop songs.

GEOFFREY: What was it like to be the most famous teenage girl in London there for a while?

HOPKIN: It didn't occur to me that I was.

GEOFFREY: Did fans approach you?

HOPKIN: Yes, yes, but I was never impressed by that. It became more of a nuisance than anything else. I didn't lie in bed at night thinking, "Oh, isn't it wonderful to be so famous?" I just thought, "Oh God, I wish they'd leave me alone!"

GEOFFREY: Were there Mary Hopkin fan clubs and things like that?

HOPKIN: Yes. My mother ran me a British fan club.

GEOFFREY: If you got a new car, a new dog or something, would all that be reported around the world?

HOPKIN: Oh yeah, everything. No, I didn't like any of that. I didn't really enjoy that part of it at all.

GEOFFREY: Tell me about some of the promotional films you made, because obviously these days they are very obscure.

HOPKIN: They all sort of run into each other. Oh, you know just very corny ideas like gazing out longingly from the windows of little thatched cottages and things. I cringe at the thought.

GEOFFREY: One of the things that we touched upon was the fact that I found a certain duality in the way you were promoted because on one hand, you were the virginal, perpetually innocent, wide-eyed, lightweight Mary Hopkin. On the other, your skirts were about two inches away from your ... So I told you today—and you were a little surprised—that a lot of people thought you were rather sexy.

HOPKIN: Really? Oh, tell me more ...

GEOFFREY: Were you conscious that you were a very good-looking girl as well?

HOPKIN: Well, I mean I certainly knew I was popular and, of course, I did have a steady boyfriend.

GEOFFREY: What was it like dating after you became famous?

HOPKIN: Horrible, a real pain. It's just that I was always very suspicious of boys after that unless they were musicians themselves. For a while, I went with one of the guys from the Grapefruit band who were signed to Apple. That was fine, we were on an equal basis. We knew where we stood. But other people outside the business, I was immediately suspicious of. They always expected me to foot the bill if we went to a restaurant or they'd be off telling their mates, "Oh, I went out with Mary Hopkin." It was very difficult to figure out who wanted to know me for me and who wasn't impressed by all the rubbish that surrounded me.

GEOFFREY: Ultimately did you lose interest in the business or did the business lose interest in you?

HOPKIN: No, it's very nice to be able to say that I lost interest in the business. It's usually the other way around, isn't it? I mean, I bowed out at the peak of my career. I could have gone on to do anything I wanted to, I suppose, but I was very disillusioned by that time by the kind of music I was being pressed into doing.

GEOFFREY: Did you ever feel you were hiding behind the microphone, as it were?

HOPKIN: Yes, but isn't that what we all do? I mean, you're actually very shy and quiet, aren't you? I would have liked to be given more freedom to choose what I wanted to do. I was very restricted, of course, they went for all the lucrative things once I had agents. They said, "Oh, Mary, this is great. You'd make a fortune." Regardless of the sort of music I had to do. The quality of the music was appalling after a while, so I just gave it up.

GEOFFREY: Do you wish now you'd done at least a few horrible things just for the money? A couple of them anyway?

HOPKIN: No, because it's hard enough to live down the things I did do. If I'd have done anything worse, I couldn't take it.

GEOFFREY: Of course, you know I don't agree with you on this, but I understand what you're saying. A lot of your music was actually very good.

HOPKIN: I think you're about the only one who thinks so.

GEOFFREY: Did you ever sing backup on any Beatle records or anything like that?

HOPKIN: Yes. I sang on "Let It Be." A little part with Linda and George. I'm not really sure, though, if Paul used the original ones or if he redid them at some point, but it may well be on there.

GEOFFREY: What were you singing?

HOPKIN: Just those very high parts on the chorus, "Let it be, let it be . . ." I mean, the part is certainly still there. I just don't know if he used the one I did with Linda and George or not. We just happened to be in the studio at the time. And I was also on "Hey Jude" with the mob, in the crowd.

GEOFFREY: Where did they get the mob from, then?

HOPKIN: Just people, you know, the secretaries and security guys from the studio.

GEOFFREY: I'm going to throw out some names and you just give me impressions, okay? Let's start with George Harrison.

HOPKIN: Oh, he's a sweetheart. He bought me a wonderful guitar once, which was a great surprise. Could I tell you more about that? I went to one of the sessions. I think it was "Happiness Is a Warm Gun." I remember John strumming away. I'd been sitting there for an hour before the session started. George had this beautiful acoustic guitar, inlaid with mother-of-pearl. I thought it was wonderful. A while later George left. John and Paul were working out "Happiness Is a Warm Gun." They were just going through the chords and things. Later, when George returned, he went back to his guitar and started talking to the others. So, anyway, the Beatles' roadie Mal said, "Mary, come with me for a minute," and he led me out of the studio. There, sitting on the reception desk, was this beautiful classic guitar, a Rameares, which is absolutely wonderful. It was a present from George. He'd just spent an hour hunting around town for a guitar for me and didn't say anything. It was the day of the premiere of *Yellow Submarine,* so when I saw him later that evening I thanked him. But he's always been a sweetheart. Good man.

GEOFFREY: Ringo?

HOPKIN: Well, he's lovable, Ringo. Everybody knows Ringo.

GEOFFREY: Mal Evans.

HOPKIN: Oh, I loved Mal. I was horrified when I heard about the shooting.* I don't know what really happened, of course, but it was awful. Couldn't the police just have shot him in the knees or something? God, they're trained to shoot. They could shoot any part of the body they want. They didn't have to kill him. I mean, he was the gentlest person I've ever known. My sister and I used to go out for drinks with him in the evening sometimes to clubs. He was a darling. I got to know him and his family very well.

GEOFFREY: Linda McCartney.

HOPKIN: Oh, I like Linda very much. She wouldn't think this, but I

---

*On January 5, 1976, Beatles minder, Mal Evans was shot to death by Los Angeles police after they were called to his apartment by a distraught girlfriend. Evans was holed up in an upstairs bathroom with an air rifle, and when the cops burst in he made the mistake of pointing it at them.

think of her like a big sister. Although I hardly ever see her, but I feel very comfortable with Linda.

GEOFFREY: Derek Taylor.

HOPKIN: Yes, I like all these people. Derek was especially wonderful. I used to be terribly in awe of Derek because he's just so wonderful. His command of English is superb. He's a good man, very clever.

GEOFFREY: Allen Klein.

HOPKIN: A creep. A real creep. I didn't like him at all. He's very smarmy.

GEOFFREY: Why? What did he do to you?

HOPKIN: Nothing. He didn't need to. His personality was enough. I was never directly involved with him financially, thank God. I just didn't like the man. I don't like people that try and patronize me.

GEOFFREY: So he was sort of transparent, then, in telling you how wonderful you were.

HOPKIN: Yeah, trying to manipulate me. He'd say, "Do this and that." I remember walking away from him in the middle of a meal once. I just don't like him. I like to think I'm a good judge of character. Maybe I'm not. Maybe that's why I'm divorced now. Certainly with him, he was very transparent.

GEOFFREY: Not only did the Beatles eventually disintegrate, but Apple disintegrated as well. What do you put that down to?

HOPKIN: To optimism, really. I think it was a lovely concept. Typical of the sixties to have this wonderful idea of one big happy family and giving everybody the opportunity to be a success. But it attracts all the hangers-on. I think they realized that after a while. After a lot of money had already been spent and had gone down the drain.

GEOFFREY: What's your life like today?

HOPKIN: Well, sadly my sister and my father died within a week of each other. Then I was seriously ill with hepatitis. That was awful because that came shortly afterwards. So that was a very rough time. I've finally come out of that now. I'm healthy again, everything's fine. I'm feeling settled for the first time in years. I'm sort of at one with myself.

GEOFFREY: Do you have any professional aspirations?

HOPKIN: Well, I really want to sing. I enjoy writing songs. I'd like the opportunity to record my songs and other people's as well. Just do good music and work with good people. I'd like to do one-off projects rather than a full commitment to one thing. I don't really want to be a member of a band. I don't want a full-time career anymore. But projects with people I respect I'd love to do. Yes, I do want to be heard, but it's not for the fame. I never enjoyed that side of it anyway, just the music.

GEOFFREY: Do you still play the guitar and sing?

HOPKIN: No, I play piano and sing. I hardly ever touch the guitar at the moment. I may pick it up again one day, though.

GEOFFREY: You're very private and I know you make it a point to be that way. Do you have to struggle for that?

HOPKIN: Not as much now, I'm thankful to say. A lot of people think I live in the States. A lot of people are surprised that I've lived here all these years. Probably because of Tony, marrying an American. So I suppose in some ways it's been a help. The thing that bugs me now and then is the press, because every time I have a relationship or something, they love to exploit that side of things. They won't mind their own business about my private life. So next time around, if there ever is one, I don't think I'll be quite as polite with the press as I have been.

JACKIE LOMAX

Los Angeles, 1991

QUESTION: John Lennon once said that, as a band, as players, he considered the Beatles to be "just average." What do you think?

JACKIE LOMAX: No, he was wrong. Before the Beatles were writing original material, of course, they were playing other people's material. They were the first band I ever heard onstage that sounded like a record. They used to do Buddy Holly tunes, for instance, and they would have the harmonies down *great* and this was very hard to do, early on. The concept of harmony wasn't really the thing. It was singing "Hound Dog" at the top of your range, or something like that. But they would have great harmony and George Harrison—who was the youngster at the time—would learn the guitar solo *exactly*. And it really did sound like the record. People thought that was incredible and they liked to dance to it. It was all dancing in those days, see? People didn't sit around so much and watch the band. They danced all the time and if they liked it and enjoyed themselves, they clapped. If they didn't, they'd just stand there and stare at you and maybe throw things. Because Liverpool was a rough town, a rough town to play.

Singer/songwriter Jackie Lomax recorded one album and several singles for Apple Records. None of them reportedly did a thing. He makes his home today in Los Angeles.

QUESTION: When Brian Epstein took over managing the Beatles and they later had their first hit with "Love Me Do" and they became a national sensation, did the other Liverpool groups like the Undertakers believe the same could or should happen for them too?

LOMAX: I thought that was great for them, but I'm not sure we felt that was going to have a trickle-down effect. Yet we would be offered more money to go play somewhere just because we were a Liverpool band. And people thought there was some special kind of music, something new, coming out of there. But it wasn't new, really. The German promoters came over to check out what we were doing and said, "The Beatles have got a record coming out. We're not going to be able to get them as many times as we'd like. Could you come over and play?" This was a direct result to the Beatles putting out a record. In four and a half years of touring, we covered the whole of England, Scotland, and Wales. We did every gig there was to do. We had some great times, we did some great gigs. Certain nights can be remembered forever. That's the important part of music. We had no idea at all about business. It came down to us having a chance to go to New York in 1965, and by doing that we kind of broke up the band. Because the guy who made us the offer asked us not to get any gigs. We stopped gigging for a while and our manager was paying us a wage each month. We had no concept of what we were doing, I don't think anybody did in those days. We went to our manager and asked him to split up the money among us that we'd made over the past four and a half years and, of course, he said, "Well, there isn't any."

QUESTION: How did you become a solo artist and how did your association with Apple Records come about?

LOMAX: I met Cilla Black at a party and she said, "Brian Epstein's looking for you." Well, Brian was a big name, this was 1966. I said, "Well, where is he?" She told me and I got in touch with him. He said, "I'm looking for a solo singer. Are you interested?" You got to be a fool to say no! This is the biggest guy in the world right now. So, I said, "I have a band here right now. Come down and see us rehearse. If you like the band, take the band. And if you don't like the band, I'll go with you anyway. No problem." We were rehearsing in some cheesy, funky dance studio on Eighth Avenue in New York and he actually agreed to come down and hear us. When I think about it now, to get Brian

Epstein to come hear a band rehearse, it was like *impossible*. Why I didn't think it was impossible, I don't know. Anyway, he came and he liked us. We went back to London and started doing gigs there. We were called the Lomax Alliance. That's when Epstein had the Saville Theatre, we played it. That's where Hendrix made his debut, Cream, all this stuff going on. It was a great time. But then, of course, Brian died. We had recorded an album, produced by John Simon, with all original songs, but it was never released. I don't think it was a great album, but we had all started writing.

QUESTION: What happened after Brian died? As far as you were concerned?

LOMAX: He left me as a legacy to NEMS Enterprises, his company which was run by Robert Stigwood. And Stigwood wasn't particularly impressed with me. So I couldn't get an album out. He gave me a chance for a single, provided I record a Bee Gees song on the B-side, which I did. I put out a single, written by an American, called "Genuine Imitation Life." And the other side was "One Minute Woman" by the Bee Gees, my version. Nobody knew what to do with it. I don't think it was released over here. So I was kind of hanging around, waiting for something to happen.

QUESTION: That was when George Harrison suggested you do a solo album, with him producing?

LOMAX: Right, but he told me he just wanted to produce it, not talk to the press about it or anything. We came to Los Angeles and stayed in Zsa Zsa Gabor's house in Beverly Hills, which was great for me. We recorded seven tracks here with great musicians. Hal Blaine played drums, Joe Osbourne played bass, and then there was me and George messing about as well. I played guitar on all of them, but George would play the *significant* guitar and overdub all the lead stuff. The title cut was "Is This What You Want," and Larry Knechtel's piano is great on that. We did some stuff back in London, too. Clapton did like five tracks with us. Which was, to me, incredibly generous. I knew Eric quite well, but I could not have used my influence to get him into the studio to record with me. George could, of course. So it was a great opportunity for me and I'm still very appreciative of that. Eric was great, he worked for hours. We had Ringo on drums, Paul played bass on one thing, this was going on during the same time the Beatles were recording the White

Album. So George might say, "We'll work on your songs." Well, of course, it would run over and I'd be sitting there hearing stuff that was blowing my mind. The White Album is very special to me because I was at a lot of those sessions. I was there for "Revolution" and "While My Guitar Gently Weeps," and I actually sing on "Dear Prudence." When the Beatles say to you, "Why don't you come out here and sing?" it's like, all of a sudden, you ain't got no voice! I ended up singing really low, which is unusual for me. I've got a high voice. It works good on the record. We were trying to get a single to break out for me. "Sour Milk Sea" was released at the same time as "Hey Jude" and the Mary Hopkin song, "Those Were the Days," so mine didn't get much notice. I did a song with Mal Evans called "New Day Dawning." It was added to the album later on a second release. I was quite proud of that. George came back from India and put some great guitar work on it. I even did a session with Paul as producer when George was away. He picked this Drifters song "Thumbin' a Ride" for me. But that song was never released. George also came up with this tune written by Mickie Most's brother, "How the Web Was Woven." We had Leon Russell involved in that, who I was quite fond of. He played almost all the instruments on that. Later on Elvis Presley recorded it and he must have used my record for the demo, because I don't think anybody else did it but me.

QUESTION: How did things wind up with Apple?

LOMAX: Allen Klein had taken over and nobody knew what the hell was going on. I tried to get in to see him three times, but each time it was canceled. So I joined a blues band called Heavy Jelly. We went on the road and I wrote a whole bunch of new tunes in the blues vein. And it was fun! During that period I received a letter from Jackie Simon and he said, "I'm living in Woodstock and I have all these musicians, but no singers. Can you get over here?" Well, that's a big question, right? So, I ended up in Woodstock with Jackie Simon and this record deal with Warner Brothers cropped up. I met the Band, Bob Dylan, all those people. I ended up producing the first Warners album myself, which was a heavy responsibility at the time. Simon worked on the second one. I felt good because I was touring nationally, mostly clubs. But I really like clubs, it's much more of an intimate atmosphere than theaters. Touring was good for me, because it gave me a perspective of this country.

QUESTION: Why did you choose the life of a musician when you surely knew that unless success happened for you that was something like what happened with the Beatles, your life would be full of uncertainties and insecurities?

LOMAX: My life has always been insecure. But I come from a very poor background. But even in that there is a kind of security, maybe not a monetary security, but more of a spiritual one. Do you know what I'm saying? You *know* that's what you're supposed to be doing. That sometimes frightens people. Especially your old lady, who's telling you to get a job. If it's not your mother, it's your old lady. You've got to have a sense of humor, it's very important to keep laughing.

DONOVAN

Toronto, 1986

GEOFFREY: I have many pictures of you in Rishikesh at the Maharishi's ashram. Can you give me just a quick feeling for that time?

DONOVAN: Here's a nice story that comes to mind concerning my time with the Beatles. It was 1968 in India, we were all gathered together in the Maharishi's bungalow, four Beatles, one Beach Boy, Mia Farrow, and me. Maharishi was on the floor sitting cross-legged, but the rest of us were all still standing around as we'd just arrived. Anyway, there was a kind of embarrassed hush in the room and John Lennon—always the funny one—decided to break the silence, so he walked up to the Maharishi, patted him on the head, and quietly said, "There's a good guru."

GEOFFREY: How do you remember Lennon?

DONOVAN: John certainly had a wicked tongue all right, but he was honest to a fault. His work proved that. Therefore, many people considered him to be very hard and forward. Actually, that's how he protected his sensitivities, by saying exactly what he felt. He was a very sensitive man inside and it was a great loss to the world. Everyone remembers ex-

---

Popular sixties singer/songwriter Donovan Leitch was one of the select few to be invited to accompany the Fabs to the Maharishi's mountaintop ashram in Rishikesh in 1967. He has recorded individually with at least three of the Beatles, who have graciously returned the favor by showing up as backup vocalists on one or two of his tunes.

actly where they were when it happened. As far as I'm concerned he ranks with Kennedy, Martin Luther King, and Gandhi as a figure for peace in the world. His passing produced a great shock wave across the world and people felt it right to the bone. You never know what you've got until you lose it. Like in the old blues tune they sing, "You never miss your water till your well runs dry." And that's what happened. We didn't miss John until he'd gone. We didn't really appreciate him until he'd gone.

RAVI SHANKAR

London, 1968

QUESTION: When and how did the sitar boom of the midsixties come about?

RAVI SHANKAR: What I term the great sitar explosion began in early 1966. At least, that is when I became aware of it, when I went to England. All the big publicity came about when the Rolling Stones and the Beatles used it on some of their records.

QUESTION: How did you come to meet the Beatles?

SHANKAR: I must tell you I never actually heard any records by these groups, but I suppose I vaguely knew they were immensely popular young musicians from the west. Then, in June 1966, I met Paul McCartney and George Harrison at a friend's home in London. I found them to be very charming and polite young men, not at all what I expected.

QUESTION: And what about George Harrison?

SHANKAR: He told me how very impressed he was with the instrument and my playing. I then asked him if he would show me what he'd learned on the sitar and he very humbly told me it was "not very much." I was struck by both his sincerity and his deep humility. Tapping

Virtuoso sitarist Pundit Ravi Shankar was great friends with all of the Beatles, but especially George Harrison.

262

into his knowledge of the guitar, he had experimented a bit on his own but expressed the desire to properly learn to play.

QUESTION: But surely learning to play the sitar "properly" is a lifelong process. It seems doubtful that a young pop star could ever muster the devotion necessary for such a high ideal.

SHANKAR: Of course I explained all this to him, making sure he understood that before even a single note is played one must spend years learning all the basics. He said he understood and so I invited him and his sweet wife Pattie to India to spend some time with us. Before he left, however, I joined him at his home in Esher where I gave him his very first lesson. Actually, I visited Mr. Harrison once more before returning home and played privately for the other Beatles.

QUESTION: And how did the two of you finally get together in India?

SHANKAR: After I returned to India, George wrote and said he would be able to come and spend six weeks with me. I wrote back telling him to grow a mustache and cut his hair a bit so that he would not be recognized. When we went to pick up George and Pattie in September, we found that trick had worked and no one recognized either him or Pattie although there had been a lot of publicity about their visit in the press. They registered for a suite at the Taj Mahal Hotel under a false name, but as it turned out, a bellboy happened to spot them and within twenty-four hours, all of Bombay came to know that one of the Beatles was there.

QUESTION: One imagines it rather quickly became complete chaos.

SHANKAR: Huge crowds of teenagers gathered in front of the hotel, headlines appeared in the papers about George's arrival, and my telephone started to ring nonstop. One caller even pretended to be "Mrs. Shankar" and demanded to talk to George. She changed her mind when I took the telephone myself. I couldn't believe it when I saw this mad frenzy of young people, mostly girls from about twelve to seventeen. I would have believed it in London or Tokyo or New York—but in India!

VIVIAN STANSHALL and "LEGS" LARRY SMITH

Chertsey, 1983

GEOFFREY: How did the Bonzos' appearance as the house band in *The Magical Mystery Tour* come about?

VIVIAN STANSHALL: Brian Epstein used to own a place called the Saville Theatre, and Paul and John used to sneak in occasionally to see us, because we supported Cream a couple of times and the Bee Gees. Yes, I think the *Mystery Tour* was just dropped on us. Paul suddenly phoned up and said, "Do you fancy it?"

"LEGS" LARRY SMITH: We were doing a week's cabaret in somewhere wonderful like Darlington, which is up in the north of England, and our roadie came rushing back from the telephone and said, "You're not going to believe this." It was an almost definite confirmation that we'd gotten the *Mystery Tour*. The Beatles had personally invited us to perform.

STANSHALL: Someone nicked all our instruments, though, didn't they,

---

Vivian Stanshall, the otherworldly headmaster of the fabled Bonzo Dog Doo Dah Band, costarred in the Beatles' *Magical Mystery Tour* film, going on to become chums with John Lennon and George Harrison.

"Legs" Larry Smith was a founder member of the Bonzo Dog Doo Dah Band. Today he is exceptionally close with George Harrison, having worked on the cover art for his solo *Gone Troppo* LP and other Harrison ventures.

from outside that alley, don't you remember? All the saxes went, your kit went, we had to hire everything to do the film.

SMITH: It was pretty rushed because, as I said, we were doing a week in Darlington. And believe it or not, the manager we had at the time was wondering whether we could get out of doing the gig, if I recall. And we had to rush around to find a substitute to play. We got Gene Pitney, as he was flying over.

GEOFFREY: You must have been personal favorites of the Beatles, or you wouldn't have been asked.

SMITH: Surely, yeah. That's very nice to know.

GEOFFREY: Were you around on the bus with them and all that?

STANSHALL: Oh no, we just did that one bit, and it was finito. Then they had that ruddy great party wherever the hell it was, where they all—

SMITH: At the Lancaster Hotel.

STANSHALL: Oh, we had a great jam that night, didn't we? God, I wish I had that on tape.

GEOFFREY: Who was involved?

STANSHALL: Well, I was up on stage with Lennon doing vocals on "Lawdie Miss Clawdy," "Long Tall Sally," you know, all the oldies. We screamed our heads off. Who was on the kit? Must have been Ringo, I should think, and Klaus Voorman playing bass.

SMITH: George got up and blew some saxophone.

STANSHALL: That's right. By god, it was a great row!

SMITH: I remember going out into the lobby and overhearing Lulu speaking on the phone: "Hello, Mother? I'm in London having a great time. I just can't come home just yet. I'm with the Beatles!" For me the most wonderful costume event of the evening was George Martin and his wife storming the cocktail area as Prince Philip and the Queen. For a moment everyone thought, "Can it really be them?" I mean, they just looked so right.

GEOFFREY: Tell me how Paul got involved in producing the band.

STANSHALL: Well, they wouldn't let him back into Poland. Actually I was more chummy with John myself, riding around in that absurd psychedelic Rolls of his. I think I just phoned Paul up and said, "Look, I think we could do with a hit record." So he said, "What have you got?" And so we sent him over some stuff, and when he heard "Urban Space-man" he said, "That's the one. I'll come and do it, you fix up the studio," and he came down and we did it. Just to put us at our ease, he sat down and said, "I've just knocked this song off, what do you think of it?" and he played us "Hey Jude." So I said it was all right, apart from the verse!

SMITH: And I told him religion will never be a hit. You can't write about that! Anyway, we worked really efficiently, it was quite nice. We did the whole thing in about five hours. I don't know why he wanted to be called Apollo C. Vermouth on the record, though.

STANSHALL: That was my idea. I didn't want the thing to sell on his name alone. It was nothing to do with anything contractual on his side, he was quite happy to have it out there with his name on it, but I just didn't think that would be a fair measure.

GEOFFREY: Do you know he put out a few tunes under the name of Bernard Webb? He also penned several songs for other artists that Epstein had under assumed names, just to see if they would sell on their own or if everything was just selling because he was Paul McCartney. And he had a big number-one hit. Tell me about this relationship with Lennon.

STANSHALL: There's not a lot to tell, really. Just the absurd anomalies of the time. We'd wind up at the Speakeasy or some other godawful club, get sloshed, and he'd say, "Want a ride home, wack?" I'd say, "Okay, John," so he'd drop me off in my crabby basement in Islington that I was rat-hunchbacked in, and he'd be in his Rolls full of birds and things and just drive off!

SMITH: And I'd have been up two hours worrying where he'd been all night.

London, 1984

GEOFFREY: You actually met the Beatles at Abbey Road during the Bonzo's first session there, didn't you?

NEIL INNES: Not to talk to. It was those days when they looked like the Blues Brothers—they all had dark glasses on, dark suits, and they're coming through the wall grinning . . . "Did you see that? That was the Beatles!" "Oh yeah, that was the Beatles," blah blah blah.

GEOFFREY: What do you remember about the filming of *Magical Mystery Tour?*

INNES: I remember Ringo was filming his own version, he called it *The Weybridge Version*, and George was saying that we ought to release "Death Cab for Cutie" as a single. I said, "They'd never play it, George, come on, what are you talking about?" Paul was very nice about the album—he particularly liked the "Music from the Head Ballet." John was a bit quiet that day, I seem to remember. I don't think John was very keen on the film . . . as it turns up in *The Rutles*, which was "not the best idea for a film—four Oxford University professors on a hitch-hiking tour of tea shops in Great Britain," or whatever. But I thought

---

Bonzo Dog alumnus Neil Innes is a longtime associate of the Beatles. He later starred in *The Rutles*, the top-drawer parody of the Beatles' incredible life and times, and was long known as Monty Python's "musical member."

it was a good idea. It had some terrific songs in it—I've always loved "Fool on the Hill."

GEOFFREY: It stands as one of the very few appearances of the Bonzos on film.

INNES: I know, the irony of it. The Bonzos were such a visual act, and there's very little evidence of that and a whole new generation has grown up, it seems, listening to the records, never having seen them.

GEOFFREY: Tell me about Paul's involvement in producing "Urban Spaceman."

INNES: Viv [Stanshall] met Paul McCartney at a club one night—Viv was always one for the clubs and things—and was bemoaning our sorry plight in the record business. Everyone in the business had rather enjoyed "Gorilla," people like Hendrix and Clapton, and all those folks we'd rubbed shoulders with over the years. Paul offered to produce "Urban Spaceman," so we said, "You're on." So the great day came, the magic man arrived and was very quick at putting everyone at ease—he sat down at the piano and said, "I've just written a song," and was going (sings) "Hey Jude, don't make it bad." And I'm looking at my watch, saying, "Come on, Paul, who needs a ballad at a time like this, can't we get on with it?" Only when the record came out did I realize, "Hey, that's what he played us in the studio that day, isn't it funny how you don't really listen?" But it was perfect, because when we got to make the thing, Paul just got on the controls . . .

GEOFFREY: You mean Mr. Vermouth?

INNES: Apollo C. Vermouth. Paul was playing Viv's ukelele on the rhythm track, and afterwards our manager's wife said, "What's that you've got there, a poor man's violin?" He said, "No, a rich man's ukelele." Anyway . . . when Viv wanted to do his big garden hose plastic funnel trumpet sound at the end, the engineer was saying, "Well, I don't really know how you can record a thing like that." Paul said, "Yes, you can, you just put a microphone at each corner of the studio." So it went down. We wanted to keep it a secret that Paul had produced it because we wanted to see what the record would do on its own merits. It did grab a few peoples' attention, got quite a lot of airplay, and it sort of crept up the charts. We were in Holland somewhere and heard it was number 36, came back and it was number 32; then it got to number 24 or something then the powers that be couldn't resist it and leaked the fact that Apollo C. Vermouth was Paul McCartney and it immediately shot up to number 4. But it was in the charts for a long, long time—in England I think it sold well over 250,000. But that was it, that was our hit, the one that got away.

GEOFFREY: Tell me about how the Rutles project came about and specifically how you did the sound track music?

INNES: By the time we'd formulated the idea of doing the Rutles, I'd made a couple of inroads in the songwriting brief. We needed about fourteen Beatle-style songs which ran the whole gamut of the Beatles' stuff, from "I Want to Hold Your Hand" to the psychedelic stuff—the whole bit. A curse in a way, because I've been labeled as a parodist ever since. But it was a real labor of love, because I listened to nothing—I just thought, "Ah, I remember that kind of song," and I just started writing them up . . . The group, the Rutles, got together and I thought this is one of the few astute things I've done in my career: to insist that we rehearse together for a fortnight as a group in a grotty little place in Hendon, so we more or less went through the experience . . . the rags-to-riches thing. By the time we left the rehearsal place, we felt like a group, it was really good, because we had none of the inhibitions about desperately having to make it . . . we knew we were going to make it, because we were going to make a film in a few weeks' time! So everyone was very up—we made the record in two weeks—in fact, the only part of the project that came in under budget was the album!

GEOFFREY: Certainly George being involved in the production validated it, didn't it?

INNES: George liked the idea of it, I think, because . . .

GEOFFREY: It burst the bubble of the myth?

INNES: In many ways, the story needed to be told. There's lots of things that are too heavy about the real story to make it entertaining at the end of the day. So the Rutles, the Pre-Fab Four in *All You Need Is Cash* was a pretty good way of saying from their side what it was like, but without making it too heavy. It must be quite grueling, because you've made some popular records and you're a rock'n'roll band that people will bring people in wheelchairs up to you so you can touch them and make them better, you know. On the whole it doesn't make for a very healthy ego, but I think all the Beatles survived the madness of it really quite well. You can't do it with any other group—people were saying, "I suppose you'll do the Rutland Stones next." We said, "Nope." "What about a live gig at Shea Stadium?" "Nope." People couldn't understand why we weren't going to rip this thing off. Because the Beatles hold a very special plateau in the history of the sixties.

AUNT MIMI

Bournemouth, 1983

QUESTION: How do you remember your nephew?

MIMI SMITH: John liked to run along the sands. Sometimes I imagine I see him. Is it him? I like to think it is.

QUESTION: Why is it that you raised John instead of your sister, Julia?

SMITH: Do you believe in fate? Because I knew the moment I saw John in that hospital that I was the one to be his mother and not Julia. Does that sound awful? It isn't, really, because Julia accepted it as something perfectly natural. She used to say, "You're his real mother. All I did was give birth . . ." I brought him up from a few weeks old until he was twenty-one. My husband George adored John just as though he were his own son. And like all dads he spoiled him. Sometimes when John had done something wrong and I sent him up to his room, I'd find George creeping upstairs with the Beano, John's favorite comic, and a bar of chocolate.

QUESTION: Did John ever have it tough as a child?

SMITH: All this talk about John's hard upbringing in a Liverpool slum is a fantasy. He wasn't pampered, but he had the best of everything we could provide.

QUESTION: To what do you attribute his early interest in music?

SMITH: I couldn't understand it. Here was a nicely spoken boy, attending church three times on Sunday of his own free will in the church choir,

271

suddenly taken to twanging a guitar. I told him it was awful and that it was distracting him from his studies as an art student. Nothing would have convinced me that John would make his fortune with that boy at the front door [Paul McCartney]. But in the end I had to concede that music was far more important to him than the career as an artist and illustrator I had mapped out for him.

QUESTION: Didn't John's half sister Jacquie live with you for quite sometime?

SMITH: Yes, but one day she didn't turn up for work, so I looked in her room to find her clothes had gone. No note, nothing to say where she'd gone. After weeks of worry she turned up on the doorstep crying bitterly, "I'm pregnant." After that she stayed for a while but eventually vanished again. I only heard from her when she got herself pregnant yet again and wanted more money.

QUESTION: And what did you think of Yoko?

SMITH: I have to admit Yoko was a good wife and mother and, thank goodness, I told John so long before. Sean is a darling, he's the living image of John. He has his mannerisms and his sense of adventure. We are very good friends. He tells me what he's been up to and I tell him all about his dad. He's very interested and can't discover enough. When he's twenty-five he'll be a very rich man, but for now he needs a good education. Yoko is a sensible girl and is seeing to that.

QUESTION: And your other grandnephew, Julian?

SMITH: I think Julian ought to get a real job. I've heard him sing and it's not my cup of tea. Julian doesn't keep in touch, not that it worries me too much.

QUESTION: How did John and Cynthia come to be married in the first place?

SMITH: One day I came home to find John moping around with a long face—he would have been about nineteen. "It's to do with Cynthia," he said at last. "She's coming round to see you. She's got something to say." Then he went up to his room. I knew Cynthia had been keen on John ever since they studied together at college, I knew she was making a play for him, but I didn't know exactly what was going on. When she arrived I let her in and called upstairs for John. He came down crying his heart out. "Whatever is the matter, John?" I said. Then clinging to me just like he did as a child he blurted out, "Cynthia wants us to get married. Please, I don't want to get married." I asked Cynthia if it was true and she nodded. Cynthia said she'd called round to ask my permission because John wasn't yet twenty-one. I got John on his own and asked him outright if he loved her, he shook his head saying he wasn't sure. That settled it. I went to Cynthia and looking straight into her eyes I said I would not give my consent. I said when he's twenty-one he can do what he likes, but until then I was still responsible for him. Of course she got him in the end, although she had to wait another three years.

I told Sean what happened. I showed him the picture of his father on the cover of the paper and explained the situation. I took Sean to the spot where John lay after he was shot. Sean wanted to know why the person shot John if he liked John. I explained that he was probably a confused person. Sean said we should find out if he was confused or if he really had meant to kill John. I said that was up to the courts. He asked what court—a tennis court or a basketball court? That's how Sean used to talk with his father. They were buddies. John would have been proud of Sean if he had heard this. Sean cried later. He also said "Now Daddy is part of God. I guess when you die you become much more bigger because you're part of everything."

I don't have much more to add to Sean's statement. The Silent Vigil will take place December 14th at 2 P.M. for ten minutes.

Our thoughts will be with you.

Love,

Yoko & Sean
Dec. 10 '80
N.Y.C.

New York, 1983

GEOFFREY: John and Yoko are legion in Toronto. I recently ran across some photographs of you and John at the Science Center where you gave your press conference in 1969. You had the big floppy hat on and everything. Do you remember that day?

YOKO ONO: Oh sure, I remember. We often thought of Canada, it's very lovely and, as you know, we did the Bed-In there.

GEOFFREY: They had a television special on it all. My mother wouldn't let me watch it. My father wanted to see something else.

ONO: Those were the days. John liked the Skidoos so much that we just went on riding until very dark. I was a bit scared, of course, it's a bit rough, isn't it?

GEOFFREY: I met a man in London and he said, "Yoko Ono lived in the same building as I, and I had a little stepladder that I used to get into my apartment with . . ."

ONO: Oh, it's that, I remember.

GEOFFREY: ". . . You know, I went there one day and it was gone and I found a little note under the door that said, 'Please come see your stepladder at the Indica Gallery,' so I went and it was painted white." Did you do that, did you steal someone's stepladder?

ONO: No, well, we didn't steal. We borrowed his stepladder.

GEOFFREY: Was that for the Indica Gallery [where John and Yoko first met in 1966]?

ONO: Yes. I think some of the gallery people said, "Well, we can pay for this, it's just a ladder, isn't it? Aren't you pleased it's in an art exhibition?" But he wasn't very happy about that. He was saying, "No, I would like it back and I don't like it white," and all that, you know. We paid for it, but it was very strange. I think the gallery people thought he'd be delighted that suddenly his ladder was an art piece.

[The sounds of children playing in a nearby hall filter into the room.]

ONO: Excuse me just a second. Shall we let these people go somewhere else?

GEOFFREY: Is that young Master Lennon?

ONO: Yes. Sean. Sean!

SEAN LENNON: What?

ONO: Would you mind coming here?

GEOFFREY: Well, he snaps to the whip, doesn't he? A well-trained boy.

ONO: He's thinking about it. [Sean enters] Hi. You're back now. He was just at a country place called Iron Gate. So how was it?

SEAN: Yeah, it was wonderful. I went sledding every day.

ONO: Oh, I see. That's very nice. These days I am resigned. "All right, all right, so we were a couple for how many years, how many decades?" So when he was alive I used to always try to keep my independence because he was such a strong, powerful energy. With the whole world behind him as well, by the way. So if I didn't keep my independence, I would have been swallowed up. Whenever somebody calls me Mrs. Lennon I used to say, "Mrs. Lennon? I'm Yoko Ono, thank you."

John also encouraged that in the sense that it was good I was independent so we can have a dialogue. Then after John died, somehow, when people called me Mrs. Lennon I felt good about it. People write to me saying, "We grieved over John's death, and just wanted to know how his widow was doing." That would have maybe made me feel a bit strange two years ago, but now I'm grateful people are writing because they love John and are concerned about his family. Whenever I do something now I feel my first concern is, "Do you think John is liking this?" I don't want to do anything that would shame his name or embarrass him. When I'm doing something and I know John would have approved, I feel better. Let's say all this has mellowed me in a way. As Yoko Ono, I am very mellowed to the point that, yes, it's all right I am Mrs. Lennon. So that independence thing is rapidly disappearing. . . . When I'm making music I didn't really care so much about how people were going to take it. This time around it was really in my mind I was carrying on what John and I did together. So I didn't have a partner who was taking care of the mass media side. In those days I thought, "Okay, he can take care of that side and I'll just do my own thing, thank you." But it wasn't like that this time. I was really talking to his fans as well. Because they were the ones who were really concerned about us and sent us their love and prayers, which really helped us get through the hard times. That's another new discovery, I didn't really think that would happen.

GEOFFREY: You're talking to us about how you've grown through the whole damn thing.

ONO: Oh yes, it's really amazing. Initially when my assistants showed me piles of letters and telegrams I said, "Oh, too bad that John's not here," meaning I automatically thought that they were sent for him. And they said, "No, no, these are for you." I actually checked all those envelopes to see who they were addressed to and they all said 'Yoko Something,' you know? And that was the start, from then on there was a nice dialogue going on.

GEOFFREY: I heard that you actually read a good bit of that mail.

ONO: Yes, I do.

GEOFFREY: Do you ever answer any? Once in a while you send out a letter from you and Sean to everyone.

ONO: Yes. That was an attempt to say thank you, and by the way, hello. It's hard to send a reply to each letter. When I made that attempt, of course, a lot of people were happy about it and thanked me for it. Also, some people were upset it was just a set letter to all of us. It wasn't an individual reply and some people were saddened by that. They just have to understand that with so many letters and telegrams I just couldn't answer each one of them.

GEOFFREY: "Approximately Infinite Universe," the song, is fantastic. Did you ever think of rereleasing anything?

ONO: Probably one day. When I'm not making a new record, you know. John was a very direct person, open—well, there was the other side, too, very shy and not open—a complex person. But that side is what woke me up in a way. I was like most end-of-the-fifties crowd, getting more and more complex, becoming a little bit out of touch with your own body, shall we say. That sort of bag. And here comes this man who doing very simple chords most of the time and saying, "What do you really mean? Don't give me all this roundabout tiptoeing." "Oh, I see, okay, well, uh, what I meant was, probably, well, I love you." You know, we never say, "I love you," we always say, "Well, spring is here and it was very beautiful outside and somehow it made me feel good," or whatever. That's what he did for me and now Sean is doing the same kind of thing. Again I was into my bag of being shy and not communicating or if I do communicate, communicating with a little symbolism, and here comes Sean saying, "Wake up! Come on, wake!" I don't know whether it was him, or whether it was him *and* John, together.

GEOFFREY: You showed a lot of people, my wife and I, for example, that I can be yin sometimes and she can be yang, and we can go back and forth like that. That's a very nice thing that John and Yoko gave to a lot of people growing up around you.

ONO: It has a lot to do with John, too. I mean if he didn't have the material, I couldn't have worked on it, you know? John was an Englishman, and you can imagine an English couple, the strong-headed woman, independent, but caring . . .

GEOFFREY: Like Auntie Mimi, right?

ONO: Yes, you know, saying, "It's time to get some milk for the cats, dear," or whatever, and the men tending the garden. That's how it was in a way, and that's all right. John had that side of him. Making tea was very natural for him to do, so he'll make the tea for me—it was very nice . . .

GEOFFREY: And bake the bread!

ONO: Yes. So there was nothing new about that, really. But we were trying to state that, yes, we can do that too if we want to. He had a very vulnerable side, and I had the tough side, I suppose, as well—just as much as the vulnerable side. So we can all exchange roles once in a while and that was very natural for us. Maybe because of how I dealt with the situation after John died it lets people think I'm a very strong woman and therefore I am different, so when they say, "It's all right for you, you're especially strong!" No, nothing like that. I consider myself just normal. If somebody says something nasty about me, I get hurt and think about it for the whole day. And the way I coped with the situation was almost a miracle! Part of me was ... well, part of me is *still* in shock ... and the other side of me was like a little baby. I felt like I was five years old, saying, "Oh, why did this happen?" And "I need a big teddy bear" or whatever. So when I look back on what I did last year—the videos, or the album, and the announcements, that's when I think, "Wow, how did I do that?" So there are several people in me, and they somehow organized it, you know? That put me in a situation and I just coped with it; if you were in that situation, you would've done the same, or maybe even better, I don't know ...

GEOFFREY: There was a lot of talk when the eighties came around that they were going to be far-out like the sixties. Then this thing happened with John, and people said, "Oh, shit, there goes the decade." But now I see the work that you're doing and we're all trying to do ... is to make that thing happen. You're getting on with your work to help make the eighties the thing that John wanted so that the "crazy man" up in Washington doesn't have his way. We're just getting on with life and making that promise of the decade come alive, right?

ONO: You mentioned "the crazy man," so I will say this: each time there's a president, we tend to say, "He's not good enough, let's wait for the next election." I think that when you really look into the system, it has an automatic operation that stops anyone who's there, regardless of his personality, from going too far afield from what the people want. Now, it's our responsibility to give him a definite sign of what we want and a unified opinion. Even in a man-woman relationship, we know that we are giving many conflicting signals to each other, and that's made it very difficult. We are getting wise on a individual level, so why don't we get wise about communication with the government? Now, if we do have a unified opinion, *he* has the responsibility to carry it out. The problem is that we don't have a unified opinion, or we're not expressing it. We have to be very thankful we have a system like that. In a dictatorship, they don't have to care about people's opinion. So since we do *have* to, we should use that. What I think is that this time around we have to really voice it. When I say "express it" I don't mean a million in Central Park so that they can say, "It was five hundred thousand and by the way there were ..."

GEOFFREY: "Several arrests for drunkenness and marijuana."

ONO: Well, "It was minority," and they're right to say it's minority, because a million people *is* a minority . . . though we can say, "A million represents ten million," or whatever. So this time around it has to be all three hundred million of us, really giving the vote. And I'm suggesting a peace poll. Done on the congressional level. Every city, every town in the United States, all the states, do a peace poll.

GEOFFREY: That's not a new idea for John and Yoko either. There was your Peace Vote of 1969 . . .

ONO: Yes, but this time we should do it on a level that would be understood by the people we want to communicate with. The point is, they may feel we're not communicating with them yet, you see. "When in Rome"—it's that one; you go to Japan, you try to talk in Japanese, not English. That's how it is. So we have to talk in their language—which is the congressional vote. We have to put it there.

GEOFFREY: Work through the system, then?

ONO: Yes. Because the system is still usable; it's a very good system, actually, if it's used right, but we have to know how to use it.

GEOFFREY: One of the things I liked about what you and John said in one of his last interviews was, "What's all this 'Star Wars,' projecting war in space with lasers? Don't you understand that all these mind projections add up? They calculate karmically or whatever . . . so let's just project a positive image. We can create other things to entertain our children with than lasers and Star Wars and all that!" It's very important that everything we do has this consciousness, to project this peace principle.

ONO: Yes. Since John died, in the past two years there were many things that happened in my life I just never expected, very cruel, heartbreaking things, and it was an experience, I just had to learn another lesson. Because I thought when that happened in 1980, the rest of my life, just coping with that emotion was almost . . . big enough for me. But then there were many unexpected incidents. I thought, "How am I going to deal with this?" What happens usually is that the good people usually confront these negative attacks, and then they start to get busy just coping with that, trying to fight the negative. And they spend the rest of their lives fighting with a negative. Instead of doing that, let's *ignore* the negative, just forget it. It's hard; but just forget it and meanwhile create positive things. While we're fighting with a negative, we're going to be on the same level as them, and nothing positive will happen while we're doing that. So don't put your energy or attention into negative matters.

GEOFFREY: Just leave it alone and it will go away?

ONO: It'll go away when the positive becomes large enough. Now, there's no chance of the positive becoming large if we don't *do* anything, you know, and we're just fighting them. So that's the trap we fall into.

GEOFFREY: At least we're still alive. We thought we might be blown up by now, didn't we?

ONO: Yes, that's true too, therefore I'm saying it's going to be all right. One day we can all laugh about it, I suppose.

GEOFFREY: Yoko, do you believe in God?

ONO: God or Goddess? No, it's just a joke. Well, look, I do believe there's some kind of big power that is beyond us . . . and in us, right? But you can explain it in a way that agnostics could understand—it's like a mass dream, a human-race dream. We had a dream that we realized: we always wanted to fly, and for centuries people tried to jump off the . . . whatever, and finally, yes, we have airplanes. And, of course, this is not quite the way we were thinking of flying, we were thinking of flying without anything, but . . . still we're flying. There was always talk in poetry about what would it be like to be on the moon. We always talked about the moon. So we went to the moon. So there's always a collective dream that we have as the human race. And this time around, I think there's another dream we've always had, which is to survive. That's a very strong one. There are three things we all want, which are: to love and be loved; to be happy; and to survive. There's nobody in the world who doesn't want that. Even the people who are saying, "I want to commit suicide"—it's a kind of reverse expression of happiness—and wanting happiness, wanting love, wanting to survive in that way. And anybody who thinks they can somehow con us into thinking otherwise, *they're* the dreamers. We are the realists. Because there are billions of us thinking the same thing and that is our collective dream. That's what I call the "great design" that is above us.

GEOFFREY: On the back of [your album] *Approximately Infinite Universe* you said, "The dream we dream alone . . ."

ONO: ". . . is only a dream. But the dream we dream together is reality." In the sixties we waved flags and everything. The eighties, however, it's a bit dangerous to even go on the street, even. And most of us—it's not just me, it's not just old ladies on Amsterdam Avenue, even the kids— they're sort of frightened of going out: they're basically all sitting at home watching the TV or something. So I thought, what can we do now, because the eighties has its own way of doing things—that we can't do in the way we did in the sixties. It's not gathering at Wood-stock, because to go to Woodstock on the subway might be dangerous.

GEOFFREY: Besides, there's no good bands anymore either, no one to lis-ten to.

ONO: Oh, there might be music, but it's impractical because oil is ex-pensive, and you don't want to travel that far, you know.

GEOFFREY: And we all live in suburbia now and wear ties all day. No one would show up anyway.

ONO: So where could we connect, where could we gather all together and make this thing big enough that it would actually change the world? Dream power!

GEOFFREY: I got a bootleg the other day of "What a Shame Mary Jane Had a Pain at the Party." It's the funniest thing I've ever heard, and you're in there. I heard Magic Alex was at that session and John wanted to release the song on Apple.

ONO: Yes.

GEOFFREY: Is it the same song as "What's the New Mary Jane"?

ONO: Yes. I don't know how to tell you, it was just one of those . . .

GEOFFREY: Do you remember who was there?

ONO: The usual crowd. I don't think Paul was there; I think probably George was . . . I don't particularly remember that. I do remember we did it, but I don't particularly remember it as a very great time.

GEOFFREY: John said he'd like to be remembered as a great peacenik. How do you think the world can find peace today?

ONO: We'll do it. We just have to do it step by step and it will happen.

GEOFFREY: I don't think the bomb's going to go off, do you?

ONO: No. But that's not the problem. The problem is more in the way we think. It's not good that the economic situation is so bad and there's a lot of people suffering, which is making the world very tense and vi-olent. That sort of thing can be solved rather easily through the political system we have. It's no longer true to say that war is economically viable.

GEOFFREY: "Let's have a war and get the economy going."

ONO: That one. There's that sort of feeling still in some of us, and that's why there's only a million people in the peace march rather than ten million, some people are still not quite sure. We have to understand the reality of that.

GEOFFREY: "We'd like to be peaceful, but the Russians will never be peaceful with us, so we'd better keep up this macho image . . ."

ONO: But that's what the Russians are saying too!

GEOFFREY: If only we could get together and say "Game over, let's just be peaceful," but to do it is tough.

ONO: Well, no, it's not really that tough, and there are ways of doing it. As you say, it's obvious that everybody wants peace, but it has to be voiced. And not just voiced through a few hippies, or whatever.

GEOFFREY: Will you continue to voice it for us in a way, and with us?

ONO: I'll be doing my share, whatever that is.

GEOFFREY: But we need leaders, don't we?

ONO: No . . . I think each of us is very important in that sense. Naturally, because of the particular environment I'm in I have my share of doing, I suppose . . .

GEOFFREY: We can trust you, I think . . .

ONO: Well, you can trust me as what I am, whatever *that* is, you know. It's coming to a point that the thing is so important, and we don't have much time. And to make the real turn round, the most important people are really just *people*. Numbers count now. Maybe they can conveniently hide one spokesman. If it's one spokesman, it's easy to deal with.

GEOFFREY: I heard that you and John were going to a march with Cesar Chavez near that terrible time in 1980, weren't you?

ONO: The plan was we were going to go to San Francisco that Thursday to join a march the next day for equal pay for Oriental people in San Francisco. It was announced, we sent a statement there, and John was very happy to do this, because John had a son who was half Oriental. So he was envisioning carrying Sean, and saying "Here's . . .

GEOFFREY: Living proof of the harmony.

ONO: Yes . . . that was one of the things we were going to do. And that probably indicated we were going to do a few things in that direction.

GEOFFREY: May I ask, do you still own your cows?

ONO: Yes, I do. Or rather, the cows are still with us.

GEOFFREY: Are you vegetarian? I heard you don't kill any cows.

ONO: No.

GEOFFREY: When they get old and don't give milk, you don't cut them up for meat do you?

ONO: No, of course not. That's not why I got them. It just was suggested to us as one of those business situations. But since then, we've had so much involvement with that area . . . and the cow's sacred in India, there may be something going on there that we didn't know! And somehow the cows were saying, "Well, look, we'd like to be with people who won't kill us!"

GEOFFREY: A Gallup poll recently said that four out of five people believe in reincarnation. Do you?

ONO: Well . . . I think we have many lives, probably. I hate to label myself, so I don't even want to say I'm a vegetarian. I eat fish and things like that too, and occasionally I might just go off and eat chocolate or whatever. But generally speaking I do keep a vegetarian diet just because it's good for my health. But it may not be for others.

QUESTION: You don't want to dictate behavior.

ONO: No, because each person has their own karma. I don't even know what *my* karma is, so . . .

QUESTION: You're finding out—we all are.

ONO: Right. Gradually finding out, yes.

GEOFFREY: I was reading in some book that you and John actually lived with the founder of the Hare Krishna movement, Srila Prabhupada.

ONO: Yes, he was with us.

GEOFFREY: Tell me about that.

ONO: He was in one of the cottages we had at Tittenhurst.

GEOFFREY: How did you find him? Because everyone says, "They're a cult, they're going to rob you and take your mind, zombies—" but they didn't seem . . . they were at your "Give Peace a Chance" session at the Bed-In. They banged the drum and all that.

ONO: Well, I think each person has his or her own karma. So I'm not the one to say which one is which. People gather where it's naturally important for themselves. In my view, all religion is the same in a way.

If somebody understands it this way better, then they should go there, you know?

GEOFFREY: Elliot Mintz* said that in John's famous "God," which by the way, is a great song . . .

ONO: I was just saying that this morning! Somebody was saying, "What songs do you like of John's?" and of course I said that "Imagine" is probably one of the most important songs he put out, but "God" is one that I like very much.

GEOFFREY: John said, "I don't believe in Jesus, Krishna, Gita, etc.," but Elliot said John *did* believe in all that. Because when he went with you to Japan, he visited the temples of Buddha . . .

ONO: Oh, sure. He believed in all that because it's just a variation. All this is just another way of expressing the same thing. He believed in the "root," which is the big power, and any expression of that he had respect for. I do too. But what he did in "God," that very powerful song, is like a declaration of independence. "Let me be me now, and let's start from here!"

GEOFFREY: No more daddies.

ONO: Yeah, right, so it was a beautiful statement—I really like that song. Also, the myth is "The Beatles—and Yoko" or whatever. I'd like to say that until I met John I didn't really know what the Beatles were about; I suppose I heard about them like most people in those days, not as fans, but as a social phenomenon. Elvis Presley was another phenomenon I wasn't involved with, but just sort of knew about it. Since I got involved with Paul I now know what he has done . . . and it's a beautiful thing he did. After all, he's one of the Beatles and that's what John did as well, and John being Sean's father etc, so I'm part of it! I feel a family pride in what they did—it's beautiful, as opposed to—not to knock them or anything, but certain groups making their career out of only saying negative things. What the Beatles were about was just simple love and—I want to hold your hand, that's the gist of it. It's a beautiful thing and no wonder it was so popular. It changed the whole world. Working class was something to be ashamed of before that, especially in Britain. But now, even the shopkeepers know that if a young guy comes in who's speaking with an accent, you're not supposed to be

---

* John and Yoko's close friend and advisor near the end of Lennon's life.

impolite to them just because they're young and not from an aristo-
cratic family. It changed everybody's consciousness. If you can make it
when you're young, that's fine. Being young and rich doesn't mean that
you were born into a good family.

GEOFFREY: You performed with the Beatles on "Bungalow Bill." Actually
you're on a few Beatle cuts.

ONO: But that doesn't mean anything, it just could've been some girls
outside. When they needed a chorus they used to say, "Let's get some
girls in here." So it doesn't mean anything, but I would say I was definitely there when John and I started to do *our* thing. A lot of things
we did together were not a waste—it was something that spoke and will
probably speak much later, too.

GEOFFREY: We talk about John and Yoko's contribution to music all the
time, but I remember Box of Smile, Acorns For Peace . . .

ONO: Mmmm, those things.

GEOFFREY: . . . your video for "Cold Turkey," your conceptual films . . .
what about Yoko Ono's other artwork?

ONO: Well, it was natural for John and I to meet. I was in Trafalgar
Square standing in a bag, saying this was my peace statement. One day
John and I were lying together—as usual—saying, "What about this and
that, and what about the working class?" He was bringing up the working class a lot, saying sort of "Let them eat cake. What did you do for
peace?" What was I doing? "Standing in Trafalgar Square." "Oh, I see,
that's what you were doing, okay, well, look—why don't we stand in
Trafalgar Square together, in a bag?" "Well, okay, if you want to." "Well,
no, that's a bit too much, why don't we go in a Rolls, and bring out all
this beautiful picnic stuff, and just have a picnic in Trafalgar Square?"
That's more our style. I said "Well, all right." He said, "No, why don't
we just sit in bed?" Well it's easier, isn't it, as we're sitting in bed then.
"So what're we gonna do?" "Invite the reporters, tell them we're just sitting in bed for peace." "But then all these reporters will be climbing up
the windows and everything, it'll be terrible. No, we won't do that." So
eventually, "Let's go to a hotel and do it." What I'm saying is that I was
doing things on my own, and he was doing it with the Beatles in the
sense of all you need is love, etc. So when we got together we had
nothing to disagree on. That was basically the way it was. That was our
meeting.

GEOFFREY: The question is, will you make more things, more films, maybe show us what you've made in the past again . . . what else?

ONO: Well, the future's an open book. I don't know what's going to happen. I never know. Every time I turn around there's some big surprise, so I wouldn't know. The things I did before were pertinent then and not now. So I don't feel like going back to any of the things I did. It's something that's still there, and I don't have to duplicate it. So it's there, and other than that, I just go on.

GEOFFREY: Someone tried to sell me one of your original Acorns for Peace for five hundred dollars the other day. I just thought you'd like to know.

ONO: It's so funny.

GEOFFREY: Can you say anything about the night John died?

ONO: I was still shaking in bed, so to speak, and the bedroom was the old one that John and I used to sleep in, which is on the Seventy-second Street side. All night these people were chanting, or playing John's records, so that I heard John's voice, which at the time was a bit too much. What I learned was that I don't have much control over my destiny or fate or anything. Seems like it's all out there, somehow, and certain things I'm not supposed to know. John and I thought we knew all about enlightenment, so there was that arrogant side of us. And this was like a big hammer from above saying, "Well, just remember you don't know it all, there's a lot more to learn."

GEOFFREY: The video for "Walking on Thin Ice" was fantastic and very surprising!

ONO: You like that, huh?

GEOFFREY: Sexy!*

ONO: There's that part of John and me, but it's only shot from up here . . . That was taken about a week before he died. In the gallery. John was saying, "Let's show them," because people have a feeling that somebody who's married for ten years . . .

GEOFFREY: Won't get into it anymore.

ONO: Some old middle-aged couple, what are they doing, watching TV or something? When I did *Double Fantasy* with him, I had to realize yet again how much he knew. He was like a living dictionary about all the

---

* The video showed scenes of John and Yoko supposedly making love.

little licks and this and that, just *everything*. It was amazing. . . . I feel that now, John is helping me through Sean.

GEOFFREY: Same birthday.

ONO: Mmmm. You could ask his statement, because the last time some British radio people came in they said, "Could we ask Sean to make a statement?" I was sort of worried, then thought, "Look, these guys are very nice guys, they'll edit whatever. So don't worry about it, it's for the girls and boys in Britain." He was thinking so long I thought, "He's stuck, he's stuck, oh, it's not gonna work," and he just said, "Keep having fun, because it's worth it." I thought that was like John. John used to tell me about his salmon fishing. One of his aunties lived in Scotland and she had married a Scottish man, so whenever John visited them he went salmon fishing. This man really liked fishing and he did it by himself usually, but sometimes John was allowed to join him. Salmon was a big thing to him. John used to say, "Scottish salmon, there's nothing like it." When I visited this auntie with him I did get to eat the salmon and it was very fresh. Here, we used to get smoked salmon, but most of it that I get here is sort of salty and the salmon we got in Scotland were really good. I don't know why they don't export that one. Salmon was one of the things we enjoyed eating.

GEOFFREY: How profound!

ONO: Yeah, right!

PAUL McCARTNEY AND JULIA BAIRD

London, 1986

PAUL: Good morning and welcome to Radio Norwich. I have today with me Julia Baird who's . . .

BAIRD: Shut up!

PAUL: . . . got some questions she's going to attempt to read in the first part of our "Read a Question Telethon"!

BAIRD: Thank you. Well, Paul . . .

PAUL: What, Julia?

BAIRD: Would you kindly tell me about your first meeting with John?

PAUL: The first time I met your brother was at the Woolton Village Fete. I'd been invited there by Ivan Vaughn, who was our mutual mate.

BAIRD: Did you hear what's happened to him?*

PAUL: Yeah. Actually I saw him last weekend. He came to our house. I know him quite well, still. He was born on exactly the same day as me, Ivan, June 18, 1942. So we've always had a lot in common as well as with John.

Julia Baird is John Lennon's half sister on his mother's side. This was McCartney's first meeting with the forty-year-old teacher since she was a little girl.

*Several years ago, Ivan Vaughn contracted Parkinson's disease and is today a well-known advocate of research into the cause of this deadly neurological disorder.

BAIRD: You mean to tell me you and John had mutual mates without ever knowing each other?

PAUL: Well, John lived in Mendips* and Ivan lived just a garden away or something. So they were mates from where they lived. But Ivan was a mate of mine from school and so one day he said, "Don't you want to come along to the Woolton Village Fete? A couple of the lads are going to be there and stuff, and I'll take you." I think at the time John was about sixteen, so I might have been fourteen or fifteen.

BAIRD: I know my family went to that fete. Auntie Nanny came over with our cousin Michael, our other aunt Harrie, me, my sister Jacqui, and, of course, our mother Julia. We all just had to go and see John playing. So what year was that, then?

PAUL: Good question, next question. Honestly I'm hopeless on years, I really don't know.**

BAIRD: In later years, when we moved to Woolton, we belonged to that same church. You know that field where the Quarrymen played is all buildings now. Geoffrey Giuliano and I went up there recently and that whole area has been built up.

PAUL: Isn't that terrible? That's actually *regress*, isn't it? They keep right on doing it, though. So, anyway, I'd been invited by Ivan and he took me along. I remember coming into the fete and seeing all the sideshows.

BAIRD: Yes, the scouts, cubs, and everything.

PAUL: Right. And also hearing all this great music wafting in from this little Tanoy system. It was John and the band. Len Garry, Pete Shotton, Colin Hanton on drums, Griff on guitar, and maybe Nigel Whalley, who was their official manager. (He managed to get onstage!) Anyway, he was a good lad. I remember I was amazed and thought, "Oh great, I'll listen to the band." Because I was obviously into the music.

BAIRD: Hadn't you originally gone along to sing yourself?

PAUL: No, no. I'd only come as a guest with Ivan. We were just in the audience watching. I remember John singing a song called "Come Go with Me." He'd heard it on the radio. It was a lovely song by the Del

---

*"Mendips" was the name of John's boyhood home at 251 Menlove Avenue, Woolton, in suburban Liverpool.

**The actual date was June 15, 1956.

Vikings. John, however, didn't really know all the verses, but he knew the chorus: [*Paul sings*] "Come come come go with me. Little darling, go with me." The rest he just made up himself. Good bluesy lyrics like, "Come go with me down to the penitentiary." I remember at the time he was playing banjo chords on his guitar.

BAIRD: Our mum taught him to play the banjo. It was a big mother-of-pearl banjo she had.

PAUL: Right, Julia taught him to play banjo chords, but he'd got a guitar because it was more fashionable and modern than a banjo. He still played with banjo tuning, though, and only had about four strings at the time. I just thought, "Well, he looks good, he's singing well, and he seems like a great lead singer to me." Of course he had his glasses off so he really looked quite suave.

BAIRD: And his hair greased back. He must not have been able to really see too much with his glasses off.

PAUL: Well, no, he wouldn't have been able to see. Are you shortsighted, then, too?

BAIRD: Completely and utterly, I'm afraid.

PAUL: I knew through friends at the art college there was this guy named Geoff [Mohammed] who was even more shortsighted than your brother. So John used to often help him across the street. The blind leading the blind, I suppose!

BAIRD: That's right. Well, that's when he had the big, thick black glasses, wasn't it?

PAUL: The Buddy Holly look! You see as a rock'n'roll person we all liked wore those glasses, so it was great. Anyone who really needed to wear glasses could then come out of the closet, I suppose.

BAIRD: As long as that's all he was doing!

PAUL: Until Buddy came along, any fellow with glasses always took them off to play. So anyway, getting back to meeting John. He was up there jiving away and after they finished their set I met them all in the church hall. They were having a beer, I think. It wasn't crazy drinking or anything, it was more just a bit of fun. You know, we all used to really think John was pretty cool. He was a bit older and would therefore do a little more greased-back hair and things than we were ever allowed. I just didn't do it. The way my dad was, really. But John looked a bit of a ted with his drake and all. He had nice big sideboards, as we called them. I remember him on this old guitar that was laying around. I knew a lot of the words and that was very good currency in those days. That was the big thing then. It was, "How did you get the words to that, man?" "Oh, I know a fellow who lives in Bootle and if you get a bus to his house, why, he'll teach you B7!" So we'd all pile on the bus to learn a chord . . . almost. Knowing the words to a song was the same, so it really was a big deal to actually know the full lyrics to "Twenty Flight Rock," and I learned them all! It was one of the very first records I ever got. I bought it at Curries in Liverpool.

BAIRD: I remember John and I slowing records down in order to try and learn the words.

PAUL: That's right, we used to do that too. At the time I remember thinking John smelled a bit beery and was obviously a little older than I was used to. I was only still a kid when I met him and hadn't quite seen the grown-up world yet. Of course, later when George came around he was even younger. He was my little mate, you see. Nonetheless, he could play guitar, particularly this piece called "Raunchy," which we all used to love. You see if anyone could do something like that, then it was enough for them to get into the group. So what happened that first night with John and the lads, we all went to the pub for a couple of drinks and that. I had to try and kid the barman that I was really eighteen.

BAIRD: I was wondering how they let you in.

PAUL: Well, you know, I had a sports coat on and I just tried to look like one of the boys. As I recall, there was a bit of a panic on because there was a big fight brewing and suddenly the word went round that we were all needed. Apparently there was a mob forming up the road getting ready to invade the pub! I just thought, "Jesus, what have I gotten myself into here? I've only come for a day out and suddenly I'm with all these men who are about to begin hailing machetes at each other!" But somehow that all blew over and we ended up having a very nice evening. I think later the band went back over to the church hall for a jam, but I had to get home and that. A couple of weeks later Pete Shotten came up on his bike and invited me to join the group. You know, one of the interesting things about John to me was that his people always had a bit of money. I was from the trading estate like the rest of the Beatles and it was kind of like seeing another world from what I was used to. I remember being very impressed in Mendips seeing the complete works of Winston Churchill.

BAIRD: Yes.

PAUL: And John had read them! I hadn't really met people like this before, so I was very impressed with that side of him, you know. I mean, with his going to art school and that kind of thing. Of course, I went to the school next to his, so we met up there. I remember seeing him in the chippy one day, too. And you'd see him on the bus, you know. Actually, I saw him a few times before I met him. It was, "Oh, he's that fellow! He's the ted who gets on the bus at the stop." I always thought John was very hip. Then I was asked to join the group, probably on the strength of knowing "Twenty Flight Rock." I think I also sang "Long Tall Sally" for him as well. That was my Little Richard thing, which I still do. The Eddie Cochran attraction to me was in the words, "I've got a girl with a wrecking machine." There's some great words in all those early rock'n'roll songs.

BAIRD: Geoffrey Giuliano recently met an old neighbor of yours in Canada who apparently worked with your mother years ago in Liverpool. She commented to him that she thought your mum wouldn't have approved or even *allowed* you to get mixed up in rock'n'roll. What do you think about that?

PAUL: No, it's not really true. I mean, she was a nurse and was into stuff like hygiene, but she wasn't really prudish. Of course, it was in those days after the war, and she was a little strict on cleanliness and things like that. Later, I kind of rebelled a bit against it and sort of hung out in dirty jeans, but we were never really allowed to do too much of that. My mum loved to see us doing well and wouldn't have really cared how we did it. She would have loved it. That is one of my deepest regrets, you know, because obviously she died when I was fourteen, before this phase of my life. That was one of John and I's biggest bonds, you know, the fact that both our mums had died when we were teenagers.

BAIRD: I remember our mother saying, "That poor boy, he hasn't got a mother."

PAUL: God.

BAIRD: Actually, that was the thing that struck her most about you, and then it happened to us as well, which is awful.

PAUL: Yeah, God, yeah . . .

BAIRD: What did you think of the Quarrymen musically?

PAUL: Well, I thought John was good. He was really the only outstanding member. All the rest kind of slipped away, you know? The drummer was pretty good, actually, for what we knew then. One of the reasons I know they all liked Colin was because he had the record "Searchin'" and, again, that was big currency. Sometimes you made a whole career with someone just because he had a particular record!

BAIRD: Do you know anything about the supposed existence of film of the Quarrymen playing at the Woolton Fete?

PAUL: I have heard that somebody did take some home movies, but I've never seen any of it.

BAIRD: What sort of memories do you have of our mother?

PAUL: Of Julia . . . well, I always thought she was a very beautiful lady and a really nice woman, and of course John absolutely adored her. Number one, obviously, on the level that she was his mom, but also because she was a very spirited woman. As we were saying before, she taught him to play the banjo, and I mean, that's really very *gay*, isn't it, in the old-fashioned sense of the word.

BAIRD: Full of life.

PAUL: Full of life, yeah.

BAIRD: You know we used to get our fairy stories told to us with the banjo and sometimes even the piano.

PAUL: Did you? I mean, our family was musical, but there certainly wasn't a woman who could play the banjo; that was *very* unusual. It was always the men. Julia was very ahead of her time. Actually, you used to get quite a lot of that in the twenties or whatever that era was. I mean, that was one of the things I undoubtedly found very interesting about your family. I know my mother was a nurse and my dad a cotton sales-man, so we always lived in the nurse's house on the estate. Nearly al-ways it was the midwife's house we lived in. So to actually see this sort of middle-class thing was fascinating for me. Christ, I can even recall John getting one hundred quid for his birthday off your relatives in Edinburgh!

BAIRD: Yes, we all got it when we turned twenty-one.

PAUL: One hundred quid! I mean, I still say I'd like it *now*. You know what I'm saying, isn't it true?

BAIRD: Just a minute, let me check my purse . . .

PAUL: Someone just hands you a hundred quid, still feels good to me. And so I thought, "This is amazing, I've never seen people like this!" I remember John taking about people the family knew from the BBC, friends that were dentists and uncles and aunts up in Scotland, so it was very exotic to me, all that. You know we went to Paris on that money. It was supposed to be Spain, but we never got past Paris, we enjoyed it so much. We hitchhiked but suddenly thought, We can't get to Spain on a hundred quid. I don't really know if he was really fond of me or just into spending. And I would be there for the banana milk shake. I think actually I paid my own way, but, you know, in those days it was much safer hitching than it obviously is now. We soon realized we needed a bit of a gimmick to get people to stop, so we both wore bowler hats in addition to our leather jackets. We thought that might take the edge off of the kind of hoody look or ruffian image we had then. I guess people would just think, "Whoa, look there's a couple of daft kids in bowler hats there. You know, they don't really look like a threat." We got a bit drunk on the French beer. We had been drinking the British stuff, so we thought we could handle it, but this foreign stuff really went to our heads. It was all just so adventurous. I had never done anything like that. I'd hardly ever been out of Liverpool before. We'd been to Pehewli, Scagness, and Leamington Spa before, but that had been the whole of my travels. It was very exciting to get off on your own with a mate. John was a great guy because he was *never* boring. I don't actually think anyone in your family is boring. You're really a lively bunch. To be honest, John and I shared a lot of things, you know, cruel humor which we got into. I imagine I could go on for days about that . . . but, some other time. Seeing as you've got sixty questions here.

BAIRD: John used to practice in the bathroom of our house on Bloomfield Road because of the echo it gave. Do you remember that?

PAUL: It was the best room in the house!

BAIRD: Now, I remember Jacqui and I being taken out of the bath and being allowed to go outside and play again because everyone was there wanting to use the bathroom.

PAUL: How do you mean *everyone*?

BAIRD: Well, people with guitars.

PAUL: Could have been me, John, and George rehearsing. We did a lot of that at each other's houses, only my dad wouldn't always have it.

BAIRD: I remember the guitars were very, very loud.

PAUL: There might have been an amplifier.

BAIRD: Do you remember my mother joining in with you all on washboard?

PAUL: Yeah, that's right. Many a song has been written in that little room. In fact, you know, at home I used to not only stand around with one leg on the toilet, but if I had to actually go, I would take in my guitar instead of a book. So what's the difference? My dad used to say, "Paul, what are you doing playing the guitar on the toilet?" And I'd say, "Well, what's wrong with that?" Those were the days.

BAIRD: What's the first tune you ever wrote with John? Can you remember?

PAUL: Yeah. I've got an exercise book at home somewhere with some numbers we started.

BAIRD: I wonder how many great things have been started in school exercise notebooks?

PAUL: The first one I think might have been called, "Just Fun." We actually wrote a few that never got published, looking back. They weren't put down anywhere, so they only exist in my memory. Actually, it's something I want to do something with. I mean, they're pretty rough songs, but they're not bad rockabilly in a way. "Just Fun" goes like [sings],

> "They said that our love was just fun
> the day that our friendship begun
> There's no blue moon in history
> There's never been that I can see . . ."

It was really quite good, but there were some terrible lyrics. That was one of the first; "Love Me Do" was from that batch as well. "Too Bad about Sorrows" was another one. I was very proud of them, actually.

BAIRD: Would you ever consider actually writing a book yourself?

PAUL: You know, I don't know. These possibilities are really starting to kind of come to the fore. To me John's passing has really made all this nostalgia, but for me I don't feel as though it's stopped yet.

BAIRD: No.

PAUL: But now that the twentieth anniversary of *Sgt. Pepper* is rolling around, so it's beginning to dawn on me what a big nostalgic event it is. You know, I was talking to Neil Aspinall at Ringo's wedding,* and we were remembering something that happened years ago and he said, "Oh, I remember it exactly, it was in Piccadilly Circus, wasn't it?" I said, "No, it was Savile Row." We had exactly the same story, but the background had somehow changed. So it suddenly made me think *ding,* "Wait a minute, I'd better put this down because it ain't gonna get any better, the old memory." Whether I'll write it all in longhand or whatever, I don't know. But, you know, so much has gone on that to me I kind of want to try and play down the John-and-me thing. I've never really tried to say, 'Yeah, I'm the guy who wrote all the songs with him! I'm the guy who knew him best."

BAIRD: But you are.

PAUL: Well, I am, that's what I mean, it's suddenly dawning on me.

BAIRD: It was a partnership.

PAUL: You know, ever since the days you're talking about at the Woolton Village Fete, we were always trying to write these little songs. Well, we eventually succeeded on a minor level, then on a huge mega level and now, here I am. When John went to New York I remember thinking that I might never see him again. Of course, there wasn't much I could do anyway because he was getting married. It's like a song we all used to do, "Wedding Bells Are Breaking Up That Old Gang of Mine." That was one of his songs, you know, I think your mom taught him that. I'll tell you another one she taught him, "Ramona."

BAIRD: Yeah, I remember. It's a lovely song.

PAUL: To this day I remember those things. Actually, that's the kind of songs my music publishing business is into.

BAIRD: I love it. What was the other one?

PAUL [sings]: "Girl of my dreams I love you, honest I do" and "Little White Lies," "The night that you told me, those little white lies." We actually used to try and write songs like those. For instance, in "Here, There and Everywhere" we'd put the little verse on the beginning because of our fondness for those old songs. [*Sings*] "To lead a better life, I need my love to be here." We just thought that was a great old tra-

---

*Ringo married actress Barbara Bach on April 27, 1981 at the Marylebone Registry Office in London.

dition, they don't do that anymore. A few of our songs did happily manage to bring that back. You know, a lot of John's musical influence has got to be traced back to Julia and, of course, mine would be my dad.

BAIRD: Your dad was in a band, wasn't he?

PAUL: Yeah, he was pianist, you know. He played by ear, his left one. Actually he was deaf in one ear. He fell off a railing or something when he was a kid, busted an eardrum. But yeah, he was my musical influence, so that's it.

BAIRD: Yeah, that was wonderful. Nine out of ten.

PAUL: Hey, what about *ten*?

BAIRD [mock horror]: You don't give *ten*! You can't encourage people.

PAUL: Oh, she's a hard taskmistress!

BAIRD: Paul, is it true that you didn't particularly want George in the group originally?

PAUL: No. I got George in the group originally, he was my little mate. Obviously, it's so long ago now that all these little things become rumors. You see, I knew George when none of the others knew him. They were all from the Woolton set and we were the Allerton crowd. Originally, I lived in Speke—I was a neighbor of George's—and we both went to the Institute, so we caught the same bus to school. Occasionally, we'd sit together and chat. We even learned guitar from the same book, George and I. I was, in fact, the one who suggested George to the group. We were looking for a good guitar player and I said, "I know this fellow who can play 'Raunchy' ..." They said, "What 'Raunchy'? No one can play *that!*" So I said, "Just wait till you hear him!"

BAIRD: So how old was he then?

PAUL: George was a baby. You know, I have a string of memories from that time, but no idea what year or month things were. People have documented it all, however, which I'm glad of, actually, as I'm dotty about that stuff. Anyway, I'm more artistic, I'm creative, I don't need to be that specific. That's my excuse.

BAIRD: So what about George's audition?

PAUL: That was on the top of the bus. Then about a week later we kinda went, "Well, what do you think?" And they said, "Yeah, man, he'd be great." Actually, the one I had problems with was Stuart and that is a regret now because he died, but you really can't help it if you run up against problems. The main problem there was, and it's been put down as millions of other things, was that he couldn't actually play his bass in the beginning. So that when we did photos and things it was a bit embarrassing. We had to ask him to turn away from the camera because if people saw where his fingers were, he wasn't in the same key as the rest of the group. I was probably over fussy at the time, but I thought, "Well, this isn't really a good thing for an aspiring group, we have a weak link here." He was really a lovely guy, you know, and a *great* painter, but he was the one I used to have all the ding doings with. Obviously, I wished now we hadn't because it all worked out okay and we eventually went to Hamburg with Stu as our bass player. I played guitar then, but it got broken so I shifted over to piano. I was just learning how to do all this stuff as we went along. Eventually, though, Stu wanted to stay in Hamburg because he fell in love with Astrid, so there was a kind of ceremonial handing over of the bass to me. Truthfully, we had our sticky moments, we even had a fight onstage one night. I assumed I'd win because he wasn't that big, but the maniac strength of love or something entered into him and he was no easy match at all. We were locked for about half an hour. "I'll kill you. I'll bloody get you!" I think they had to pour water on us in the end.

BAIRD: What are your early memories of Jacqui and I?

PAUL: Yes, of course I remember the two of you, but because John and I were a bit older there *was* a gap. You know how it is when you're seventeen. We all had fun, you were a good laugh, and I have some very happy memories too. We used to go to the place in Woolton where your dad lived.

BAIRD: That's right.

PAUL: Occasionally we'd use his record player to play Carl Perkins records on. In fact, I think we busted one of his once and got into trouble. It's funny what you remember, you know. Back to you as a kid, though. We never really talked that much.

BAIRD: Oh no, that's what I said. If John was doing anything with us, once his friends came over we were made to go outside and play or were sent up to bed. By the way, what do you remember about your first visits to Mendips?

PAUL: Well, the porch outside was always good—like the toilets—for guitars. We learned "Blue Moon" in there. I remember Mimi as being a very forthright, middle-class woman. Most of the women I'd seen previously were off of the estate. Not to put them down, but they were rather common. Although my mum wasn't like that, she sort of aspired to talk less like the other ladies. In fact, one of the worst moments in my life was when I made fun of the way she talked, because she sounded slightly posh. I can just hear Mimi saying, "John, your little *friend* is here to see you." You know, that kind of thing when it's obvious she was belittling you. But when you looked at her like, "Hey, wait a minute," there was a twinkle in her eye, so you kind of knew she quite liked you really. Even though she often seemed to keep people at a bit of arms' length. I think she used to think that maybe I was one of John's *nicer* friends and was to be encouraged. Because, obviously, there were a few that *weren't* to be encouraged. Inside the house, he'd be writing at the typewriter in his famous *In His Own Write* style, "In the early hours of the morcambe," which again, was very classy. I never knew anyone who had a typewriter. If someone wanted to write, it was like a pencil and a little pad. We used to play together in the garden in the summer, that was nice. Next question please, Magnus.

BAIRD: How did John and your brother get on? John has said he was very fond of him.

PAUL: Yeah, they liked each other. I think John liked Mike and was kind of like an elderly brother to him. Mike certainly idolized John, he was the guy we both looked up to. The other thing was there was a sort of "literature" thing between us. You know, art school poetry and the like. It was all there, the blossoming of all that in yourself where you never really had much of a chance except at school. Then when it turned out mates actually liked that kind of stuff, it was quite good. Okay? So look through for your next question because we will have to wind this up soon.

BAIRD: How did you help John out when Mummy died?

PAUL: Oh well, it's all a bit of a blank actually. When I look back all you kind of see is the word *T-R-A-D-G-E-Y* written in big, black letters. You just don't see much more. The only way I could help was, I'd had the same thing happen to me. So I couldn't really *say* anything. But there was a funny thing, not really *funny*, you know, but rather cruel, but it's boys and it's teenage. About a year or so after it happened when he was just getting over it—not really "over it," because you never *really* recover from things like that—but the shell was returning. In other words, he could bluff it out a bit better, the act was coming back together again. Anyway, people would meet us together and often say, "And how's you mum, then?" And I'd say, "Well, actually, she died a few years ago." We knew people would say, "Oh, I'm awfully sorry. Oh my God." And we used to have a laugh about that. It was a wonderful way of masking our true feelings and it gave us both a bit of a bond. We'd say to each other, "Oh Christ, here we go, they're gonna ask!" and we'd rather enjoy watching as the person wriggled with embarrassment.

BAIRD: What do you think you'd have been if you hadn't become a musician?

PAUL: I should have been a teacher because of the GEC thing I got.* I doubt now whether I would have had the patience, but I like kids okay. I enjoy passing on information.

BAIRD: What would you have taught?

PAUL: I think the only thing I vaguely had was English. I got an A level in English literature because of this good teacher I had we called Dusty Durbin. He got me into things like Chaucer by telling us to read all the dirty bits. You know, "The Miller's Tale" and all that. He knew how to get our attention.

BAIRD: And what do you think John would have been? I would say a commercial artist. That's what he went to art college for.

PAUL: I really don't know. I think John, in fact, had a great wanderlust, a great adventurous streak. I can imagine a scenario where from, say, eighteen, nineteen, and twenty he might have worked as a commercial artist. Then from twenty-one, twenty-two, and twenty-three maybe he'd have gone off on a boat somewhere. Because, you know, he did have this rather colonial attitude. A lot of British, Liverpool and even Scottish people have this thing that they're going to colonize everywhere. We're gonna go and quell the natives or teach them a thing or two.

BAIRD: Okay, now for some quick impressions. Pete Best.

PAUL: Pete? A good mate. His mom had a club where we played, you know.** A good lad, he was our first *real* drummer.

BAIRD: Mal Evans.

---

*General Education Certificate.
**The Casbah.

PAUL: Mal was a bouncer at the Cavern. A lovely, big, huggable bear of a man, who used to always request "I Forgot to Remember to Forget," which was an Elvis song, because first and foremost he was a Presley freak. He took *Elvis Monthly* all the time. A lovely, lovely man. Terrible ending, but that's life or . . . death.*

BAIRD: Alf Lennon.

PAUL: I didn't really contact much with Alf. I doubt whether I ever met him actually.** The only thing I knew was that it was a great pity that he reappeared through a news report in Sunday's *People* or something. It was, BEATLE'S DAD WASHES DISHES IN THE BEAR HOTEL IN ESHER.

BAIRD: Yeah, I know. It was awful.

PAUL: I was with John at the time when he had to kind of say, "*Oooohhh* . . ." Luckily, we had a good, robust nature, so we would say, "Oh, bloody hell, isn't it *typical?*" We managed to laugh it off like that. Eventually, of course, John went to see him.

BAIRD: George's parents.

PAUL: Harry and Louise Harrison. Harry was a bus driver who was a great man, but forthright and very straightforward. He would run over a *dog* with his bus rather than swerve and avoid it. Quite rightly, too, probably, because he might kill people. I remember always being a little bit disturbed about that hardness in his character, however. Now, Louise was lovely, she was quite a hard lady but soft inside. I remember her pouring a pan of water on some fellow she didn't want to answer the door to. No, she'd tell you how she felt, Louise.

BAIRD: Cynthia Lennon.

PAUL: Cyn was John's original girlfriend at art school. It was the time when you wanted to turn your girlfriend into Brigitte Bardot.

BAIRD: John adored Brigitte Bardot!

PAUL: I know, we all did. We were all just at the age for a sex goddess to be there taking her clothes off. At that age there's no contest with something as gorgeous as that. We were smitten, all of us. So all the

---

*In 1977 Mal Evans was shot to death by Los Angeles police while answering a domestic disturbance call.

**Actually, Paul McCartney did meet with John's father on at least one occasion. It was at the postproduction party for the cast and crew of *Magical Mystery Tour* at the Lancaster Hotel in December of 1967.

girls, they had to be blond, look rather like Brigitte, and pout a lot. John and I kind of had these secret talks where we intimated, without really saying it, that we wanted to try and turn our girlfriends into Liverpool's answer to Brigitte Bardot. So my girl was Dot and John was going out with Cynthia. I think we got them both to go blond and wear miniskirts. Terrible, isn't it, really? But that's the way it was.

BAIRD: Bob Wooler.

PAUL: Bob was a lovely, lovely chap at the Cavern and everything. Strangest thing about him though was, late at night, we'd drop him off after a gig and he'd never let us in his house. I don't know to this day what he was hiding. We used to imagine all sorts of things. If you do another book, we can go into what I imagined. You never got into his house. Other people, they'd invite you in for a cup of coffee, but with Bob it was, "Well, good night, lads . . ."

BAIRD: Mimi.

PAUL: Well, at first you might imagine she was a bit cantankerous, but she wasn't. She was forthright and I like that in women. I like them to stand up for themselves.

BAIRD: My dad.

PAUL: I didn't meet him much, but he seemed like a nice fella. I know John had this sort of *stepfather* thing. He liked him, but he couldn't quite associate with him as his dad. It was a problem I had later when my father remarried. I think when you look back on it, it was quite strange for him, really. Your dad was a good lad, though, he let us use his record player and everything. Actually, it was more your mom John was visiting, I think.

BAIRD: Oh, very definitely, there's no doubt about it. At the height of the Beatles' success it seemed as if John and George wanted to get off the road whereas you might have liked to stray out a little bit longer. Is that accurate?

PAUL: Kind of, yeah. No, what actually happened was that with John's "bigger than Jesus" quote and all these Klansmen marching around protesting, we had kind of a rough tour. It wasn't really that much worse than any of the others. I mean, we sold out, we did great, the individual shows were great, but people were trying to knock us and stuff. I remember John and George getting pissed off at the whole thing and eventually we simply decided to give it up to work in the studio.

BAIRD: What can you say about Brian?

PAUL: Eppie? There's a book that came out on me recently* and although I only flicked through it, there's one bit where he quotes my dad as saying, "Don't get in with Jew boys, son," or something. That's exactly the *opposite* of what he actually said, which was, "Get a good Jewish manager, they're very good at business." It's a real Liverpool working-class attitude. So we did eventually, and, of course, Brian came down to the Cavern and all that story. I think people know that bit. We liked him, we thought he was good. His gay bit never really entered into it as far as we were concerned.

BAIRD: It's something you didn't really hear about until he died.

PAUL: Well, we knew about it from the off. He didn't make any secret of it. You'd have to be daft not to see the kind of people he was around. So you kind of knew he was gay, but it never interfered. It was *his* world.

BAIRD: Well, I just remember him as being so polite and courteous.

PAUL: He was a lovely man, a lovely man, Brian. I think one of his main faults, though, as I used to point out with a word he hated, was that he was a little bit "green." I think it was true, however. Some of the deals he struck, like the fact that Lennon and McCartney songs weren't our copyright, were *very* naive. He had some business acumen, it's true, but his real thing was the *flair*. Also, I would say he was good for the people he introduced us to. When we first came down to London we were meeting people like Larry Gelbart, who was the writer who created M*A*S*H. It was an artistic class of people that I don't think we would have got in with otherwise. I think probably Brian had lots of faults, but I liked him.

BAIRD: Are you a Beatle collector?

PAUL: Yeah, odds and sods. I'm not a very thorough one, though, because I haven't got all the records, for instance, which is daft. I really ought to have all of them. I've got some great little things, however, like my Hofner bass with the gig list which is still taped to it. I've got my Sgt. Pepper coat. I've got the first record we ever made, which is great.

BAIRD: This fellow I'm working with on my book, Geoffrey Giuliano, is supposed to be one of America's biggest collectors.

McCartney by Chris Salewicz.

PAUL: Is he?

BAIRD: And he was very interested to know . . .

PAUL: What I've got. Well, I have a bunch of stuff, Geoffrey. Let's just leave it at that, shall we, son? I think we'll have to wrap up now, luv. So, good night, everybody, and remember, all the little birds and Daddy Bird say, "See you!" So rock on, bye. Say bye bye, Julia . . .

BAIRD: Bye bye.

Chester, September 14, 1986

GEOFFREY: Tell me the social worker's story if you would.

JULIA BAIRD: When John was three or four, Mimi was to have said to my mother, "You're not fit to have him." That would have been just after Victoria's birth.* I suppose Mimi's concern was for John, though, wasn't it? John could have greater stability with her. My mother, of course, desperately wanted him. As far as I know, Mimi had to go away the first time she tried to take him. My father said, "It's her child, and if she wants him, then that's it. It's her son." Anyway, Mimi returned with a social worker who said, "I don't want them to have him, they're not married." The worker then said, "Well, I'm sorry, Mrs. Smith, but John's her son. Come, show me where he sleeps." They were then shown the room where John was sleeping with my mother and father. John was given to Mimi at that point. And the social worker said, "When you have somewhere for John to sleep, then he comes back."

GEOFFREY: Later your mother presumably became convinced that it was better for John to live with Mimi.

BAIRD: My mother probably thought he'd been backwards and forwards enough. The only reason she handed him over was for his own good.

---

*Victoria was Julia Lennon's second child. Born on June 19, 1945 in Liverpool, she was immediately given up for adoption and nothing further has been heard from her since.

GEOFFREY: What does Mimi say about Julia? Does she ever imply she might have been derelict in her duty to have given John up?

BAIRD: All of my family say that my mother was a most wonderful person and I remember it to be so. I think she was a bit eccentric, though.

GEOFFREY: What about this idea that your mother was of loose morals?

BAIRD: Obviously it's not something I want to confront. But I know now that first there was John and then there was another child, Victoria, before me, which I didn't know until about two or three years ago.

GEOFFREY: Would the other sisters have lit into her for that?

BAIRD: I'm sure. She already had John, didn't she? There was no money coming from his father, and Pop [Julia Lennon's father] was helping keep them. From what I gather, between my grandfather and Mimi the pressure was on to have the baby adopted. Mummy didn't go into Sefton General to have Victoria, where John, Jacqui, and I were born. She went into a nursing home, where they arranged the adoption. Mum had the baby and it was adopted by a Norwegian sea captain, as far as I know.

GEOFFREY: This Victoria would be forty-two now, with virtually no knowledge of her background.

BAIRD: Apparently Norwegian law says you don't have to tell the child anything. Now, here, if you're adopted, you get your birth certificate and you see immediately if you've been adopted.

GEOFFREY: I suppose it's very difficult to give us your first memory of John because, as you've said, he always seemed to be there.

BAIRD: I never realized he was a half brother because you don't realize such things, do you, unless the family's going to make it clear, which they didn't.

GEOFFREY: Until when?

BAIRD: I was about sixteen. I overheard two aunts talking.

GEOFFREY: But surely you knew his last name was Lennon?

BAIRD: It didn't mean a thing to me. They were always talking about Freddy Lennon and it began to wash over me when I was about fourteen, but I completely put it to one side until I heard the two aunts discussing it. We'd never been brought up as "This is your half brother, this is your half sister."

GEOFFREY: From what I can gather, your family was close to the extent that the whole clan became an extended family. John might live with

Mimi, you could stay with one aunt, and another aunt could take care of the other kids for a while. That's very different.

BAIRD: Yes, we cousins were together when we were growing up. Leila, Stanley, and John were close and David, Jacqui, Michael, and I are like a second family within the children's generation. We're all still called "the children," however. We did visit a lot because all the sisters were really very, very close.

GEOFFREY: What kind of big brother was John?

BAIRD: Obviously he didn't live with us full-time. You look back now and think, Why didn't we think it was odd? But we didn't, it was just the way it was. He'd come over weekends, we'd get up and John would be there. The older we got, the more he came round with his mates until he was there almost nightly and at lunch. When he was younger he used to take us to the park. My mother would say, "Take the girls to the swings, please, John." He'd take us out while he played football with his friends and we had a go on the swings. He used to take us to the pictures under duress. We went to see the Elvis film *Love Me Tender,* which we saw twice because we were abandoned there. He'd watch it once with us and then run off. I don't know where he went, probably to see his friends or something. Then he'd pick us up after the second show.

GEOFFREY: Tell me about John's bedroom at Mendips.

BAIRD: Well, he had this small front room which you could just about get you and the cat in. You'd open the door and he'd have skeletons and things flying about with their arms all going in the air. John made them himself. The lights went on and off and these puppets jiggled around when you opened the door.

GEOFFREY: On John's *Plastic Ono Band* album in 1970 he referred to himself as the Dreamweaver. One gets the idea that he was indeed very dreamy, but I get that feeling, too, about your mother.

BAIRD: Very much so. She lived in a bit of a fantasy world.

GEOFFREY: Did you ever personally meet Alf Lennon?

BAIRD: No. He was just sort of a mythical being. Every now and again you'd hear the name and that would be it. We all realized he'd run away. We thought he'd jumped ship in America. He didn't turn up again until John was about five. I've heard since he came back when he was eighteen months old.

GEOFFREY: Do you feel that Julia did indeed love Alf Lennon?

BAIRD: Nanny says they were determined they were going to get married. If anything, it was my mother who was more determined than he. All she needed was an attic to live in. She just wanted to be with him. Mummy was always an incurable romantic, I'm afraid.

GEOFFREY: People often comment on your mother's alleged promiscuity in the period between leaving Fred Lennon and meeting your father, John Dykins. Recently we've also learned that a female child was born to Julia around that time. How do you think John might want you to reflect now on those early years?

BAIRD: Well, it's really got nothing to do with what John would want me to say, as she was my mother too. I do know that she was deserted by Alf and was therefore forced to bring up her little boy by herself. Eventually though she moved into my grandfather George's. As for Julia's love life, what might be called promiscuous in those days certainly wouldn't be now. Look, she'd been deserted by her husband and was therefore not eligible to remarry. You see, in those days the husband had to disappear for seven years before a divorce would be granted. So she was in a very difficult position and the mere fact that she had a boyfriend I don't think is promiscuous by any standards. I feel great sympathy for her.

GEOFFREY: How did your parents actually meet?

BAIRD: Aunt Nannie told me that Julia had taken a part-time job and she met him there. She didn't dare bring him home to Pop after all that had happened, so they met together secretly for quite some time.

GEOFFREY: Why did your mother decide to give John to Aunt Mimi to raise?

BAIRD: I think it was really a very gradual thing that happened because my mother had met my father.

GEOFFREY: I met a taxi driver yesterday who was a childhood friend of John's, and I was very surprised to learn that neither he nor any of the other neighborhood kids realized that Mimi wasn't actually John's mother.

BAIRD: Well, John was certainly very aware of it.

GEOFFREY: Yes, but Mimi apparently didn't go out of her way to tell people, "Look, this isn't really my son."

BAIRD: Oh no, of course not. Anyone who really knew the family would have known, but everyone else would have seen her walking John to school and assumed that he was her child.

GEOFFREY: Tell me something about John as a boy.

BAIRD: Happy as a lark, whimsical, always dancing up and down, very good with us girls. Really just a lovable big brother hanging around the house, we were all great friends.

GEOFFREY: People say that he was rather aggressive, though.

BAIRD: He wasn't within the family. He was always a very family-oriented person.

GEOFFREY: What about his relationship with Mimi? It was rather tempestuous, wasn't it?

BAIRD: Not always. I think as a teenager he was certainly a rebel. He rebelled against school as he didn't really like the uniformity. He also rebelled against art school by not working when he finally got there. I don't really know what he would have done if he hadn't broken into music so successfully.

GEOFFREY: Tell me about John singing to you girls.

BAIRD: He'd sing to all of us, not just Jacqui and me. He'd perform for all the children in the road. My mother would do exactly the same.

GEOFFREY: What did he sing?

BAIRD: Very simple stuff on the piano. And later Elvis songs just banging away.

GEOFFREY: Did John and Mimi argue much?

BAIRD: They started having great rows about John's clothes and things. Mimi was doing the bread and butter and looking after us. My mother was the fun girl. It must have been a difficult position for Mimi to be in.

GEOFFREY: You've commented that your mother and John had a great thing going, humor wise?

BAIRD: They both had a fantastic sense of humor. There was a terrific rapport between them. There was a lot of wit flying backwards and forwards.

GEOFFREY: You've said it really wasn't like a mother-son relationship at all. It was more of a friendship.

BAIRD: Well, I mean, this is how it is when you got older, isn't it? She would still do the washing for him, though.

GEOFFREY: Did he always call her Mummy?

BAIRD: Always.

GEOFFREY: What kind of trauma did Uncle George [Smith] dying create in the family?

BAIRD: John would have been very upset about it. Uncle George worked nights and we never really knew what happened. He gave John lots of love, affection, and time. John would have missed him desperately.

GEOFFREY: What's all this "Twitchy" business?

BAIRD: It's a name I take very great offense to.

GEOFFREY: How did it come about in the first place? John must have called your father that at one point.

BAIRD: He probably did to his friends, but not to my father's face. People have said he called him Twitchy, and I'm very cross about it, it's just not true! Daddy did have a nervous cough and was highly strung. I didn't even know about this nickname until I read it in a book. I can't see how it was derived, John always called him "Bobby" because that's what my mother called him.

GEOFFREY: Did your dad pay a lot of attention to John?

BAIRD: Yes, he did. I don't ever remember Daddy shouting, "Get out and take all your guitars and your friends with you!"

GEOFFREY: Was there a piano in the house?

BAIRD: Oh yes, we had a piano and Mummy taught John the banjo. I re-member she use to teach him all the chords. It was a mother-of-pearl banjo. Of course, everyone was madly enthusiastic because of Elvis, weren't they? I also remember he'd come over with his guitar and his mates would come with him. The last years in that house, it definitely became *the* practice place for John and his pals. John and Paul used to practice in the bathroom because it echoed. My mother loved it all, she use to be in there with them.

GEOFFREY: So Paul met your mother then?

BAIRD: Yes, he did. In fact, I remember mother saying to John, "It's such a sad thing to lose your mum. It's so awful not to have your mother."

GEOFFREY: What was John's first public appearance like?

BAIRD: I think we were more interested in the coconut showers and run-ning off, as it was a garden fete at Woolton Parish. Paul and John first met there. It just seemed to us it was only what was going on in the bathroom at home. It was exciting, though, because there was more equipment. We once saw him play in Roseberry Street as well. Jacqui and I went on a Sunday-school outing to a place called Casberry Hill. When we got back to the church Mummy was there waiting for us. Instead of going home we got the bus into town. My mother decided to take us to see his group Johnny and the Rainbows. We got off the bus at Princess Avenue. I ran on ahead, and she was saying, "Look for Roseberry Street." We were shouting, "Here it is, here it is!" John and Paul were playing on the back of a flatbed lorry. John pulled Jacqui and I up onto the back because we were going to be squashed in all this crowd of people. The lady of the house brought us out a cup of tea and said not to get frightened.

GEOFFREY: Do you remember John bringing George around?

BAIRD: I remember George was dead skinny and he came from Speke. That's all I knew about him.

GEOFFREY: Was John very much the leader of all these guys?

BAIRD: I couldn't really say. I saw them at our house, but Paul lived quite a walk away. I don't know if they went to Paul's house. As far as I know, most of the rehearsals were at our place.

GEOFFREY: Do you remember John's first girlfriend?

BAIRD: The girls always liked John. This one girl, Barbara Baker, appeared a lot. She lived up in Woolton near Mimi. John was coming down more and more, so she used to show up as well. We would all be playing and there she was. I remember once she asked us to go and fetch John. We did and my mother came out and shouted, "What do you want from him?" The next thing I know, John was walking down the road with her. They would cuddle together in the grass.

GEOFFREY: I've heard that Mimi once wanted John to accept a job as a bus conductor.

BAIRD: It must be very worrying to see somebody you're responsible for living on a dream when their whole life is stretching out in front of them.

GEOFFREY: Did you ever go to the Cavern to see the Beatles?

BAIRD: Everybody went to the Cavern. I didn't go as much as I might have, as we lived quite a long way out of town. The last bus back was ridiculously early so we couldn't really stay out very late.

GEOFFREY: You must have talked to Paul back then. Would he talk with you a little bit?

BAIRD: He would sort of speak. I remember at Mimi's they would all say, "Yes, hello," but they would mostly just talk business.

GEOFFREY: Tell me how John first got involved with Cynthia.

BAIRD: That was at art school. We all knew John had this girlfriend, and then she started appearing. We were greatly impressed by her. She was a beautiful blonde and John use to bring her round Harry's house while Jacqui, David, and I were living in the cottage. They'd sit holding hands, chatting, and drinking tea on Saturdays, after school, every day really. She became a fixture, definitely.

GEOFFREY: When I mentioned you talking to Cynthia now, you intimated you might not want to. Why? Has time created hard feelings?

BAIRD: Cynthia was always very good to us. When we went to Weybridge to stay it was always Cynthia who took us shopping and all the rest of it. When John split with her and started living with Yoko she had her own life to live. She had a brother in South Africa and her mother had come back from Canada and was living in Esher. So she had her own family. We just saw less and less of her. The next time I saw her was at Harry's funeral. She turned up out of the blue.

GEOFFREY: She lives around here, doesn't she?

BAIRD: Her roots are here, twenty miles up the road at Hoy Lake. When she came back from the Italian drama, she returned there. Julian was at school. At that time I was in touch with John, 1974 or '75. He kept asking in letters and on the phone, "Will you please go and see Julian? I haven't heard from him. Will you please go see what's going on?" I didn't really want to because you just don't bounce in on people. Eventually, though, Allan [Baird's husband] persuaded me that I should when we got another letter asking, "Have you been to see Julian yet?" Allan said, "Look, he's never asked you to do anything else. I think you should go." So we went. It was just six miles around the corner. John had given us the address. She seemed very embarrassed to see me. In fact, so much so that I backed off and said, "Is Julian there, please? I would like to see him." She said, "No, he's gone out," and I just said, "Well, good-bye, then." It was very odd.

GEOFFREY: Was she doing okay?

BAIRD: Well, she lived in a very nice bungalow. She wasn't married again at the time. She did subsequently marry John Twist. She didn't get in touch again. I do regret that I didn't see Julian because perhaps we could have formed some sort of relationship. Like John said, "His auntie was living just round the corner and I'd like him to know my family." I think that's very true.

GEOFFREY: You could *still* see Julian, you know.

BAIRD: I've got my own children now. It's a different matter altogether.

GEOFFREY: Would you like to see him?

BAIRD: I don't know. I'm still his aunt. I'd make him welcome. But I don't see much point, he's made his own life. He doesn't really know that much about our side of the family.

GEOFFREY: How did it affect your life when the Beatles became very successful in Liverpool before they went to America?

BAIRD: At school it was nice. We spent quite a few double A level lessons sitting and chatting about the Beatles. Still, the school, like me, had grown up with it and we were all a little blasé about the whole thing. I went down to London on shopping trips and it was all very exciting. Kenwood* was just being renovated.

GEOFFREY: Do you remember when the Beatles went to the States for the first time?

BAIRD: Oh yes. That's when John really departed from our lives.

GEOFFREY: Didn't Mimi go on one of those trips?

BAIRD: Mimi went on a world tour. She went to Hong Kong and brought us all back watches and things. We have family in New Zealand and she went to stay for about six months, but that wasn't a Beatle thing. She went to see her family and stopped off in Hong Kong on the way and brought us all stuff back.

GEOFFREY: Do you remember what it was like at Mendips when the fans were going nuts in the garden?

BAIRD: Oh yes. That was awful. Poor Mimi. I really felt sorry for her. She was beleaguered by people camping in the garden.

GEOFFREY: How did John change when he got money?

BAIRD: He was still very family-minded.

GEOFFREY: People have told me he never really cared that much about money.

BAIRD: I think anyone who asked for it got it. Which prevented a lot of people who maybe would have liked to have done from asking. John

---

*John and Cynthia's home in Weybridge, Surrey.

was very family-minded and lovable. The Beatles were doing shows at the same time. He did a gig once and we all went to watch it. We were in the dressing room and Mick Jagger was there. People would come in to wish them well and everyone was drinking Cokes. Jacqui and I were put in the front row. We wanted to go out front so we could see the show. When it got a bit raucous John said, "Get the girls," and we were hauled onto the stage and watched from the wings because we didn't realize everyone was raging forward.

GEOFFREY: You must have felt very special going up onstage when all the other girls were clambering about.

BAIRD: No, it wasn't as glamorous as that. We were just hauled up bellywise into the wings to get out of the way.

GEOFFREY: Where did John and Cynthia stay when they first got married?

BAIRD: I was there chatting with Mimi in the morning and she said, "John wants to see me this afternoon. I know what he wants, he wants to move in, and I'm going to let him." I said, "What are *you* going to do, Mimi?" She said, "I'm going to live upstairs," and that's exactly what she did. John's bedroom was converted into her kitchen. Just a tiny little cooker where John's bed was and she made the front bedroom her sitting room.

GEOFFREY: How long did they live there?

BAIRD: I don't know. A couple of months or something. Then I don't know where they went. I remember them moving in, though.

GEOFFREY: How did Mimi react to John's initial success?

BAIRD: At that stage you couldn't really argue with it, could you?

GEOFFREY: When he first got money, what did he do? Did he run out and buy a big car?

BAIRD: He couldn't drive until he lived at Kenwood. He didn't have a license, so he didn't buy a car. I don't know when he bought his Mini, but I know that Harry borrowed it for a time because John couldn't yet drive.

GEOFFREY: Do you remember Julian being born?

BAIRD: Yes, I do. I remember Cynthia coming home from the hospital and going into Mimi's morning room. Mater and Stan were there. We were all gawking at this baby. He was called John Charles Julian Lennon and he had a birthmark on his head. Of course it's covered by hair now, so perhaps I shouldn't say. When a child is born you can see a parent in them and to me he looked very like Cynthia.

GEOFFREY: I heard John was away on tour at that time.

BAIRD: No, he wasn't around. I think he probably saw him first by himself.

GEOFFREY: Did Cynthia cloister herself at Mendips?

BAIRD: She stayed with her mother initially. Her mum had been a nanny in Canada. After John made it and Cynthia had Julian, her mother came back.

GEOFFREY: When the Beatles first started to happen, did John say anything to you like, "Hey, I did it!"? Was he very excited?

BAIRD: He was around the corner at Mendips. Then he was away more and more. Gradually, it would just be reports of what John was up to rather than John himself reporting in. In school everyone was very interested in what was going on. Jacqui and I started writing to some of the fans. The letters came to Mendips, there were thousands of them. We were just scouting through the letters and one girl sounded very interesting. She lived in Castleford near Leeds and I actually wrote to her for about six or seven months.

GEOFFREY: When was A Hard Day's Night?

BAIRD: 1965. I was eighteen. We all went to the premiere in Liverpool as a family. It was a place [the Liverpool Town Hall] we had gone by for years and suddenly, there you were on this balcony looking out at thousands of people, wondering what it was all about. We were told not to eat all the sandwiches and things. We actually lost John there. I think we were at the whole thing without seeing John at all apart from on the balcony before the film. He shouted out, "Where's my family? Are you still here?" It was so mad and we just waved and said, "We're up here!"

GEOFFREY: What about John's early relationship with Paul? Mike McCartney told me recently that they used to argue a lot even back then.

BAIRD: They would have done because they were two very strong personalities, both trying to assert themselves. Still they made a very good team.

GEOFFREY: Do you recall hearing the Beatles on the radio very early on?

BAIRD: We'd come home from school and John was always there to inform us when the Beatles would be on the radio. At that time they did a big concert in Liverpool and we all had front-row seats. That was our first experience of the wildness of Beatlemania. We were locked in the dressing room, unable to get out. I think that's when it really hit me, I thought, What *is* going on?

GEOFFREY: Tell me about these wild shopping sprees John and Cynthia took you on.

BAIRD: We had whatever we wanted. Jacqui got a pair of beautiful leather trousers. It was just clothes beyond what you would have normally been able to afford. Expensive jumpers, records, and things.

GEOFFREY: What about your visit to George Harrison's house?

BAIRD: We went to Esher not long after George moved in. John said, "We're just going across for a visit." Cynthia drove. It was John, Cynthia, Julian, Jacqui, and me.

GEOFFREY: Was he married to Pattie Boyd at the time?

BAIRD: I don't know. All I could think was that she was the Smith's Crisps girl and she had a lisp. The house was very bare, but nice. There were cushions on all the floors. I think it was the last time I've ever personally seen George. We'd seen Pattie once before at Woolworth's in Liverpool promoting Smith's Crisps.

GEOFFREY: Tell me what John said when he rang you in 1970 in Ireland after you were with Allan.

BAIRD: I asked him what he was doing. It was during the macrobiotic period. Harry said he was a veritable skeleton of the boy he was. He had lost so much weight and she didn't feel it was a good diet.

GEOFFREY: Tell me about the time you went to Apple.

BAIRD: It was on one of my trips to London. I used to go and help Leila with her three children when she was doctoring in the hospital. After she returned from Germany she was living initially in one of John's flats in Sloane Square and then she bought her own house in London. On one of those occasions I was literally strolling on Savile Row and I thought, "I'll just nip in," and I did. I stepped into Apple's main reception area with millions of people, walked up to the desk, and asked, "Is John here?" And the girl said, "Yes, he's upstairs. Who are you?" and I said, "I'm his sister, actually." She said, "Mr. Lennon hasn't got any sisters." I said, "No, of course not," and walked out. I just wasn't prepared for the fight, if you like. If the place had been empty, I would have said something, but because there were people hanging around I just thought it didn't matter and left. I told John about it later and he said, "You silly fool, you should have come upstairs." I said, "Well, I was just so flung when she said he hasn't got any sisters."

GEOFFREY: How effective do you feel John and Yoko's various peace demonstrations were?

BAIRD: I was very glad I was in Ireland and that nobody knew John was my brother when he was cavorting around in black bags. I don't doubt for one second, however, that he was one-million-percent sincere about the whole thing. But I was glad no one knew about us. I guess it embarrassed me.

GEOFFREY: Do you think John was crazy?

BAIRD: No. John was by then a very powerful figure and he genuinely thought, "If I do something as outlandish as this, perhaps people will sit up and take notice. They'll discuss it and even if they ridicule it, they're taking notice and listening." In any sort of protest, you make an idiot of yourself. Walking along in the rain with a placard isn't the nicest way to spend a weekend, but people will sit up and take notice even if they say, "Look at that damned idiot walking along in the rain with a placard." And John had real clout.

GEOFFREY: What do you feel about John's inferred philosophy that soft drugs stimulate creatively and help people tap into their own innate spirituality?

BAIRD: I'd say that many creative people like Byron, Keats, Shelley, the great artists, often perform under the influence of these mind-expanding aids. The very fact that a lot of artists perform, write, paint, and think under the influence of these drugs says something. For years people have been chewing on stuff, it's just different types of stuff. So what can you say about John doing it?

GEOFFREY: What did you think at the time?

BAIRD: You'd think things like, I hope he knows what he is doing. I hope he's not doing himself any physical harm. Obviously, it was Cynthia's refusal to take part in John's LSD trips that was the beginning of the end for them. Whether Yoko was more willing, I don't know. But for Cynthia, it just wasn't her lifestyle, that's why she lost John. He tried to get her to do these things and she didn't want to. Personally, I didn't want to do it either. John had to entrench himself in the company of like-minded people. She made her choice, I made my choice, and John made his choice.

GEOFFREY: What do you think John's overall contribution was?

BAIRD: I think he was a genius. A bottomless talent. Just beautiful. I could have see him writing poetry and highly imaginative books. Of course, there was also his artwork as well. He was just maturing as an artist when he died.

GEOFFREY: How do you think future generations will regard him?

BAIRD: I think he will always be highly regarded. I can't see it any other way. Particularly being cut off in his prime. From what I hear, Yoko has many more tapes of John. I'm sure in time we'll hear those as well.

GEOFFREY: Do you feel that he was the driving force of the Beatles?

BAIRD: Absolutely. I would say he was the driving force in terms of both personality and talent.

GEOFFREY: How do you feel about John's decision in the midseventies to embrace the role of a househusband?

BAIRD: It was very admirable. They'd obviously made the decision between them that Yoko was going to be the businessperson.

GEOFFREY: Did you ever meet Yoko?

BAIRD: No. The family has met her, but I didn't. John rung me in 1970 in Ireland. That's when I went home and just missed them, when Yoko left me her silk blouses.

GEOFFREY: Did he keep in touch with anyone in the family between 1970 and 1976?

BAIRD: I think Mater might have heard from him, as did Stanley, Leila, and Harry.

GEOFFREY: What did you think when he and Yoko went to LA in the early seventies and got into the whole primal-scream trip?

BAIRD: John was trying to get rid of the agony of Mummy's death in one way and I was getting rid of it by throwing myself into my children.

GEOFFREY: How did you and John get back together again after all those years?

BAIRD: Mater rang one night just after John had gone back with Yoko in 1976. He told Mater, "Get in touch with the girls." He said that he wanted to see us. He told her that he had been thinking about Mother a lot and wanted to make it up to us. He said he could set Allan up in business and if we needed anything we were only to ask. Probably, if he hadn't been such a megabucker, we'd have been in touch before. If he had immigrated to Australia and become a sheep farmer, I would have gone and stayed, but his financial position put him out of touch with just about everyone. Allan was saying, "Are you going to ring him?" "I need time." I said, "I need to think about it."

GEOFFREY: Did Allan want you to call?

BAIRD: Yes, but he wasn't a money-grubbing idiot. The first time I phoned I didn't know what to expect. A woman answered and said she'd been expecting my call for some time. She asked all kinds of questions, my maiden name, who had given me the number, my father's middle name. After a few minutes I said, "Forget it, just forget it, it's all wrong." As I put the phone down I heard John shout, "Hang on, don't hang up! I'm sorry about that, but you have no idea how many sisters, cousins, and aunties I've got." Then we had a long, long chat. Mostly he was going on about, "Do you recall laughing with Mummy and do you remember her spotted dress?" He said he had a new baby and asked about ours and Jacqui's and wondered if ours looked Irish. He wanted to know if my daughter Nicki had red hair like Mummy's. We didn't talk about being famous at all.

GEOFFREY: Were there any tears?

BAIRD: Oh yes, he cried and I cried. We spent a lot of money crying! John said, "I've thought a lot about you over the years. Really and truly I have." We were talking about how he felt about Mummy and how he felt now that he had a baby. He said he'd screwed things up with Julian, completely. "I've been looking for a family and now I realize I've had one all along," he told me. I said, "Yes, you have, but we're here and you're there." Then we talked about his green card and how the US government was trying to boot him out of the country. There was so much he wanted to do in America, and if he left, they wouldn't let him back in. "You'll have to come over," he said. But nothing ever materialized. Ironically it was John who said, "We'd better get off this call. Next time call collect." "You mean reverse the charges?" I said, "Speak to me in English, you've gone American on us!"

GEOFFREY: Didn't John ask you to send him some family photographs?

BAIRD: He asked if I had any of Mummy and I said yes. There was one in particular where she was pregnant with Jacqui and I had this big, furry hat on. Leila, Stan, and John were also in it. Allan did a twenty-by-sixty black-and-white print of it, but with only Mummy and John. I eventually snipped John off it because I only wanted a photograph of my mother. John said, "Send it to me, please. Send it to me." I said, "You must be joking. You must have far more photographs than I. You should send me what you've got!" He said, "The stupid reporters took them all and I never got any of them back. I haven't a single one of Mummy." The next day we packed up loads of photographs and sent them over.

GEOFFREY: How long did that first call last?

BAIRD: Two and a half hours. Allan paid the bill. It was enormous. After that I called collect.

GEOFFREY: What would you say to John if he were here now?

BAIRD: I'm very sorry that I was out of touch for so long. I would love to be with him and I'm sorry I have been away. I could kick myself for not seeing him before. I should have made more of an effort to stay in touch with him. It's easy to say, "*He* should have done it." But *I* could have done it as well.

GEOFFREY: What do you think John's greatest achievement was, musically?

BAIRD: The song "Julia" I'm very proud of.

GEOFFREY: Did you hear from John when your father died?

BAIRD: No. I don't know if he even knew about it. Later, when we were phoning, he said, "I'm sorry about Bobby dying. I'm so sorry you lost Bobby as well. You've had a very hard time." When I was talking to John about looking after Sean he said he was really going to throw himself into it and be with him twenty-four hours a day. I said, "You're not going to spoil him terribly or indulge him, are you?" He said, "No, I'm not." That's when he said he regretted not having been able to do anything with Julian because he was on tour all the time. Julian was pawned out a lot to people. When Julian was small, we all gathered at Mimi's because John was there. We sat for years listening to idle chit-chat. But this time we were really listening because John was there. I don't know what Nanny said to him, but John insisted that his child wasn't going to be a stuffed dummy, he was going to be a wild spirit! A couple of years later he was ringing Mimi, pleading, "Can you please take Julian and do something with him!"

GEOFFREY: Did you tell John the story about that boy who claimed to you that he was your brother?

BAIRD: I told him on the phone. He said, "What a load of rubbish. You don't know how many brothers and sisters I've got." About phone call number nine I thought, "I really want to do something for him." Allan and I talked about it. You couldn't really buy him anything he doesn't have bigger, better, and ten of already. So I decided I would get an elegant Irish tablecloth and embroider it for him. It was taking a long, long time. I was doing a bit and then putting it down. I thought, "He's keen on food, he likes presenting it well," you can tell that by listening to him. I worked on it for two years and, of course, it still wasn't finished when he died. I remember thinking that him coming over would spur me on. That was my present for John. I'm going to finish it this summer.

GEOFFREY: Was it difficult getting through to John on the phone?

BAIRD: Sometimes I got through to John, sometimes his secretary, and sometimes to Yoko. Initially it was all, "Yes, I'll go get John, and, yes, here he is." Sometimes, however, Yoko just broke in on a phone call. That was fine. We never said anything she wouldn't have already known, I'm sure. The next thing I heard was that he was coming over in January of 1980, it was on the family grapevine.

GEOFFREY: Tell me about the letter you got from Yoko.

BAIRD: In the midst of John writing me letters, after I sent some photographs over, Yoko wrote me. It just headed, "Summer of '75, New York City." It was just a chatty letter saying that Jacqui looks like John when he's in good condition, chatting about Sean and what they did together. I was quite surprised, though, to see that it was from Yoko and not John.

GEOFFREY: What did John tell you he'd been up to during all those years he spent away from the music business?

BAIRD: I asked him what he did with himself and he said he was a househusband. He looked after Sean. He was going to give him the years he hadn't given Julian, which he always regretted. He was steeped in things like changing the baby and seeing to his needs. He also learned how to bake bread and was always asking me how to cook. He asked me how hard my loaves were and how soggy bread was supposed to be in the middle. He said he always wanted to look at them when he knew he shouldn't open the oven. "Wasn't it lovely eating it straight out of the oven?" and things like that. As children none of us cooked. We always came in from school to a full delicious meal every night. We never had to do anything. So we left home not knowing how to boil an egg. Now John was learning on his own. He told me that at first his bread was rock hard and couldn't be eaten. Then he talked about cooking meat. His favorite must have been lamb. When he came home to Harry's with Yoko in 1969 she cooked him a leg of lamb when he was all macrobiotic and he loved it. When Cynthia and he were entertaining at Kenwood he particularly wanted her to cook a leg of lamb. Then he asked me, "How do you cook lamb?" And I was saying, "I just roast it, I don't do anything particular." "Do you put it in baker foil or not?" It was like two old women exchanging kitchen news. He was making me laugh saying, "You've no idea how exhausting it is looking after a baby." I said, "I'm on my second one now, of course I know." He seemed to be thoroughly enjoying life. He said he loved going to the park with Sean and Yoko, pushing the baby.

GEOFFREY: You heard through the grapevine that he was coming over just before he died?

BAIRD: I thought, "This time I'm *definitely* going to see him." I thought about the tablecloth. I must get some work done on it so I could show him.

GEOFFREY: How long was it after you met Allan Baird that you told him John was your brother?

BAIRD: Oh, a long time. Months. He was actually bragging to me that he knew the drummer for Them.

GEOFFREY: What did you say?

BAIRD: "Well, actually, I can go you one better. I am John Lennon's sister." At first he said, "Pardon, what was that?" Then he said, "Oh," because he had just been bragging. I just told him and that was it.

GEOFFREY: You were all obviously very close and yet for so many years no one really knew you or your sister even existed. Did John go out of his way to insulate you from all the madness of Beatlemania?

BAIRD: I think he tried very hard to keep his family life private. Only Mimi has really chosen to be interviewed thus far.

GEOFFREY: What prompted you to write your book, *John Lennon / My Brother?*

BAIRD: I just wanted to set the record straight because of all the many misconceptions about my mother and John. I've simply told the truth as I know it. Remember, I was there.

The Shirley Show
Toronto, February 1993

SHIRLEY SOLOMON: Did you read Geoffrey's book *Blackbird?*

FREDERIC SEAMAN: Yes. I thought it was quite good. He confirms the story that Yoko had a hand in having McCartney busted in Japan in 1980, which Paul denies.

GEOFFREY GIULIANO: He may not even know.

SEAMAN: I think he knew long before any of our books were published. He just denies it, because he has a business relationship with Yoko to protect.

SOLOMON: Tell me about that.

SEAMAN: McCartney was on his way to Japan in January of 1980 when he called the Dakota and wanted to hang out with John, whom he hadn't seen in about two years. Only he didn't get through to John. Yoko saw to that. But in his conversation with Yoko he told her that

May Pang was John Lennon's lover during his notorious 18-month "Lost Weekend" in the mid-seventies.

Frederic Seaman was Lennon's personal assistant from the late seventies until the singer's tragic death in December of 1980.

Shirley Solomon is a popular Canadian TV talk show hostess.

325

Linda had scored some dynamite marijuana. He also said that he was on his way to Japan and that he and Linda were planning to stay at the Hotel Akura, in the presidential suite. Which is the same room where John and Yoko always stayed. When Yoko heard this she became very upset, because in her mind it would forever spoil their good "hotel karma." She told John that something had to be done about it. She said she was going to put a spell on Paul to insure he'd never move into that hotel room. The following day she went into a meeting with one of her psychics and, indeed, the next day Paul was busted at the airport in Tokyo.

SOLOMON: They [the McCartneys] really liked grass a lot, didn't they?

SEAMAN: Yeah, they're really into pot. You see, as far as John was concerned, Yoko was a very powerful magician, a sorceress, and she put a spell on Paul. In fact, what she actually did was place a call to a relative who was a high official at Japanese customs. They knew Paul was carrying, but they didn't really want to bust him. They asked if he had anything to declare. If he had turned it over, perhaps they would have let him go. But Paul became very belligerent. So they had no choice but to search him. Anyway, they found the drugs and carted him off to jail. John was very fascinated by the whole thing. He asked me to get all the British papers and enjoyed rumors that Paul was being forced by his Japanese captors to play "Yesterday" over and over again on the guitar. So the whole thing was very amusing to him. He knew nothing would really happen to Paul. They would keep him in the slammer a few days and then deport him.

GEOFFREY: But Paul himself was worried, because there was a possibility he could get up to eight years. The Japanese don't fool around with this stuff. They wouldn't even let him take a shower. He was apparently washing his face in the toilet. Finally, they said, "Do you want to take your bath alone or with the others?" So he said, with the others. Anyway, he stripped down and they were all just staring at him. The guards, everyone in the whole place was there. Being the eternal showman he is he broke into song and started singing "Mull of Kintyre." And they all jumped in in Japanese.

SOLOMON: Fred, you were John's personal assistant.

SEAMAN: Yes. My book* is a personal memoir. It's based on my own ex-

---

*The Last Days of John Lennon, published by Birch Lane Press in 1991.

perience and my journals. So I stand behind it one hundred percent.
Because I know what I experienced.

GEOFFREY: I stand behind it as well, by the way.

SOLOMON: Yes, but it's only his perception of Yoko Ono. Really, truthfully, it is.

GEOFFREY: No, it's *many* people's perceptions of Ono. I personally don't
know anyone who has had dealings with Yoko who walked away feeling
good about it.

SEAMAN: Well, the people who are making a lot of money off her and
still on her payroll, they feel good about her.

SOLOMON: May, do you like her?

MAY PANG: I don't really have a relationship with her anymore. I don't
have a very high opinion of her. Because I know things that happened
in the past in my relationship with John and what was going on there.
I mean she called every day.

SOLOMON: You and John were living together for a while when things
were rocky in their marriage, right?

PANG: Absolutely.

SOLOMON: I don't know if she was actually that unhappy about him
moving out with you.

PANG: No, she was glad.

GEOFFREY: Yoko was having her own fun. Believe me.

SEAMAN: It was Yoko who suggested that May become involved with
John, because she had lost interest in John sexually and wanted to re-
cruit May as a concubine to "take care" of John.

PANG: And unfortunately for her, John and I fell in love and we moved
in together. And she thought, Oh, after two weeks it will be over, I'll
get him back, he will be satisfied. But he didn't come back.

SOLOMON: Fred, you say that Yoko was happy to get rid of John, that
sexually she wasn't interested in him anymore. In your book you talk
about his insatiable sexual appetite.

SEAMAN: I merely mentioned that he had a healthy sexual appetite.

PANG: I can vouch for that.

SEAMAN: He talked about it a lot.

SOLOMON: Maybe he was an "all talk, no action" guy.

PANG: Hold on. I will take that one. John had a very healthy sex life.

SOLOMON: Was he great in bed?

PANG: Yes.

SOLOMON: It's funny, you know, because there has been so much written about John Lennon. Every part of his life is chronicled except this. It's like this is taboo. We can write about his drug use. We can examine everything about him except what kind of man he was in the sack.

PANG: Well, I don't really want to get into details, but he was wonderful. He was gentle with me. I didn't understand a whole lot about sex, because I was very young and I was not a promiscuous person. I only had a couple of boyfriends and I was always working. So he took me under his wing and it was lovely. I learned a lot from him.

SOLOMON: Sex aside, what did you learn from John Lennon?

PANG: I learned that two people can be very much in love. He would have loved to have gone back to his teens before he was actually famous to do things. And I tried to give him that when the two of us were together. I learned that he loved just being a friend to somebody.

SOLOMON: He was actually a man of very simple needs in many respects, wasn't he?

SEAMAN: Well, John craved affection. And I think from May he got a lot of affection and devotion. I think May really loved John, which was a big change from what he got from Yoko.

SOLOMON: Which was what?

GEOFFREY: The cold shoulder.

SEAMAN: Yoko basically used John for his money, his fame, and his power.

GEOFFREY: The last years of John Lennon's life he was a bird in a gilded cage. I believe he was a virtual prisoner in the Dakota, if not physically, then certainly psychologically. Yoko with all her nonsense about spells and power. John was just naive and spiritually inclined enough to go along with it. And that was enough in his vulnerable, emotional state to keep him prisoner.

SOLOMON: Were they both on heroin, or was it just her?

SEAMAN: Yoko was on heroin during much of the time I was there, 1979 to 1982. John was definitely off heroin.

SOLOMON: Who got him hooked?

SEAMAN: Well, Yoko hooked him initially, I think. And when I got there he was doing some marijuana. He did mushrooms.

SOLOMON: Did McCartney or Ringo ever do heroin?

GEOFFREY: Not to my knowledge. Paul has certainly done some coke. There's a million drug stories, luv—I mean who hasn't, in a way?

SOLOMON: I haven't.

GEOFFREY: Well, jolly good. Listen, there are a lot of people in the music business, particularly those who grew up in the sixties, who have taken drugs, myself included.

SOLOMON: But that's not the same. Because Fred implies in his book that she took it every day. She walked around like a zombie.

SEAMAN: Heroin was actually quite good for Yoko. It mellowed her out. It relaxed her.

SOLOMON: Oh, great. Let's tell people heroin is good for you now. Come on.

SEAMAN: Well, for Yoko it did make her more human and easier to get along with.

SOLOMON: I want to talk about Paul McCartney. I didn't realize the vindictiveness in the Beatles. Here they were singing about love.

GEOFFREY: Well, their hearts were certainly always in the right place. Imagine being twenty-one or twenty-two and having the whole world thrown at your feet. You have entrée to any level of society you want. Any car, any chick, anything you want is right there instantly. George Harrison, in particular, I respected for the fact that he basically rejected all that and wanted to go inward and develop spiritually. I think John was potentially a very spiritual person as well. Let us not think for a moment, however, that the Beatles' great work as artists was in any way negated by their messy personal lives. I could never understand Picasso's work until I saw a documentary on his life and realized how obsessed he was with his wife, Jacqueline. Sometimes he would beat her, then he might make love to her on the floor. Hearing that pulled into focus his work for me. So it's okay to take a good hard look at these artists that are so important, indeed invaluable to us. And by the same token to understand what is going on inside of them that helps inspire this great work they do. So we mustn't ever cast stones at the Beatles' work.

SOLOMON: I'm not. I am merely asking you because to all of the fans that bought the records . . .

GEOFFREY: They're not Christs. They're not gods. They were just four talented working-class kids from suburban Liverpool.

SOLOMON: Let's be realistic. You give us a look at their lives we otherwise wouldn't have. We know all these personal things about them because you choose to tell us and Fred chooses to tell us. And, May, you've written a book as well about your relationship with John.*

PANG: Only because I got really tired seeing stories about myself and my relationship with John being told in such a weird way. Yoko would come out and say things in the press like, "Well, I certainly didn't know John was leaving me. He left to go buy cigarettes and he never returned." I mean, that's a lie.

SOLOMON: Look, I'm not saying let's not take a long hard look. But if you guys would stop writing books about them . . .

GEOFFREY: And *you* wouldn't have us on your show. If we just wrote jolly little books and said how wonderful it all was and retold the myth, you just flat out would not have us on! So we *all* play the game. We're all guilty of the same charade.

SOLOMON: Yeah, but you write them . . .

GEOFFREY: Look, you want ratings. I want book sales. What's wrong with that? For many people, the Beatles are an important social issue. Personally, the Fab Four were my wake-up call in this incarnation. Here I am, twelve years old, after listening to Bobby Darin, the Beach Boys, and all this sophomoric garbage. I put the headphones on and heard George Harrison singing, "We were talking about the space between us all and the people who hide themselves behind a wall of illusion." This is imperative. This is important. The Beatles pushed forward the boundaries. They stretched the parameters of what we heretofore understood to be popular music.

SOLOMON: But, Geoffrey, you don't just talk about the music. You get into the nitty-gritty details of their personal relationships. The fact that John threw a brick through Paul's window because he was angry at him.

GEOFFREY: All part of the dance.

SOLOMON: Do we really need to know about them warts and all?

GEOFFREY: Okay, let's cancel the show, then, and go home.

PANG: Look, I will give you my side of the stories of things that are written about me and what my relationship was with John.

GEOFFREY: Do you think my book was exploitative, then?

SOLOMON: You know this was your fifth Beatles book.

---

*Loving John, published by Warner Books in 1983.

GEOFFREY: And I'm doing several more. Should I apologize?

SOLOMON: Fred, I felt you went through a heartbreaking experience in many respects and writing this might have been cathartic for you.

SEAMAN: Yes. But the interesting thing about the Beatles is that it's a case of the runaway myth. The Beatles had an enormous impact on popular culture. And what we're finding is that the reality behind that myth was very different.

GEOFFREY: The work is above all of this, however, the music stands forever.

SEAMAN: The music ultimately will survive, and the fact that it was created by four imperfect human beings . . .

SOLOMON: I don't think that bothers anybody. Let's face it, we're fascinated by the kind of men they really were. I want to talk about McCartney for a moment. When they broke up, McCartney got together with Wings. Geoffrey, you wrote about the relationship he had with them . . .

GEOFFREY: Well, he didn't pay them properly for a start. Isn't it interesting how with Wings and this new band of his he picked virtually unknown guys who really needed the job? They needed the gig and they would do what they were told.

PANG: I just want to disagree with that.

GEOFFREY: Well, listen, Denny Laine lived at my house for six months, so I think I really ought to know.

SOLOMON: Who's Denny Laine?

GEOFFREY: Who's Denny Laine! Well, that really says it all, doesn't it? Mr. Laine was McCartney's collaborator in Wings for ten years. While John Lennon worked very closely with Paul McCartney, he never lived in his back garden, which Denny did in his beat-up old caravan for years.

SOLOMON: And what does he say?

GEOFFREY: They all say that they didn't get the money they deserved. I have seen the invoices from MPL proving how much Denny was making during Wings. I know for a fact that Laine wrote the majority of the lyrics for "Mull of Kintyre." That *Band on the Run* was not a Wings album, it was a Laine/McCartney album. The other two guys split before they went to Lagos, Nigeria. These two guys sat down and wrote those songs, and Laine simply did not get the credit. He didn't get the royalties, he didn't get the accolades, and today he is driving around England in a caravan camping out. He's like a Vietnam veteran that never came back from the war of Wings.

SOLOMON: So why would Paul McCartney not treat him as an equal if he was writing music with him? Why did he treat him as an employee?

GEOFFREY: You'd have to ask McCartney. All I can think of is that Paul, like many very aggressive, successful people, gets into a state of mind where making money becomes an end unto itself.

SOLOMON: You have other stuff in the book about his stinginess too.

GEOFFREY: Even more than money, it's about *control*, knowing that you're the gaffer; you're the big boss.

SOLOMON: I understand his father was also a stingy guy.

GEOFFREY: No, James was wonderful. Old Jim McCartney was a great old guy. He was a cotton salesman. He never had two nickels to rub together, so he had to watch the pennies, but Paul didn't. At one point Denny was getting just thirty-five pounds a week for being in Wings and writing with Macca during the period of *Band on the Run*.

PANG: I'm not saying I'm on Paul's side, but why didn't Denny just leave?

GEOFFREY: Denny needed the gig. Just like Hamish Stewart needs the gig.

PANG: But Hamish Stewart came from a very well-known band.

GEOFFREY: *When* was that?

PANG: The Average White Band; people still remember him.

GEOFFREY: I remember a lot of people. It doesn't mean they're particularly doing well. The money often runs out a long time before our remembrance of what they've done.

SOLOMON: Do you like Paul McCartney?

GEOFFREY: I respect Paul McCartney's body of work.

SOLOMON: As a man, though, do you like him?

GEOFFREY: I like the fact that he's interested in animal rights and he's a very strict vegetarian, as am I. And I like the fact that he loves his children very much and tries not to spoil them.

SOLOMON: Do you think he's a man of integrity?

GEOFFREY: I think in business he's an extremely ruthless fellow.

SOLOMON: I want to ask you, Fred and May, about the relationship between John Lennon and his sons. John was apparently a man who didn't have much of a father figure in his life. His mother was very young and beautiful from what you say in the book. She died fairly young but was forever trotting men home. He didn't have a terribly stable life. Interesting that he ended up calling Yoko "Mother."

PANG: Well, he also had a very strict relationship with his aunt Mimi. That's where Yoko comes into play, that strictness. Mimi would pull him back all the time, but his relationship with Julian started to happen more when I was around. He hadn't seen his son in three years and Yoko told me, "I know John is going to have to see his son at one point. I don't get along with him. So I hope you're around to help him out with that." Cynthia and Julian came over to visit in 1973, for Christmas. Which was the first time Julian had seen him in three years.

SOLOMON: From what I gather, you allowed them the kind of relationship that Yoko was very threatened by. Because she wanted John to be very involved with Sean . . .

SEAMAN: She didn't even want John to be very involved with Sean. She didn't want John to be involved with Julian either. She didn't perceive Julian as a threat, but she did Cynthia. When I was there Yoko did whatever she could to keep Julian and John apart. Only once during a two-year period in March 1979 did Julian visit John. It was a very tense and awkward time they spent together because John really didn't understand Julian. You can't just make up for so many years of neglect overnight. John was very acutely aware of this. He felt he had failed as a father and that he was repeating the pattern of his own youth. It really haunted him. With Sean he tried harder because . . .

SOLOMON: Sorry, you mean John didn't have a close relationship with his own father?

SEAMAN: No, not at all. He tried to make up for it. He tried to be a better father to Sean. But there again he was limited by his own emotional shortcomings. You see, John was a man who was not able to really open up emotionally and there were a lot of barriers there. So at least he tried. He spent time with Sean. He tried to educate his mind. John believed, perhaps, in a naive utopian way, that if Sean survived to the age of eight or nine, he would be able to heal himself. Because John knew he was being raised in a very unhealthy environment. But at least John tried. Yoko didn't even bother.

SOLOMON: In your book you call her a zombie.

SEAMAN: Not just that. I don't think it had much to do with the drugs.

The fact was, Yoko didn't believe that women should have to be mothers. She felt that was something society imposed on women. Yoko didn't consider herself to be good mother material. In fact, in her famous quote after she gave birth to Sean, she turned him over to John and said, "Well, I did my part, now it's your turn." She pretty much washed her hands of his upbringing.

SOLOMON: Are you ready for this? She takes the placenta from the birth and puts it in the freezer.

SEAMAN: Yeah. Well, Yoko read somewhere that it had rejuvenating qualities.

PANG: They sell placenta in Europe.

SEAMAN: If you eat the placenta, it keeps you young. She was obsessed with staying young, because she was eight years older than John. She instructed that the placenta be frozen and that she was going to eat it. Unfortunately, one of the maids left the refrigerator door open, so the placenta spoiled.

GEOFFREY: Aw, shucks.

PANG: In my relationship with John I tried to make him understand that he needed to be with his son, and John realized it. When I was with him, John called Julian every week and we had Julian quite frequently. There was a relationship. Julian loved coming to America to see his father. We had no problems.

SOLOMON: Is Sean a nice boy?

SEAMAN: When I was there you could already see there were a lot of discipline problems. He would go running around the house hitting people. Sometimes it was really surreal. He would storm around the house screaming Beatle lyrics because he was becoming aware of the Beatles. He would scream, "Do you need anybody? I need somebody to love." It would drive John crazy sometimes. It was very strange. But there were times he was a very sweet boy. He looked very angelic.

SOLOMON: He's a beautiful young boy.

SEAMAN: He is. And he's a very smart kid.

GEOFFREY: But he's been pushed into the singing by Yoko with that awful version of "Give Peace a Chance" he was involved in during the Gulf War. I think he might have inherited John's looks but, regrettably, Yoko's talent.

SEAMAN: That's a cruel thing to say.

GEOFFREY: Well, did you see the video?

SEAMAN: Yeah.

SOLOMON: Yoko was a real problem to the Beatles. There's a story about when she was pregnant and confined to bed.

GEOFFREY: That was in 1969. The Beatles were still together and were recording. She had a miscarriage with a little boy. He was named John Ono Lennon II.

PANG: I think she was quite well on. Somewhere between five and seven months.

SOLOMON: Is this when the White Album was out, or have I got my time frame wrong?

GEOFFREY: Right after that. We're talking about the breakup now. An ambulance arrived at Abbey Road. Two uniformed guys got out, took a hospital bed, not a gurney, but a proper, big hospital bed into the studio. And not in the control room either, but right in the center. John instructed them to hang a microphone overhead. Yoko was then brought in on a stretcher and placed on the bed so that she could be with John, literally every minute. The mike, of course, was there in case she wanted to contribute something to the Beatles' recording.

SOLOMON: Like sing?

GEOFFREY: Like sing.

SOLOMON: God forbid.

GEOFFREY: Well, she did actually sing on "Bungalow Bill." When he went into the other room to do an overdub, the guys would wheel her down the hall after him. As you can imagine, the Beatles didn't exactly cotton to this.

SOLOMON: They really hated her, didn't they?

SEAMAN: They sensed a great threat from Yoko because they saw a complete outsider coming in who really had a strong hold on John. Certainly the Beatles, who knew John better than anybody, were his *real* family. They knew that this woman had control over John and I think they sensed she was going to take John away and, in fact, she did.

SOLOMON: Did they like Paul's wife, Linda?

PANG: John liked her, but she was not out in the foreground.

GEOFFREY: Well, she would sit in the control room. The Beatles were very chauvinistic. John Lennon once made a great quote that rivals anything Oscar Wilde ever said, "Women should be obscene and not heard."

SOLOMON: Did you, in writing this book, Fred, put everything in there? Are there some secrets you kept?

SEAMAN: Well, yes, I didn't put everything in there. A lot of it I couldn't substantiate. I also went out of my way not to take out any gratuitous swipes at Yoko. I knew that the book would be scrutinized very closely. I didn't want to be accused of Yoko bashing and I don't think I did. The book takes a very sympathetic view of her. In my experience, she was a very difficult person to work for.

SOLOMON: We haven't talked about poor George and Ringo.

PANG: I think the last time John saw George was when we attended his *Dark Horse* tour in 1974. John offered to go onstage because the tour was failing miserably. We attended a couple of the concerts Bill Graham had organized for George.

SOLOMON: I'm not talking as a Beatles fan, but I think the perception on the part of the public is that George was just somehow there.

GEOFFREY: Well, no, not at all. George was very much overpowered artistically by the other two. Even John admitted that during the *Playboy* interview at the end of his life. Lennon and McCartney were egomaniacs and it was virtually impossible for George to get a word in edgewise.

PANG: George was always following in John's footsteps anyway. John always said, "George is like my kid brother. I'll always take care of him."

GEOFFREY: A few years ago George Martin actually apologized to Harrison, saying, "If only we'd realized how very talented you were, we would have given you more room on the records." Which is evidenced by the fact that as soon as the Beatles broke up George recorded a triple album set [*All Things Must Pass*].

SOLOMON: Now, what about Ringo?

GEOFFREY: Ringo's like the guy who won the lottery.

PANG: Ringo is talented. He's certainly got my son's attention as Mr. Conductor on *Thomas the Tank Engine*. But during the time I was with John, the period considered the "Lost Weekend"—which was a year and a half—many things happened to John. He was more open to his own peers. When you go back and look at it, he was no longer in that hiding shell.

SOLOMON: I really want to get to Ringo for a second.

PANG: But that's what I'm saying. Ringo was always with John.

GEOFFREY: Ringo is a great guy. He's a great old hippie. Everybody loved him. He was a good solid drummer, but certainly, compositionally, he did not possess the innate talent of the other three. I don't think anyone can argue that. No one wants to take anything away from Ringo.

AUDIENCE MEMBER 1: I have a question for Geoffrey. Today you mentioned that Paul only employed people who needed the gig. Still, someone like Robbie MacIntosh is a very respected session player.

GEOFFREY: But he ain't Jimmy Page. They don't have a lot of money, these guys.

SOLOMON: I've got a question for you, Geoffrey, it has to do with Ringo. I understand sometime in the eighties Ringo was really broke. I don't understand how a former Beatle could ever be broke. How can a Beatle be broke? They made gizzillions of dollars. And he was contemplating selling off his shares of the Beatles holdings to an Arab?

GEOFFREY: I'll tell you what happened. I got hold of a tape of a conversation between Paul McCartney and his attorney. Now, I was the first person to ever have this tape. It was subsequently published in *Spy* magazine. I put a small excerpt of it in the book after clearing it through my solicitors very carefully. This is fairly recently. Paul's comments on the Beatles were pretty darned uncomplimentary. He said, "All right," and I'm paraphrasing. "Ringo is always looking for a handout. I will help you with one more set of promotion fees, Ringo. But this is the last time and you had better go along with me on anything to do with Apple, as well."

AUDIENCE MEMBER: Fred, I was wondering if you can tell me how involved John was in the occult and what influence it had on Sean's birthday?

SEAMAN: Well, John got all the stuff about the occult largely from Yoko. Yoko was the one who was really very heavy into it and used it to run her life.

GEOFFREY: And his.

SEAMAN: And his. Yeah. The heaviest thing I found out having to do with the occult was the fact that John and Sean shared the same birthday, October ninth. And that was no accident. It turned out that Yoko believed, because she had been told through her psychics, that if a son was born on the father's birthday, when the father died, the son would inherit the father's soul. So Yoko deliberately gave birth to Sean by cesarean section on October ninth, the same birthday as John because she believed that way when John died Sean would inherit his soul. I think that's why she also had a miscarriage on October 9, 1969, because she probably tried to give birth prematurely or induce the labor.

GEOFFREY: May I ask Fred a question?

SOLOMON: Absolutely.

SEAMAN: And I will ask you one after that.

GEOFFREY: How long after John Lennon's assassination did Yoko's current live-in lover, Sam Havitoy, move in with her?

SEAMAN: Well, Yoko was very close with Havitoy and he moved in to the Dakota in the summer of 1981, about six or seven months after John's death.

GEOFFREY: But he was there virtually every day.

SEAMAN: Yeah. He was with Yoko on a daily basis.

SOLOMON: Were they having an affair before John was assassinated?

SEAMAN: Actually, yes, they were. And before that she was having an affair with a man named Sam Green, who was suddenly dropped in favor of Havitoy.

GEOFFREY: I guess it's okay to tell you that I was contacted recently by John's gardener. John was so rich he had a gardener in his apartment! And he told me, "Look, I want to do this book. I was having an affair with Yoko. While I worked for the Lennons I was sleeping with Yoko."

SOLOMON: Is there anybody . . .

GEOFFREY: Who hasn't slept with Yoko Ono? I don't know.

SOLOMON: No, who hasn't written a book about the Beatles who has worked for them, who has slept with them, who delivered milk to the house? It's interesting you mention that the person who was John and Yoko's gardener was watering more than the plants.

SOLOMON: This is my final question to you. I'm sure that people could say unflattering things about me. I mean, I hope they wouldn't, but I'm sure they could.

GEOFFREY: Who is out to say unflattering things? We are just out to set the record straight.

SOLOMON: Oh, come on. Get real.

GEOFFREY: No, you get real! I'm interested in understanding who these artists *really* were so we can place them in history. That's it. You don't make any money from books. TV maybe, but publishing's not such a big business anymore.

SOLOMON: Fred, are you glad you did it?

SEAMAN: Absolutely.

SOLOMON: Do you feel disloyal to John for doing it?

SEAMAN: No, not at all. I think he would have wanted me to write the book. Because John was a man who was fiercely devoted to the truth.

SOLOMON: But if John wanted to write a book, wouldn't he have written it himself?

GEOFFREY: He can't. He's dead.

SOLOMON: Well, no kidding.

SEAMAN: Even while he was alive, you have to realize he was trapped in a relationship where he had very limited choices. He couldn't have written anything if he wanted to. The sense I got was that he would have wanted the truth to be told after his death. I think he knew he was living on borrowed time. Literally. I have a question, though, for Geoffrey. I heard you used to dig through John and Yoko's garbage.

GEOFFREY: Absolutely untrue. Never, ever once. I mean, there are limits, aren't there? Even to a job like this.

JO JO LAINE

Buffalo, March 30, 1990

GEOFFREY: When Wings was up in Scotland at the McCartneys' farm, was the entire band living together?

JO JO LAINE:* There was one big house sectioned off, but we never had to sleep there because we had our own caravan we were living in twelve months out of the year.

GEOFFREY: What were the living quarters like at the farm?

LAINE: Give me a Volkswagen van any day. There was no hot water—in fact, no running water, only outhouses. They had this outhouse we were told we could wash in. There were two places, the house on the hill where the roadies stayed and the big outhouse where we were. We brought a caravan up, though, and had it hooked to the Volkswagen because we wanted to have our own living space.

GEOFFREY: Was there a kitchen provided?

LAINE: No, not at all.

GEOFFREY: How were you all supposed to eat?

LAINE: We had to go up to the roadies' house to eat.

GEOFFREY: Describe the interior of this place.

LAINE: Cement ceilings, walls, floors, no carpeting, the odd chair, an old

---

*Former super groupie Jo Jo was married to Denny Laine. She now resides in rural England and is linked romantically with the colorful Marquis of Bath.

mattress. It was like a barn. And the cottage where the roadies lived at the top of the hill had absolutely no decor, although they decorated it about four or five years later. I remember one night the roadies were so stoned and fed up that they drew a TV on the wall and everybody was pretending to watch it.

GEOFFREY: So Paul brought everyone up there and put you in this bunkerlike cement garage with virtually no furniture, no cooking facilities, and no bathing facilities?

LAINE: Well, there were toilets, but you had to heat your own water. There was no *hot* water.

GEOFFREY: It isn't really what people would expect of a multimillionaire rock star, is it?

LAINE: I thought to myself, I bet Paul and Linda are living in luxury over the hill, but their place was actually *smaller* than the one we were living in! All they had to their advantage was a TV. They didn't really live much better than us except that they had hot water.

GEOFFREY: Why do you think Paul, with all his many millions, would set things up like that?

LAINE: Some people just have so much money it's like a sickness. They have to pretend and go out of their way to make it look like they're not being extravagant. Their children would often have odd socks on. I know that the dresses Stella wore were the same ones I had seen Mary in. There was this famous red-and-white-checkered dress. Still, the kids were always happy, the McCartneys were great parents, and the kids were brought up so that they didn't see themselves as any different.

GEOFFREY: Tell me about living in this van of yours.

LAINE: I was pregnant with Laine, so it must have been 1973. I'd just come back from America.

GEOFFREY: Had *Band on the Run* come out yet?

LAINE: No. They didn't start recording that until September 1973, just after I had Laine. So Laine and I left the house on Kenway Road as the lease was up in May and Denny didn't want to be in a house anymore. He wanted to be on the move. I was in America when he bought the Volkswagen.

GEOFFREY: Isn't it funny that somebody who was in a band like Wings would live in a vehicle?

LAINE: When I was five or six months pregnant, we were driving around bouncing all over the place and I thought I would have the baby in the van. We had everything we owned in this caravan. We were luxurious about it, though, we did it all in black.

GEOFFREY: So you really lived the hippie lifestyle then.

LAINE: Yes, but at least we wore the same color socks!

GEOFFREY: What kind of money was Paul paying Denny back then?

LAINE: When I first met Denny in 1972 he made £35 a week. It wasn't until *Band on the Run*—which was a couple of years later—that he started seeing any big money. He got one raise to £50 a week. Everyone got paid the same. I remember an article when Linda was busted for something and she said she couldn't pay the fine straight away because she only earned £50 a week. Knowing Paul, that's probably all he was giving her!

GEOFFREY: Why wouldn't McCartney give Denny a proper contract and a piece of the profits?

LAINE: Well, Denny always wanted something on paper, but Paul would say, "You've got to trust me, man. This is a gentleman's agreement." And Denny would say, "Yeah, but it's been a long time, the tax man will be coming soon, and I'd like a bit of security." And Paul would just say, "Listen, trust me, I'll take care of you." Even at the straight fee of $100,000 which Denny later received he was still being ripped off.

GEOFFREY: The point is, later on maybe he got a $100,000, but Wings records were steadily grossing untold millions.

LAINE: Paul was clever because he paid the guys the $100,000 *before* the album came out saying, "Hey, listen, man, take your chance. Either take the $100,000 now *or* . . ." He made it sound like, "What if I give you a percentage of the royalties and the album doesn't sell? I'd feel really bad if you guys got ripped off." So Denny and everybody were feeling hungry for the money because they were skint, and Paul would just say take it or leave it. Personally I would have called his bluff.

GEOFFREY: So you're saying he payed them a poverty wage when they were the biggest rock band in the world and then dangled $100,000 over them because they were so broke.

LAINE: Yes. I'm sure somewhere along the line he'll meet his match.

GEOFFREY: What did Paul and Linda give you when you and Denny were married?

LAINE: The wedding present didn't come until weeks later. It was still in the bag from the store, a set of bed linens.

GEOFFREY: What else did they give you over the years?

LAINE: They gave Denny a beautiful black Steinway grand piano one year for Christmas. That actually impressed me very much. All of a sudden there was a knock on the door and we were told it was a Christmas present from Paul and Linda. One year we were given a beautiful jukebox and another year we had a £10,000 bonus.

GEOFFREY: Do you feel that Linda ever had a crush on Denny?

LAINE: Well, she didn't have a crush on *me*, that's for sure! Yes, I do.

GEOFFREY: What makes you think that?

LAINE: Denny was the only other male who spent so much time around her. Even Denny wouldn't tell me the personal things she discussed with him. Sometimes she'd be upset about how she didn't really want to be in the band and wished she was at home.

GEOFFREY: You're telling me Linda didn't want to be in Wings?

LAINE: Once in a while she would say that. Even Rose told me that.

GEOFFREY: Who's Rose?

LAINE: Rose is their housekeeper, the nanny that's been there ever since the Jane Asher days. The housekeeper, slave, everything. Good old Rose.

GEOFFREY: So why do you think Linda had a crush on Denny?

LAINE: Just the way she confided in him. I remember one time I called up the hotel when they were on tour in Europe and she was in his room. This was around the time my father was dying and I called saying, "Is Denny there?" and she tried to make it look like he was preoccupied, not necessarily with her, but she *was* in Denny's room and answered the phone. So she said, "Well, he's really kind of busy right now, Jo," and I said, "Oh, well, he's a good fuck, isn't he, Linda?" She immediately said, "Hang on a second, I'll just get him." She was playing games so I would get paranoid, but I was beating her at her own game. As soon as I said that, Denny was on the telephone. I don't think for one minute they ever had an affair, but there was definitely a flirtation there.

GEOFFREY: How did Linda treat you?

LAINE: Like a total outsider, like I was nothing, a groupie. I love music and I'm also a singer myself. So was Linda, but no one ever called her a groupie. That's apparently another word for a whore. The first time I ever met her she asked if I knew Jane Asher, at a petrol station in Europe. I remember we both went to the toilet together, she probably thought it was the only time we could talk privately. She was trying to be real nice, washing her hands saying, "Oh, do you know Jane Asher?" Now, at this time my hair was red and she probably thought I was trying to groom myself to look like Jane so I could make Paul fall in love with me.

GEOFFREY: Would you say she was jealous?

LAINE: *Insanely* jealous would be a mild expression.

GEOFFREY: What did she do to you that was so horrible?

LAINE: The funny thing about it was, of course, I loved Paul McCartney. He was the man of my dreams, but once I met him and then Denny, I fell totally in love with Mr. Laine. The first time I saw Denny I thought, now there's a sexy man. Paul was like a little boy. I'm sure Linda couldn't really believe I liked Denny more than Paul, so they tried to get him on their side when I wasn't around. They'd intimate that I was always looking at Paul when no one was watching and things like that.

GEOFFREY: How do you know Paul said that to Denny?

LAINE: Because Denny told me so.

GEOFFREY: How did Paul treat you?

LAINE: Actually, Paul never treated me badly, I can't say that he was ever really rude to me. It's just that Denny told me Paul would say things. Anyway, it was really Linda.

GEOFFREY: Was Linda at all bitchy?

LAINE: No, but she talked down to people.

GEOFFREY: What part did pot play in the lives of the McCartneys?

LAINE: That was their thing, every day. They weren't that generous with it, either, except when we were on tour. But what could they do? They had to get rid of it before we went over the border.

GEOFFREY: Was it powerful stuff?

LAINE: They always had good pot.

GEOFFREY: So they must have been pretty fucked up then most of the time then?

LAINE: I wouldn't say "fucked up." It would give them energy. I've never

ever seen Paul and Linda sitting there stoned. Often they'd be nicer when they were high, which is actually a very normal thing.

GEOFFREY: Tell me about smuggling drugs in their kids' clothes?

LAINE: We were crossing a border and I knew there was a bag of grass put in Stella's little hood, though I didn't see who did it. We just knew it was being done.

GEOFFREY: How old was she?

LAINE: She was about five years old, so that would have been around 1975 or 1976.

GEOFFREY: Stella was used to take drugs through customs then?

LAINE: Yes, a bag of grass. Can you imagine if they had gotten caught? That's even worse than *them* getting busted!

GEOFFREY: Denny told you that happened a lot?

LAINE: A few times. I'm sure it was in Europe, because it's difficult to get grass there. Especially when you go to Holland or Norway, places like that.

GEOFFREY: Tell me about throwing away the drugs when you got to the border.

LAINE: When we were on the tour bus, with the open top, we had to smoke it as fast as we could. As we were approaching the border I was tempted to keep a few joints but Denny said, "Don't you dare!

GEOFFREY: Would Paul say, "Look, lads, we're coming to the border so we've got to get rid of the shit."

LAINE: Yes, you'd hear that conversation going on and Denny would tell me to smoke as much as I could.

GEOFFREY: How much did you guys have?

LAINE: A big bag. They did get caught in Sweden once. I was safely at the hotel with a boil on my chin. I had to have the doctor come in because the poison was going to my brain. Anyway, when we were reaching one of the borders, we had to do our little ritual. The McCartneys were downstairs, but we were having to get rid of whatever we had from the top of the bus as we were reaching the border. It was as if it were a funeral, the ashes of somebody dying flying in the wind. And then, of course, we'd get some more once we were over the border. One of the roadies would take it across for them.

GEOFFREY: Tell me about the time Paul hit Jimmy McCulloch?

LAINE: Well, Jimmy was really upset and frustrated about being on the farm under such uncomfortable living conditions. This was before they painted the cottage. Jimmy was an arrogant little sod when he was high because he was so tiny. He could be very funny, but he also had a mean streak in him, so he picked up a dozen of Linda's chicken eggs and chucked them all up against the wall of the cottage.

GEOFFREY: Did any animals used to come in there?

LAINE: Not in that one, but at Paul and Linda's place the sheep and chickens did. A lamb came into our caravan once while I was sitting there having a piece of cheese with Linda. It went right into my bedroom and pissed on the bed, and she started laughing.

GEOFFREY: Let's get back to Jimmy McCulloch throwing the eggs. Did he do it in front of Linda?

LAINE: No, but she knew he had done it and then Paul found out. He went over to calm him down and saw the eggs all over the place. So Paul said, "You apologize to Linda or get off the farm!" And Jimmy said, "Fuck you, I'm getting off your bloody farm. I've had enough." By that time Paul had him by the throat. That's how Jimmy and Henry [McCullough] left the band.

GEOFFREY: Why did Henry leave?

LAINE: It was July 1973 when Henry split. They were rehearsing in the barn and there was something Henry wanted to play and Paul said, "No, play it this way." Anyway, the way Paul wanted to play it was a bit bubblegum and Henry said, "No, man, I want to play it like this." And Paul said, "No, you play it the way I want." Henry said, "No." So Henry just said. "That's it. Sheila, get the car packed, we're getting out of here."

GEOFFREY: What was Paul's reaction?

LAINE: He wanted to say, okay, do it your way, but he wouldn't, so Henry just stormed out, never to be seen again.

GEOFFREY: Tell me about the second time Paul laid into Jimmy?

LAINE: It was in my hometown of Boston. I had seventy relatives all in one room waiting to meet Paul and Linda. Jimmy wouldn't go back and do an encore. Something pissed him off, the sound went wrong or something, and he said, "I'm not going out." So Paul said, "Get out there." And Jimmy said, "No, I'm not going out." They were both swearing and Paul had him on the ground and whacked him in the face. I'm pretty certain he went onstage after that. They had already done one encore and it was the second encore that everybody wanted.

GEOFFREY: Tell me about Wings's wives being kicked off the farm. Why do you think they weren't wanted?

LAINE: Well, if you had a boat race [Cockney for "face"] like Linda's, would you? Some people say she's got a nice body, pity about the boat race! One of the times Denny and I split up was because of the incident that happened in 1977 or 1978. Denny and I weren't getting along. I knew he had to spend the summer in Scotland and that we would be separated because I refused to go there anymore. They were rehearsing for a video of "I've Had Enough." By this time, the cottage and the farmhouse had been done up. There was actually nothing wrong with the way they were living then. I just didn't want to go up there because I knew this was just too good to be true. Denny called a few times begging me to come up saying, "You don't have to see the McCartneys, they are three hundred acres away. Just stay on our part of the farm and go to the beach." I said, "No, you know I'll have to see Linda, then there'll be some stupid game played. I just want to stay in London with the children." I finally gave in, however, and went up. Now, Steve Holly's wife, Sharon, who was a very good friend of mine, was already up there. She got on the phone and said, "Hey, Jo, come on up." I'm sure Denny winded her up to ring me. So anyway, I arrived and everything was beautiful. I thought, Great, it's actually wonderful being up here. So one night I made this fantastic spaghetti supper with homemade apple pie in this tiny kitchen, and Paul and Linda came over and ate. This was like my homecoming present to everyone. Even Paul complimented the meal, and I'm sure Linda was probably shitting herself. Later that night Denny went into the recording room and started playing guitar. I got on the mike and we started singing a couple of numbers he had written. So Paul walked in and started jamming—it was Paul, Denny, and I. Linda just sat there in the other room picking at her hair instead of joining in. It's not as if Paul and Denny were singing and I came in. We were having a ball, singing a couple of old Beatles and some Wings. Paul must have picked up on the vibe because Linda hadn't come in to play her tambourine or organ. The next day there was a knock on the caravan door and it was Alan Crowder, who was the McCartneys' personal road manager. He had a word with Denny, and Den came back and said, "I don't know how to tell you this, but tomorrow they're doing a video and you're going to have to leave when the film crew arrives." I said, "That's no problem, I'll just go to the beach." He said, "No, you'll have to go back to London." So I said, "Does this have anything to do with last night when I *might* have gotten a compliment from Paul, and Linda *might* have been jealous? Or was it because we all sang together?" He said, "You and Sharon have to go back." "I don't believe you, I've only been here two days," I said. "If I have to go back, I will take the children and go to America. I will leave you, the farm, and all of this crap forever!" If you confronted Paul and said, "Fuck you, my wife is staying," I'm sure he would say all right, "I'm sorry, just keep her out of the film crew's way." So I said, "Right, I've got to go, then." He said, "Yes, darling, I'm so sorry, I love you and I'll see you back in London." To top things off, Denny called me a few hours later and said, "You know what? As you were driving away, Paul and I had a joint and he was sitting there saying, 'You know I'm really sorry. Jesus, I feel really bad now that she's had to leave.'" I said, "Sure, he said that once I was gone. And you fell for it!"

GEOFFREY: Would you say the McCartneys were manipulative?

LAINE: Yes, with a capital M.

GEOFFREY: Do you think they used people?

LAINE: Maybe not now, but in those days.

GEOFFREY: Tell me about the McCartneys and cocaine.

LAINE: Once on the airplane during the *Wings Over America* tour I had some coke. We did some in the ladies' room, Linda and I. She said, "Do you have some coke?" I said, "Yes, do you want a snort?" Linda said, "Yes." So we went into the ladies' room and had a snort. That was one of the good memories I have of Linda, she was like a buddy and genuinely so. That's what's so confusing about those people. When you got a good feeling from them it went right through your soul, but the next day they'd look down at you again. That was the only time I ever did it with Linda. One time in Liverpool, for one of the New Year's parties, though, I had some and we all had a snort. Even Paul. Denny and I, Jimmy and Paul. He didn't do a lot, but I remember thinking he's not as straight as everybody thinks he is!

GEOFFREY: Do you feel that being in Wings contributed to the death of Jimmy McCulloch in any way?

LAINE: I'm sure [it did] by the way Jimmy had to live for those couple of years. He couldn't really have proper girlfriends because of the conditions, they couldn't be around. I fixed Jimmy up with two of my girlfriends, but he lost those relationships because they were subjected to the same thing I was. All the women were treated like this. It happened to me the most because I was around it the most. Jimmy could never retain a relationship because he would get so frustrated, and the girls couldn't handle the vibes from Linda and Paul. He also got into very heavy drugs. After the Wings split he didn't do anything, he left the farm and drank even more. He really did love the band, but living on the farm and being treated like a child was just too much.

GEOFFREY: So the other members of the band were treated by Paul as employees or second-class citizens, then?

LAINE: Paul once told Denny, "You weren't anything when I pulled you out of the gutter and invited you to join Wings and you can't be anything without me."

GEOFFREY: Jo Jo, do you feel the McCartneys busted up your marriage?

LAINE: Yes.

GEOFFREY: Do you think they are evil people?

LAINE: Yes, I do. One minute the magic is there—which keeps people around—because their magic is like no other.

GEOFFREY: But his image is so clean and sweet. You're saying the image does not match the man?

LAINE: No. I used to think he was wonderful as well before I met him. I used to write letters to him when I was a kid, letters he obviously read and kept because Linda told Denny about them.

GEOFFREY: She accused you of being a groupie, then, on the basis of those letters?

LAINE: Yes.

GEOFFREY: How did they treat Rose?

LAINE: Paul was always an angel to her because she was like a mum to him ... To be honest, I think Linda deeply resented Rose because she was there during the Jane Asher days and Rose always spoke very highly of Jane to me. She use to say how beautiful she was and what a lady she was and I think that deep down Linda knew Rose would rather have seen Paul marry Jane than her.

GEOFFREY: Now, of course, Paul is a very radical vegetarian, but I've heard from Denny that he would often cheat a bit when Linda wasn't around.

LAINE: Oh, sure. He'd have the odd hot dog or hamburger. I remember once Denny said that when Linda wasn't around, Paul wouldn't say no to a burger.

GEOFFREY: Tell me about the *London Town* trip to Jamaica. I understand you weren't invited along.

LAINE: That's right. Because they were in the Virgin Islands (with all those beautiful virgins running around) and Linda was very pregnant. Obviously, I would have worn a gorgeous bikini plus Jimmy's girlfriend was the Playmate for February 1976, and I believe Linda thought it was just a bit too much competition. Now, when most people are pregnant, they don't wear a bikini, but Mrs. McCartney sure did, lounging around with her dog hair hanging out. When Denny told us we couldn't go we decided to go up to the Playboy Mansion for the filming of the Play-mates of 1980.

GEOFFREY: Tell me about your lifestyle when you and Denny actually had money?

LAINE: Being strung out on lifestyle is the worst drug of all. There was nothing we didn't have. We had a Ferrari, an Austin Martin, a Rolls Royce, a Bentley, and a Mercedes.

GEOFFREY: Is it true that Paul used to get Denny to drive his livestock up to Scotland in his Rolls?

LAINE: That happened just once that I know of.

GEOFFREY: Tell me about Paul's Japanese drug bust and how Wings finally came to an end.

LAINE: Well, I was on my way to Medam to promote my record, "Dancin' Man" . . . It was completely my own project. It wasn't through any of Denny's connections. I was still in England and it was all over the papers about Paul getting busted when Denny called and said they didn't know what to do.* I was having a nervous breakdown and Denny was due to go to Monserrat to work on *Tug of War* with Stevie Wonder and Paul. Denny told me that I was going myself, but because I had been in the hospital they said it would be really bad PR and I thought, "You bloody hypocrites," with all the publicity of Paul being busted I had

---

*This refers to McCartney's unfortunate marijuana bust in Japan on January 16, 1980.

good reason being in the hospital over the shooting of my father. I expected they would understand. But no, they flatly told Denny I was not allowed to go. It was the final straw when he didn't stick up for me. So I turned to a friend who happened to be a man and eventually we had an affair. It was a very open affair as well because at that point I really didn't care what Denny, the media, or Paul and Linda thought.

GEOFFREY: How did Denny find out?

LAINE: When Paul, Linda, and Denny arrived, the guy in the studio accidentally dropped my name. So Alan Crowder called me up and told me off saying, "You naughty girl, your husband's devastated. He didn't even know you were with this guy, let alone in Monserrat." And I said, "I don't care what any of you think, I wasn't allowed to go to Monserrat with you guys, so I was invited by him. It's nothing to do with you, Paul, Linda, Denny, or anybody." Because I had that attitude, Denny really knew our marriage was finished because I had always denied any affairs, but this was very open.

GEOFFREY: What happened next?

LAINE: That's when Denny realized that if they had only let me go to Monserrat I might not have turned to somebody else. So I would say that Denny had a slight breakdown. I was still living with him, but we had separate rooms. Denny was very depressed and he was supposed to be in the studio that day. [Roadie] Trevor [Jones] called and Denny kept saying "I'm not speaking to *anybody*. That's it. I'm finished with the band and I'm finished with *Tug of War*. I'm leaving Wings." Eventually, of course, Paul called. I answered the phone and he said, "Is Denny there?" I said, "Sorry, Paul, he doesn't want to speak to anyone right now." I loved being able to say that to Paul McCartney. "It's not me that's saying it, Paul. Denny's asked me to give you and everyone else the same message, because he finally realizes the damage all of this has done. He's lost me now and it's too late. He can go to the studio with my blessings, but he doesn't want to." So then Paul said, "You fucking cow," like it was my fault! "No, sorry, luv," I said, "this time I think it's *your* fault." I hung up on him and that was the last time Denny had any connection with Paul right up until a few weeks ago when Macca called looking for him.

GEOFFREY: You answered the phone?

LAINE: Yes, I knew exactly who it was.

GEOFFREY: What did he say?

LAINE: "Hello. Is Denny there?" And I said, "No, he's not, he just left a little while ago with his girlfriend and their baby. They went to his house in New Hampshire. Is there any message?" And he says, "Oh, this is a friend of his, Paul." So I said, "Well, I've got the number somewhere, but I just came back from New York. If you ring back in an hour, I'll give you the number." And he says, "I can't, luv, I'm going onstage in an hour." And I said, "Is this Paul *McCartney*?" And he said, "Yeah." And he said "Well who's this?" "It's your old friend Jo Jo." He was silent for a few seconds and I thought he was going to immediately say, "Well, I've got to run, tell him I rung and I'll speak to him later." But we stayed on the phone for a couple of minutes. He was actually much nicer than I thought and he said, "Jo Jo?" And I said, "Yeah, this is my place. Denny and I are better friends now than when we were married. I hope you know the articles Denny did on you [in the London *Sun*] weren't really his words. He was tricked into it. It wasn't him talking and he feels terrible about it." Paul agreed with me. He said, "Yeah, I realize that." I said, "You know, Denny would love to see you. All I can suggest is that you ring back. If I'm not here, I'll leave Denny's number with Laine and Heidi." And he says, "Okay, that's fine." [Their roadie] John Hammel called the next day. He has always been a sweetheart and we got into a conversation about his children. I've always been close with his girlfriend and his kids.

GEOFFREY: And he made the arrangements for Denny to go see Paul?

LAINE: Well, Denny was late getting there. He saw the show, it was a great gig. Afterwards, Denny was backstage talking with Mike Walley. He's been around the McCartney organization for many years.

GEOFFREY: Why did Denny leave without seeing Paul?

LAINE: He said he didn't want to look like a fan. After Paul came off, Denny would have had to wait because he was doing an interview in the dressing room and was leaving on a plane that night. Still, I'm sure they would have had time for a chat.

GEOFFREY: But Denny got paranoid and split.

LAINE: He just said to Mike, "Listen, we'll be in touch, then. Possibly after the tour if Paul's in New York, we'll all get ahold of one another." Denny did mention that John Hammel said, "Jesus, Paul was really taken aback when Jo Jo answered the phone." Paul commented to John about it, but it wasn't like, "What the hell is she doing?" Because Alan Crowder had always said, "If Jo Jo's around, Paul won't ring in a million years." I thought to myself, "I hope I haven't blown it for Denny by being around."

GEOFFREY: Do you think Denny is bitter about the way he was treated? He was once a very big rock star and now he's trying to make it back at forty-five.

LAINE: Yes, he's always been a very generous man and he probably is bitter about how nice he was to everybody. He's been ripped off left and right. I think he came out on the shitty end of the stick without really deserving to.

GEOFFREY: Is he bitter against the McCartneys?

LAINE: Not now. He probably thinks they've changed. I wonder if they have, I don't know. I think Denny would probably stick up for Helen* more now because he realizes he lost one family because he didn't stick up for us.

GEOFFREY: Tell me about the downside of Paul and Denny's partnership. Obviously they wrote all these big Wings hits together, and Denny didn't get the money he should have. Right?

LAINE: A lot of the songs Denny wrote Paul added on a few oohs and aahs to. There's several tunes I remember Denny writing at home and he didn't need any other lyrics and Paul would add bits just to get his name on there. I'm sure a lot of people thought, "Oh, aren't Paul and Denny a terrific team on that song!" Well, that's a lie.

GEOFFREY: Did it work the other way around? Did Paul McCartney allow Denny to do a few oohs and aahs on his stuff and give him half the copyright?

LAINE: I'm sure there were more songs that Paul got credit for than Denny ever did. The ones Denny actually got credit for were ones he really pitched in on because there were a lot of songs that Paul would just have his name on. I would say that if Denny's name was on there, it's because he really helped out.

GEOFFREY: So do you think Paul basically ripped Denny off for a lot of these compositions?

LAINE: Yes, I do.

---

*Helen Grant, Denny's longtime live-in love with whom they had a little girl.

GEOFFREY: Deliberately?

LAINE: Deliberately, because they were good songs and he freely took credit where credit was *not* due.

GEOFFREY: How about "Mull of Kintyre"?

LAINE: That was definitely a split between them. Denny did half of that, that was pretty mutual.

GEOFFREY: Do you think Denny feels betrayed by Paul? Is there a place in there where he thinks, "Hey, I was your friend, man, you screwed me and now I'm really fucked."

LAINE: He's over it now because he's so used to not having any money. But at first he felt betrayed by me, I still got blamed for everything in the end.

GEOFFREY: What about the tax situation? Paul was supposed to pay off Denny's taxes, right?

LAINE: That was the deal. If Denny didn't ask for a percentage on the records, the deal was, "I will pay your tax when it comes in." And it was supposed to be for all those years ...

GEOFFREY: Did it come in?

LAINE: It came in ...

GEOFFREY: And did Paul pay it?

LAINE: He did not pay a dime of it. In fact, because Paul knew that Denny was desperate, that's when Denny sold him the rights to "Mull of Kintyre."

GEOFFREY: Wait a minute. He said, "Hey, man, I'll pay your tax." And he didn't do it? So Denny was very desperate and then he said, "I'll tell you what ..."

LAINE: "Sell me the songs."

GEOFFREY: "That we wrote together."

LAINE: All of the Wings songs.

GEOFFREY: How much did he get for them?

LAINE: "Mull of Kintyre" was sold for ninety thousand pounds. That may sound like a lot, but it isn't really ...

GEOFFREY: Not with new CDs coming out now. Tell me about losing the house, the boats, the butler, the Ferraris ...

LAINE: Even though Paul put us in the tax shit, I really believe that Denny didn't have to leave the country and run off to Spain. Denny just freaked out because we split up. Our manager, Brian Adams, said,

"Jo Jo, you've got to sell the house and go to America because the tax man will take it off you." Denny didn't know which way to turn. So he got on his yacht and pissed off to Spain just to get over the break with Wings. I now believe we could have stayed and faced the music.

GEOFFREY: Didn't Denny go to Paul and say, "You said you were going to pay my taxes. What's the story?"

LAINE: Sort of. Brian Adams was the liaison on that. Paul used the perfect excuse saying, "Well, Denny. You left us in the middle of *Tug of War*. You let me down, so I've let you down ..."

GEOFFREY: What did it do to Denny psychologically when he went from being a millionaire to a pauper?

LAINE: Total disillusionment and loss of self-esteem. Remember, he didn't just lose his position, he lost me as well.

GEOFFREY: And the children ...

LAINE: And that meant *everything*.

GEOFFREY: Do you think Denny losing everything was Paul McCartney's deliberate, premeditated fault?

LAINE: If Denny wasn't so in the shit with the tax, he wouldn't have lost anything.

GEOFFREY: What percentage of McCartney's fault was Denny's doom, do you think? Give me a number ...

LAINE: I would say ninety percent.

GEOFFREY: What did Denny do after Wings?

LAINE: He went to Spain for almost two years and played pubs.

GEOFFREY: You mean he went from playing Madison Square Garden with private planes taking him everywhere to gigging at beer joints?

LAINE: To playing bars in Malbau, Malada, and Madrid. All those places in Spain. Yes.

GEOFFREY: How much would he get for a gig?

LAINE: A couple of hundred pounds. A lot of times he played by himself or with some of the locals. In an odd way, he enjoyed it because he always loved Spain. He was actually very happy when I used to go visit him. I suppose he thought he was his own man again. He liked it because he didn't have to ask anyone for anything. Back then I still had the house and a bit of money. I was selling things, though, so for those couple of years we didn't do badly at all.

GEOFFREY: He was living off selling the piano Paul gave you. So he had the *illusion* of good living because you were selling everything you owned, every last stick of furniture.

LAINE: I know.

GEOFFREY: Denny seemed to intimate to me that Paul drinks quite a bit.

LAINE: Scotch and Coke is his drink. I think he would probably rather have a drink than anything. I've never seen Paul out of it, but I've seen him drink a lot and not *act* out of it. You know, we went down to Tramps a couple of times together. Paul likes the old Scotch and Coke and his joints.

GEOFFREY: Did the McCartneys ever once try and help you and Denny with your problems?

LAINE: Never. No, not once.

GEOFFREY: Do you think they enjoyed your misery?

LAINE: I'm sure they did. They were the cause of it.

GEOFFREY: Tell me about Denny's bankruptcy.

LAINE: Well, he finally had to file. That was when I was living in America. It's an unbelievable story. And then I had to do the [tabloid] articles in London, the ones about the McCartneys. To put a roof over my head when I was eight months pregnant, I had to sell everything. I sold the house for one hundred and twenty thousand pounds, and eighty thousand of that had to be paid toward bills straight away. So that didn't leave me with a lot, no roof over my head, nothing. So I did the articles. My Visa card was up to ten thousand pounds. Then I sold the shop, through Brian Adams. It sold for seventy thousand pounds, but we only saw ten of it.

GEOFFREY: Denny became a recluse, too, afterwards, didn't he?

LAINE: Yeah. He's always been a recluse. That's his nature.

GEOFFREY: I've noticed Denny exhibits a sort of phony friendliness. When he's with someone, it's like, "Hey, man, how you doin'?" But it doesn't really mean anything. He doesn't have any friends. I wasn't his friend. Tell me one friend he has?

LAINE: He's afraid to get close to people. He's strange like that. I don't think he realizes sometimes the way he projects himself. One minute he'll say, "Oh, I don't want to go out. Who cares about that?" But if you catch him at the right moment, he's the biggest party person going. You have to know how to catch him to get him to participate and sit in a lounge.

GEOFFREY: He's not as bitter as you are. He's more willing to forgive Paul McCartney than you. Right?

LAINE: Obviously.

GEOFFREY: They've ruined his life, really. Is that correct? I don't want to put words in your mouth.

LAINE: I would say that they ruined his life. But I feel Paul McCartney would have never rung if he didn't like Denny. At first we all thought that because of the articles, Paul hated him and, yes, I'm sure he did. But deep down I think Paul is a bit sentimental and maybe things could still somehow work out.

I tell you, my friends, it [Beatlemania] is like a sickness, which is not a cultivated hallucinatory weakness, but something that derives from a lamentable and organic imbalance. If our children can listen avariciously to the Beatles, it must be because through our genes we have transmitted to them a tendency to some disorder of the kind. What was our sin? Was it our devotion to Frank Sinatra? How could that be? We who worshiped at the shrine of purity. What then, gods and goddesses, was our sin, the harvest of what we now are reaping? We may not know what it was, even as Oedipus did not know, during all those years, the reasons why he was cursed.

William F. Buckley, Jr., 1964

Paul and Linda McCartney are two people I sincerely like. I remember once when I was playing London I invited them up to the Dorchester for dinner when Paul said to me, "Instead of bringing you a gift or a bottle of champagne I'm bringing you a song." It was called "Let's Love" and I was very thrilled about it. Anyway, when I got back to the United States he and Linda came over to help record it with me, which was lovely. Later, in the studio, he played on the song for me and even conducted it. Unfortunately, due to an unexpected merger between my label, Atlantic, and Electra Asylum, the tune never quite made it out as a single, but one thing's for sure, that man has loads of class and we had a wonderful time working together.

Peggy Lee, 1983

I was really just so impressed with John's brain and his genuine sentiments. I remember often meeting him telling my wife I thought I'd become a "Lennonite." I was really very taken by his caliber as a man. John was very outgoing, obviously very intelligent, quite thoughtful and caring. I think he would have made a wonderful priest. He had almost a messiahlike quality about him. There's no question about that. He would look at you and listen, *really* listen intently to what you were saying. There was no flippancy at all. He was a very concerned, serious man. Almost like a religious leader.

Ivor Sharp, photographer to John Lennon and Yoko Ono's Bed-In, 1969

You can't be in India without being aware of everything. George and I went to a meeting at Benares, the holy city on the Ganges. Millions of people had come for a big festival, which went on for three days. We stood in a little compound and watched it all. It was like a Biblical film. We felt like men just arrived from outer space.

The king of Benares came into the center of the multitude riding on an elephant. He knelt down and said his prayers. The sun was going down behind him and he was just a dark silhouette. I know it all sounds very romantic, talking about it. But it had a great effect on us. It obviously meant so much to all these millions. The process was beginning, without our knowing it.

Pattie Harrison Clapton, 1967

As a person Julian is very warm and friendly. He also has a definite freshness about him that's coming through on his records. Of course, he's very young yet and you have to allow for that, but I'm sure he has things tucked inside his little head that haven't even touched the surface yet. I think there is another level to his work that will only be really known in the years to come.

Out of all the writers I've known over the years, and obviously I've met quite a few, John Lennon was to me a truly great composer. Also as a singer he was fantastic. He didn't really have a great voice in the classic sense, but, my lord, what a feeling and delivery. He was a natural-born storyteller with a great big heart.

Ben E. King; lead vocalist from the Drifters and the composer of the classic "Stand By Me," recorded by both John and Julian Lennon, 1983

The story goes that around the time Pete Best was tossed out of the band, Paul went around Liverpool trying to find the ugliest drummer he could that happened to have his own kit. In those days it was very tough finding someone with a full kit, you know. Anyway, along came Ringo, so there they were with a homely drummer and a great kit to boot! Now, to be honest, between Pete and Ringo, technically I find Pete to be a somewhat better drummer, but he probably lacked the overall appeal Ringo had. The point I'm trying to make here is that according to Pete, it was jealousy that started the whole thing, not musicianship. After I took Pete on as an artist I saw firsthand just how upset he was about being let go practically on the eve of the Beatles' great success. Whenever they came on television he wouldn't do anything but kind of hang his head and look the other way. He often tried to change the subject or ignore the situation, but deep inside I knew it was eating him up.

Bob Gallo, Pete Best's mentor and producer following Best's split from the Beatles, 1983

There's a wall, as far as Badfinger's concerned, at Apple. It was a big bad scene when we left Apple for Warners. Our [Apple] contract ran out in July '73. We'd started negotiating with Apple, or our business people had, with Allen Klein. Klein didn't even want to sign the band. He wanted us to sing with the label for nothing! We only got five percent, that's all we got anyway, and he wanted to give us less and have us pay all the costs of everything. Now, we'd had four major hit records in a row, three big albums. Our business manager went round the corner to Warners and they said, "We'll give you $3 million." So we took the deal, right? You bet your ass we took the deal. George [Harrison] said to Bill [Collins], "Why the fuck didn't you tell us? You guys fucked us. We did all that work for you." Bill said, "Hey, man, you were with the fucking Maharishi in Tibet. Don't talk to us about getting in touch with you. We talked to your people and they didn't want to negotiate with us. They didn't want to know." All we wanted from Apple was a sixteen-track tape machine, which was about $40,000, and a mixer. Maybe $100,000 total in advances. To build a recording studio for ourselves. The deal we had with Apple, they paid all the recording costs. They would have saved a fortune. We spent $60,000 a record. So they would have saved. But Klein didn't want to do it. You know what Apple did? They held the *Ass* album. They held onto it, man and didn't release it [for a year], that's how pissed off they were. And they're still pissed off to this day. And that's why the Badfinger albums aren't in the stores, man.

Joey Molland of Badfinger, 1990

I wanted to be a famous painter, that was my ambition. There aren't too many successful painters, though. Most of them ended up being very unsuccessful. So then I saw these four lads coming out of the blue called John, Paul, George, and Ringo. My God, it was simply astounding! Somehow or other they were able to conquer the entire world on the sheer force of their music. I was very impressed. Obviously this is the way to do it if you're going to become successful. I figured that music must be easier.

Cat Stevens, 1984

Regarding the sacking of Pete Best, he was frankly too conventional and didn't fit well as either a drummer or a man. His beat was too slow, or George thought so. I liked him, though he could be moody. He was friendly with John and Paul, but George didn't like him. They *all* liked Ringo, although I thought he was rather loud. Anyway, the Beatles finally said we want Pete out and Ringo in. I had to tell him and I didn't sleep that night. I hate sackings. A session man has never been put in. At the time Ringo was in Skegness at Butlins. Pete took it very badly. That night he failed to turn up at the River Par Ballroom in Chester, and Nel, with whom he lived, didn't arrive either. Pete never played with the Beatles again. Matthew Street became dangerous. Fans were roaming the streets singing, "We want Pete! Pete forever, Ringo never!" I asked Ray McFall for protection and he gave me Paddy Delanie as my bodyguard. It was very dangerous. Rory Storm was annoyed, too, that we had taken his drummer. So was his mother, for Rory now had no drummer. It was all very difficult. I remember John said, "Get rid of your beard, Ringo. Keep your sidies."

So Ring became a Beatle and started to grow his hair. They had £40 suits from Beno Dorn in Birkenhead. I chose them with them. They only pay £30 now.

Ringo did seem to complete a visual pattern with the Beatles. Pete was a conventionally good-looking lad. But I wasn't too happy about Ringo. I didn't want him, but then, as now, I trusted the boys' instincts.

Brian Epstein, 1966

I was in the Yardbirds, and we were playing a thing called the Beatles Christmas Show at the Hammersmith Odeon, in London. The Yardbirds were on the bottom of the bill, but all of the acts in between Beatles were sort of music-hall, English rock'n'roll groups. And the Yardbirds were an R&B band, or even a blues band, so there was a bit of, like, "What's this all about?" George was checking me out, and I was checking him out to see if he was a real guitar player. And I realized he was. But we come from different sides of the tracks, I grew up loving black music, and he grew up with the Carl Perkins side of things, so it was blues versus rockabilly. That rockabilly style always attracted me, but I never wanted to take it up. And I think it's the same for him. The blues scene attracted him, but he evades it somehow. He's much more comfortable with the finger-picking style of guitar.

Eric Clapton, on first meeting George, date unknown

It's still there. It has something to do with the way we wind each other up. I mean, there's always a little barbed comment somewhere in any conversation. I mean, that devastated all three of us. It was fun at the time. It really was like one of those movies where you see wife swapping, *Bob and Carol and Ted and Alice*. And everyone was saying, "Oh, it doesn't matter. We can write our own story on this." Because those were the times. But it took years, and it'll never go away, the way it actually affected our lives. We're still very much the same in the way we think about and feel about each other. Pattie is still there in the picture for all of us. It got quite hostile at times, but we always cared for one another. I'll probably get my knuckles rapped for talking about all this. I'll go home, see George, and he'll go, "Oh, running off at the mouth again." But I find it very hard not to talk about it, because it's a part of my life.

Eric Clapton, discussing his and George's continuing feelings for Pattie Boyd, date unknown

The Beatles continue to be a very big part of Liverpool's history. Whether or not you like their music you must acknowledge the incredible accomplishments of these four young men. Of course the Beatles didn't just emerge from a background without competition, as it were. Rory Storm and the Hurricanes, for example, were probably much better performers in their early days. There was a very strong homegrown music scene here then as now. If a group gets to the top in Liverpool, then they've reached a very high standard nationwide, you know.

Helen Simpson, curator of the now-defunct Beatle City of Liverpool, 1983

When I first saw the Beatles I didn't think they'd make it. I remember Brian Epstein booked me to play the Cavern with them. A couple of weeks later he had me headlining a big concert at a theater in Liverpool. They were a support band with the Swinging Blue Jeans, Cilla Black, and Gerry and the Pacemakers. The Beatles went on and sang "Love Me Do." They couldn't do my numbers, "Lucille" and "Long Tall Sally," because I was there. When they came off, Brian Epstein said to me, "Richard, I'll give you fifty percent of the Beatles." I couldn't accept because I never thought they would make it. Brian Epstein said, "Take the masters [of Beatle songs] back to America with you and give them to the record company for me." I didn't do that, but I did call up some people for them. I phoned Art Rupe and I also got in touch with Vee Jay, but I didn't take a piece of them.

So then I was booked for a tour of clubs in Hamburg for Don Arden, and I took the Beatles with me. We spent two months in Hamburg. John, Paul, George, and Pete, they would stay in my room every night. They'd come to my dressing room and eat there every night. They hadn't any money, so I paid for their food. I used to buy steaks for John.

Paul would come in, sit down, and just look at me. He wouldn't move his eyes. And he'd say, "Oh, Richard! You're my idol. Just let me touch you." He wanted to learn my little holler, so we sat at the piano going "Ooooh!" until he got it.

I threw my shirt in the audience and Paul went and got one of his best shirts. A flash shirt, a beautiful shirt, and he insisted, "Please take it. I'll feel bad if you don't take it. Just think, Little Richard's got on my shirt. I can't believe it."

I developed an especially close relationship with Paul McCartney, but John and I couldn't make it. John had a nasty personality. He was different from Paul and George, they were sweet. George and Paul had humbler personalities. You know, submissive. John and Ringo had strange personalities.

Little Richard, 1989

I had a very strange experience in 1968 of meeting John Lennon and Paul McCartney in a New York discotheque called Salvation. Three nights earlier a friend of mine suddenly said into the air, "Wouldn't it be great if we were somehow able to actually meet the Beatles?" Two days later I was visiting this same friend when he received a call from his editor asking him if he would photograph these two English guys who had started a business over here by the names of "Lennard and McCarthy." Well, we knew who he meant even if he didn't. Of course, I never thought I would meet them because it was my friend's job and I certainly didn't want them to horn in on that. Anyway, the next day I was walking down the street when I decided to drop in on some people I knew at this club. As I was going in someone came up to me who I didn't know at all and said, "How you doing? My brother's coming down and I want you to say hello to him." This guy was a total stranger to me, so I certainly didn't know his brother! Anyway, it turned out his brother was a chauffeur driving for John and Paul while they were in New York. So before I know what's happening, the two of them walk into the club, come straight over to my table, and sit down along with this guy's brother. Believe me, it was quite a shock! Since then we've all had a very on-and-off-again relationship. Which is probably the tightest relationship you can really have.

Richie Havens, 1982

When I was about thirteen my girlfriend fell in love with the Beatles, and so I was forced to watch Ringo on the telly, but soon I was in love with them too. Laying in bed at night listening to Radio Luxembourg on my tiny transistor radio I heard "Love Me Do" shoot through all the other music that was happening—you know, all the "Bobbys and Billy" that were around at the time. Anyway, the Beatles, of course, just blew them all away! Soon I had saved up enough money from my paper route to buy an old snare drum and I just mimicked whatever Ringo did. It just seemed like a good job being a world-famous pop star, and so I just kept on bashing away.

Barrymore Barlow, drummer for Jethro Tull and Robert Plant, 1982

A guy from Capitol came to see me and asked if I would allow them to put out an album of John's outtakes. After listening to them I realized that they were just too unfinished and raw for people to hear. They were mostly rehearsals and alternate takes anyway. When I told him no, you should have seen how he looked at me. It was just awful. John always used to tell me to get a lawyer to try and get the Beatles' master tapes back, so that we could burn them. He was afraid someone would remix the outtakes and put them out after we died.

Yoko Ono, 1984

We were asked, or I was asked, by a young boy for a record by the Beatles. It always had been our policy in to look after whatever request was made. So I followed up this inquiry. I didn't know anything about it, and after a week or two he told me that they were, in fact, a Liverpool group. I assumed, for some reason, that they were from Germany. Anyway, he told me they had just returned from Germany and were playing in a club called the Cavern, about one hundred yards away from my office. I arranged to go down there and I saw them one midday session.

Brian Epstein, 1966

Just being with him and having fun was the most important gift he gave me. I hope I'll meet him up there for a drink or whatever when I disappear.

Julian Lennon, on his father, 1990

John liked all these toys on his car, and although it seems old-fashioned now, I got him this Philips record player on a spring that you could play single records on in the car. We had speakers installed out of sight under the front bumpers. One morning we were going home in his big white Rolls after being out again all night. John and I were in the back and Anthony was just hanging on in the front. We never did anything in half stages, we wouldn't go out until midnight and then we'd carry on for the rest of the night and the day and the next night. Anthony had the stamina of a bull.

Anyway, this particular morning we were going down the A3 on the slope at Roehampton, approaching the set of lights at the bottom. It was about seven o'clock on an absolutely fantastic summer morning, not a thing about except for this Austin Healey Sprite with the hood down, whose driver was obviously on his way to pick up his girlfriend to go out for the day. He was waiting at the lights and as we were coming down the hill behind him, John put this sound effects on the record player—the sound of a car crashing. It was deafening: beep, beep, squealing of brakes, crashing and bangs. The kid in the sports car didn't even bother turning round. He must have looked in the mirror and seen this big white thing looming up on him and heard all the noises, and he just passed out and flopped down on the passenger seat. We pissed ourselves.

Terry Doran; longtime Beatles assistant, 1991

It was Paul and Linda McCartney's wedding day and [we were invited to a] party . . . I was at home on my own, getting ready when there was a knock on the door . . . I thought it must be just a gang of friends coming to our house on the way. I was about to answer the front door when the back doorbell rang at the same time and I had a very uncanny feeling that all was not well. I opened the door and there they were: about six policemen, a policewoman and two dogs. A piece of paper was handed to me by Sergeant Pilcher, who was gunning for everybody at the time. I knew exactly what it said without really reading it and I answered, "Look, we don't have any dangerous drugs," and then I went to answer the back door and they all came flooding in and proceeded to search the house and the greenhouse. I phoned George and said, "Guess what's happened?" . . .

... Finally Sergeant Pilcher said, "Look what our dog, Yogi, has found," and he produced this huge block of hash which I'd never seen before. I said to him, "Where on earth did you find that?" and he said, "In George's shoe." ... It was preposterous and I said, "Well, if you're looking for grass, it's on a table in the sitting room, in a little box." I also said, "I don't understand why you're doing this, because obviously it's going to attract a lot of publicity and many Beatles fans might start smoking and I thought the idea was to try and stop people taking drugs," and he said, "I want to save you from the evils of heroin!"

... Eventually George and Derek turned up, and we all went to Esher police station and the police there were very sweet ... When we got back to the house the vibes there were so bad I said, "Look, we've got to go to the party, I can't bear it, the idea of the police going through everything." So we got ready and off we went ... As we went downstairs George saw Lord Snowdon and said, "I'm going to talk to him, maybe he can stop this bust," and I was casually looking around, when suddenly I spotted my younger sister Paula puffing on a joint which she then proceeded to offer Princess Margaret ... I couldn't believe it, it was the early evening, of the same day that we'd just been busted and there was my sister trying to hand Princess Margaret a joint!

Pattie Harrison Clapton, on their 1968 drug bust, 1991

Seven months after our visit with John and Yoko, while sitting in my prison cell, I was astonished to hear the local rock station play a new song by the Beatles entitled "Come Together." Although the new version was certainly a musical and lyrical improvement on my campaign song, I was a bit miffed that Lennon had passed me over this way. (I must explain that even the most good-natured persons tend to be a bit touchy about social neglect while in prison.) When I sent a mild protest to John, he replied, with typical Lennon charm and wit, that he was a tailor and I was a customer who had ordered a suit and never returned. So he sold it to someone else.

Lennon presented his version of this misunderstanding in the final *Playboy* interviews, which were so poignantly prophetic of his own sudden mortality.

During my exile years John and Yoko always remained most generous and supportive. They sent a sum of money ($5000?) through the Weathermen lawyers. The fact that I never got the money wasn't their fault.

> Timothy Leary, remembering John composing "Come Together" as Leary's campaign song for the governorship of California, 1982

I suppose there are two things I miss: I often think it would have been nice to have had a mother when I was a little boy, and yes, sometimes I think it would be quite nice to be considered a good guy.

> Allen Klein, date unknown

If Hitler were alive today, the German girls wouldn't let him bomb London if the Beatles were there.

> Anonymous, date unknown

I never signed a contract with the Beatles. I had given my word about what I intended to do and that was enough. I abided by the terms and no one ever worried about me not signing it.

> Brian Epstein, 1966

John Lennon and Yoko Ono's services to the cause of furthering Communist aggression in Indochina and weakening this country's will to resist will undoubtedly win for them Hanoi's highest honors.

> Victor Lasky, U.S. syndicated columnist, 1969

The Mersey Sound is the voice of 80,000 crumbling houses and 30,000 people on the dole.

> *Daily Worker*, 1963

I was headlining a tour that included Kenny Lynch, Danny Williams and Dave Allen as well as the Beatles, in the winter of 1963, when an article came out with the headline IS HELEN SHAPIRO A HAS-BEEN AT 16?

It was typical of him that John Lennon, on whom I had a giant crush anyway, immediately spotted that I was a little shaken and went out of his way to be nice to me. He was actually very shy around women, but I seemed to bring out the protective instinct in him, and throughout the whole tour he made sure nobody hassled me.

I remember they wrote "From Me to You" on the coach, which was their next number one, and I would see them from time to time down at the Adlib, the first of London's "in" clubs, where they made me an honorary member of the "Liverpool" corner.

Helen Shapiro, 1982

I arranged for the Beatles to come to the gym to see Cassius Clay, and he didn't know who they were. He had some idea they were rock stars from England, but that's all. When he met them, they were all up in the ring together, talking about how much money they made. So Cassius pulls out a line he uses all the time. He looked a them and said, "You guys ain't as dumb as you look." And John Lennon looked him right in the eye and told him, "No, but you are."

Harold Conrad, fight promoter, 1988

There was a cultural revolution where the best and the popular were identical. And that is a very rare occurrence in history. Musical groups like the Beatles made music they'll be listening to two hundred years from now. The effect of something like *Sgt. Pepper's Lonely Hearts Club Band* on me and other activists, organizers, and counterculture people around the world was one of incredible impact, like starting a fire in a fireworks factory.

Abbie Hoffman, 1987

I don't think you can separate the Beatles from what was going on in the sixties. That whole period changed a lot of people and brought on some new attitudes, and I'm not saying it was all good. There certainly were excesses. I didn't think about the Beatles much, but they were always there. I grew up surrounded by them. And when I heard Lennon was dead, there was no real reason for me to feel remorse, but I did. I felt empty, like my past was gone.

Ronald Reagan, Jr., 1984

Elvis was no longer rocking, and they did the same thing Elvis had done: they unlocked the music scene. No one was playing that raw stuff he played. I think that when their real success came, the Beatles were a bit disappointed in the scheme of things because they became so big so fast. They wanted to conquer America, but we gave it to them on a silver platter.

Roy Orbison, 1984

The killing of John Lennon altered everything ... Like fifty million other people, I cared about Lennon.

Norman Mailer, 1980

If it hadn't been for the Beatles, there wouldn't be anyone like us around.

Jimmy Page, 1980

[Rubber Soul] just took hold of me, unlocked something in my imagination that I had never experienced in popular music. I can remember it so vividly. I just couldn't resist it. It was like a tidal wave of enthusiasm, ideas, and alternatives. You just had to take part in it, and before that, I was never someone who took part. I usually stood on the sidelines and watched, because I was cynical, never engaged by popular personalities. There was a certain amount of manufacture behind them. But with the Beatles you couldn't see the seam.

Bette Midler, 1984

I resented [the Beatles] at first because it wasn't a fad I discovered for myself. I wasn't a Beatles fan until I listened to the White Album and became an instant convert.

Steven Spielberg, 1978

The Beatles, the four long-haired lads from Liverpool, are offering up as their gift the Negro's body. The Beatles are Soul by proxy.

Eldridge Cleaver, 1968

For me and my generation that song I watched John Lennon creating at the Abbey Road studios ["Revolution"] was an honest statement about social change, really coming out and revealing how he felt ... It was the truth, but now it refers to a running shoe.

James Taylor, 1989

The Beatles changed American consciousness, introduced a new note of complete masculinity allied with complete tenderness and vulnerability. And when that note was accepted in America, it did more than anything or anyone to prepare us for some kind of open-minded, open-hearted relationship with each other, and the rest of the world.

Allen Ginsberg, 1984

I think the best group over the last twenty years is still the Beatles.

Chevy Chase, 1988

When the Beatles came along, I was ripe for the plucking. Basically I'm a melody freak and they were the masters. You went out and bought a Beatles album, listened from cut one to the end, and liked them all. I started writing real Beatley-sounding songs on my own.

Billy Joel, 1979

I would've thought *Sgt. Pepper* could've stopped the Vietnam war just by putting too many good vibes in the air for anybody to have a war around.

David Crosby, 1988

The sweet sounds made by groups like the Beatles in the early 1960s gave way to harder-edged music that was heavily influenced by drugs. Suddenly Sonny and Cher were no longer hip.

Sonny Bono, 1991

[The Beatles were] one of the first groups to recognize the value of black roots in music.

Stevie Wonder, 1980

What I saw impressed me. The Beatles looked sharp, especially compared to the silly, juvenile striped shirts and white pants the Beach Boys were wearing onstage. I suddenly felt unhip, as if we looked more like golf caddies than rock'n'roll stars. Mike was equally concerned. Both of us saw them as a threat.

Brian Wilson, 1991

There are plenty of people in Britain with money and open minds. But alas, they don't use their minds, and they are usually corrupted by money. People could do things but won't. Look at the Beatles, for instance.

Jean-Luc Godard, 1968

I think the Beatles are the reason I'm a musician.

Sting, 1989

He's the only person in this business I've ever looked up to, the only person.

Elton John, on John Lennon, 1989

They were doing things nobody was doing. Their chords were outrageous, just outrageous, and their harmonies made it all valid. Everybody else thought they were for the teenyboppers, that they were gonna pass right away. But it was obvious to me that they had staying power. I knew they were pointing to the direction where music had to go.

Bob Dylan, 1980

What we admired about the Beatles was that they kept their personal and artistic integrity, and all their success didn't blow them away, like it killed Elvis.

Kris Kristofferson, 1984

The Beatles were selling all the records, so the rest of us in the record business were twiddling our thumbs, saying, "What's going on here?" It hardly made sense to go into the studio and record.

Pat Boone, 1964

Look, guys, if you're just going to sit there and stare at me, I'm going to bed.

Elvis to the Beatles, date unknown

Three bars of "A Day in the Life" still sustain me, rejuvenate me, inflame my senses and sensibilities. They are the best songwriters since Gershwin.

Leonard Bernstein, 1990

What I can say about the Beatles, very simply, is that I play rock'n'roll because of them. The Beatles also did something that parallels the development of classical music, in my mind. Everything was a development of the thing that came before it, everything was innovative. There was no idea or fear that something was too far-out. Everything new they did was supposed to challenge you. The Beatles continued to be new as long as they were the Beatles.

Warren Zevon, 1989

I invited all four to pose in 1967, but only Paul came, and that because of Jane Asher. My children watched from the front bedroom as his green Aston Martin came up the road, a Beatles number blaring from it.

As I painted him he said he wanted to stay young and be like Peter Pan. He also told me he could control his fans' hysteria by relating to them calmly and by creating an atmosphere of normality.

Paul wanted to paint, so I gave him paints, a canvas, and brushes, which he carried to his car, saying he'd do something "with a little help from his friends," and departed jauntily.

When I had supper with him in a Rye restaurant last New Year's Eve I asked him to pose again. Unlike the Keith Moons of the pop world he has kept his balance, control, and his feet on the ground, for which I told him I admired him. (He walks the streets of Rye with no fuss: a technique he had when I painted him.)

John Bratby, RA, Hastings, East Sussex, 1984

In the hot July of 1969, I became an "Apple scruff," a general Beatle name for the kids who had become fixtures outside Apple's offices and EMI studios. I was sixteen and in love, in love with an American Apple scruff called Becky and in love with the sixties. It was our time—thanks to the Beatles everything was possible: world peace, an end to starvation, and a Utopian existence.

For days, at Abbey Road, kids from literally all over the world congregated to actually meet the Beatles and depending on what kind of mood they were in, as they arrived from their separate homes, they talked to the "hang-on-every-word" kids.

As the days progressed, I gradually became aware of one fact. They were fallible, human, and completely down-to-earth. But did it destroy any illusions? Indeed, no, but it *did* strengthen the belief that they engendered that "Joe Soap" *was* important and, yes, you *too* could have something to say.

I was lucky enough to watch them record and be invited to Paul's house. (Through my determined girlfriend we entered the "Holy of Holies," a Beatle *home!*) So I feel that I've been very fortunate, and although I'm now thirty and have a lovely wife and daughter, I still like to think that I'm always an Apple scruff. And what helps me to hold on to those days is to play my Beatle records, close my eyes, and remember how it was.

Alex Millen, Newark, Nottinghamshire, 1983

Dr. Timothy Leary

Obeisances to the Four Hip Evangelists.

Believe me, this essay is not an attempt to dissect, analyze, or explain that unfolding, mysterious power the middle-aged mind cannot understand. I will not patronize the Goddess and Gods who laugh out of the eyes of the young.

This essay is a logical exercise designed to suggest that the Beatles are inspired Psalmists. Wise, slick Divinity Agents who come along exactly when we need to be reminded about what's happening. My thesis is a simple one. Let's pretend that John Lennon, George Harrison, Paul McCartney, and Ringo Starr are mutants. Young evolutionary agents sent by DNA, endowed with musical powers to sing about a new breed of humans.

I rejoice to see our culture being taken over by joyful young messiahs who dispel our fears and charm us back into the pagan dance of harmony. Is that a silly hope? Is it any wilder than the ambition of an uneducated Texas schoolteacher to become Leader of the Free World?

Now if you were born before 1940 you will find it very difficult to understand the enormous, almost religious, popularity of the Beatles.

Of course if you were born after 1970 you will find it incredibly uncool when your parents babble on about Woodstock and the Hippie Days. "All you Need is Love?" Tell that to Perry Farrell and Al Jourgensen and Trent Reznor and Snoop Doggy Dogg. (Except for the millions of new Deadheads, of course.)

Today in 1994 we can watch the interplay between:

The Radio Generation (1920–1940s) and their kids
The Jazz Beats (1950s) and their children
The TV Rock'n'Roll Hippies (1960s) and their kids
The Nintendo High Techers (1970s)
The new Whiz Kids (1990s)

The Generation Gaps between these live breeds are enormous. Communication and dialogue becomes more interspecies. The worst insult an alternative rocker can scream at some kid in the mosh pit these days is "Fucking Hippy." The worst putdown a 45-year-old Boomer can direct towards a High Techer is "Yuppy Scum!"

For example, please read the following flowery, pious gush I used to praise the Beatles in the late 1960s:

It starts in God's mind. Continually in touch with the planet earth. He sees the suffering and rigor mortis of mechanization. The metallurgic cancer. Decides it's time to reincarnate as a Divine Agent.

Wait a moment. We run into semantic problems here. You don't believe in God, reincarnation, and Divine Agents?

Good. Here we have stumbled on a basic difference that divides the generations. The young revolution today is a religious renaissance. Turned-on kids believe in living, down-to-earth God because it's more fun than being an atheist or a humanist. God? Superior intelligence that designs and operates the whole business. The DNA code is its agent. The fact of the matter is that it's a twenty-four carat stone gas to believe in a celestial conspiracy. A simple trick of faith that immediately charges everything you see and do with multiple meaning. Believing in God is a mind-blower, baby. The cosmic mystery thriller. Do you prefer to believe that the ultimate power you can conceive of resides in Washington, or Moscow, or in the secret English tobacco cartel, or in a bunch of Swiss bankers? We are limited only by the poverty of our paranoias. Think very big, baby.

And reincarnation. The turned-on kids today tend to accept the theory of endless rebirth. Again, it's more fun, it's more graceful, it's more modest, it's more aesthetic to believe in the Cosmic Theater to which we repeatedly return to play out parts. Do you really prefer to believe in one divine person two thousand years ago or a clockwork, Darwinian, one-shot struggle-for-survival? Or maybe you'd rather not think about the whole thing. But the turned-on kids are thinking about it because there's nothing better to think about. Is there?

OK. Put yourself, if you will, in God's place. Christ! What a mess down there! Time for another avatar. Another Divine intervention to loosen things up and restore the beauty and laughter and harmony of the natural order. You gotta come back down and cool out the feverish planet. How to do it this time?

First of all, to whom do you appear? That's obvious. To the Romans or the Americans or whatever the rulers of the machine-empire call themselves today.

And in what form you do appear? Do you drop, full-grown, from a spaceship? Incarnate, incandescent in a pool of blinding light? Careful, now. You are God coming back in human form. Remember the rules. You made them yourself. You gotta manage to fuse the single DNA strands of a healthy male and female within the maternal body. Choose a womb and then the genetic-coded instructions begin to unfold like a cellular teletype machine chattering out the amino-acid instructions.

Choose a congenial womb in a country related to but not part of the dying empire. Canada? England! Excellent!

Of course you have to wait for twelve years. Patiently learn the rudiments of the primitive language and culture. Study the customs. Learn all you can from Mary and Joseph. Locate the holy underground. Prepare to act when the time is right.

Whom do you address? Do you walk right up to the White House, the Vatican, the UN building on First Avenue, you, the teenage visionary ready to confound the elders by the announcement of your mission? Never! Your genetic-coded instructions warn you that a direct, open announcement to the power-holders will burn down your scene right up front. Tell the bosses of the establishment that you're a Divine Messenger come to cool things out and they'll wipe you out with one reflex swipe.

So whom do you address? Who are the key people who will listen to the revelation, open up to it, are eager for it? We won't kill you or imprison you for declaring the joyful news that this is the Garden of Eden, right here and now? Obvious. The adolescents. The arising suns. The teenyboppers. Zap them with the word before their minds are frozen, while they are still fresh, trembling, alive. Then, once you've contacted them, grow with them, tenderly nurture their blossoming wisdom. In ten years the planetary mutation will have been accomplished.

And how do you announce the revelation to the fresh flower heads? Proclamations? Nope. Pass laws and resolutions? Nope. Books? Nope.

You use music. The mythic voice of the epic minstrel. Sing it. The old refrain. In tune.

And what about the mathematics of it? If you come down to run a number, what is the number?

Four thousand years ago it was the duality. Krishna-Radha. Yin-Yang. Siva-Sakti. The Blessed Union of the Divine Couple. Two. The twin-serpents. The Seal of Solomon. The maha-mudra.

Then came the single messiah trip. The model for the last two thousand years has been the lonely light bulb. The single candle. Odd man out. One. Three. Five. Seven. Nine. Eleven. Thirteen. The only Son. Jesus, Mary and Joseph. The Holy Trinity. The thirteen reduced by the cops to eleven.

This time let's go it in even numbers. Let's make it heterosexual. Let's bring back the balance.

Then with a clap of electronic lightning the Beatles are born. The Liverpool quartet. The living pool four. The four-sided mandala, the four-petaled lotus. Each with His mate. Laughing octet. Ready to multiply.

Over the electric noosphere of the global village come the first message. They want to hold our hand Yeah. Yeah. Yeah. They love us. Yeah. Yeah. It's all young, and good and fun. And they love us.

Are they really Divine Agents? How can anyone know? What's the criterion?

Miracles, of course.

And so it came to pass that in one year the Four Evangelists, brash, uneducated carpenters' sons from Liverpool, became the most powerful VOICES the world has ever listened to.

Holy minstrels. Electronic instruments of the divine current.

The first message. Yes. Yes. Yay. Yay. Love. Dispel fear. Yes. Laugh. Yeah. Yeah.

Then comes the first public ordeal. The test. What do they do with this power? Do they become successful, career-oriented, ambitious show biz stars? Culture heroes—living out the material dreams of the rest of us? Cadillacs and swimming pools and yachts? Pop stars or messiahs?

Did the Beatles use their power like the minstrels of last year? Bing Crosby, genial owner of a chain of corporations? Elvis Presley, leather upholstered? Frank Sinatra smashing golf carts through plate glass windows of gambling casinos in Las Vegas? Nelson Eddy singing the National Anthem at the World Series?

No. The Beatles flow with the evolutionary current and it's flowing fast.

There came that time when every promoter and hustler in the world wanted to get the Beatles to endorse his product. Man, it's worth a few million dollars to get the Beatles to endorse your beer or your soap. Sign 'em up, offer them anything. What do they want?

Then comes the first endorsement. The first message to the millions of followers. Do as we do. We don't drive Cadillacs or have golf tournaments named after us. We turn on!

Please notice the incredible neurological power that the psychedelic rock group has available. Electronic equipment does to the hand musical instrument what the machine did to the horse-drawn buggy. The electronic recording studio makes it possible to take any sound that man has ever produced by hand and complicate it infinitely in volume and quality. What was a simple vibration of air becomes the center of a network of electrical pulsation. The listening ear drum trembles to, and become one with an interstellar harmony of new tonics.

The *Sgt. Pepper* album, for example, compresses the evolutionary development of musicology and much of the history of Eastern and Western sound in a new tympanic complexity.

Then add psychedelic drugs. Millions of kids turned-on pharmacologically, listening to stoned-out electronic music designed specifically for the suggestible, psychedelicized nervous system by stone-out, long-haired minstrels.

This combination of electrical-pharmacological expansion is the most powerful brainwashing device our planet has ever known. Indeed, if you were an observer from a more highly evolved planet wondering how to change human psychology and human cultural development (in other words if you were a divine messenger), would you not inevitably combine electrical energies from outside with biochemical catalysts inside to accomplish your mutation?

The stereophonic machine plus psychedelics (and throw in an acid-light show for good measure) provides an instrument for evangelic education, propaganda that few people over the age of thirty comprehend. And the message of the Beatles, the Rolling Stones, Country Joe, and the Grateful Dead, and the Moody Blues is revolutionary.

Do you get the picture: the Beatles and the Stones goofing around all night in a London studio high on *attar* arranging rhythms and psychedelic lyrics to be picked up by millions of teenagers goofing around, lying down opened up like exultant flowers in their rooms. And Mom and Dad in the parlor drinking martinis and wondering about the smiling serenity of the kids. The quiet conspiracy of the turned-on young.

They get high with the help of their friends. They found God in acid. They're on the religious trip and there's no Madison Avenue mileage from acid and no advertising budget for the grass industry. They are telling us to relax. Turn off our minds. Float downstream. This is not dying. They'd love to turn us on. No golf carts and no Academy Awards. It's beyond all that. They must be mad. They'll never sell an album. It's the old reincarnation merry-go-round of Mr. K and Mr. H. The act we've known for all these years. And they're selling more albums than ever. They've been in and out of style for a long, long while. The Beatles receiving intimations of immortality. We're more popular than Jesus, said John. And most priests and ministers had to agree. They'd like to take us home with them. They hope that we will dig their song. It's the one and only message with a new rock beat. Turn on. Tune in and . . .

Drop out! Wait a minute! First the Beatles dropped out of cute mop-top pop stardom and now they're dropping out of drugs. They're laying down a new revelation. The journey to the East.

George is humbling stumbling at the feet of Ravi Shankar. Ringo's wearing Hindu beads. They're all meditating with the Maharishi.

They're off drugs and into mantras. A hundred million youngsters are suddenly asking, what's meditation? and what's satori? and what's reincarnation? and where can you find a guru? and how do you get a mantra? and can you really get high from praying?

The Beatles have endorsed disciplined yoga. Oh no, baby, it's not just pop-a-pill and find God. It's the ancient, mysterious process of the spiritual search, perplexing, paradoxical, demanding. There are dozens of complex yogas developed by God-seekers over the centuries and the Heavenly Quartet had cut out on the pilgrimage, started the yoga of diet, of mantra, of obedience to the guru, of humble renunciation.

Far out! In 1966 the Beatles at the pinnacle of fame and influence threw it all over to sit at the feet of a little, bearded, brown man who might be able to teach them something about God. The Search for the Miraculous. It's the unmistakable mark of a turned-on Divine Messenger that he continually humbles himself in search of a more Direct Connection. The difficult position of the turned-on Divine Agent of this planet has rarely been appreciated. He's like a spaceship traveler from another galaxy dropped off here millennia ago, the return ship centuries overdue, separated from the other members of the crew, the original mission instructions half forgotten. The hipper you are, the wiser you are, the more eager you are to contact anyone who might be from your ship, someone who might have a fresher memory of the original plan. Hello, Maharishi. We want to believe in you. Take us to your leader. Do you want to find God's Agent? Don't look on the episcopal throne or even around the church. Search for the fellow who is sitting looking up into the faces of children, studying the clouds, or little Hindu holy men. Or wandering up the dusty trail to Rishikesh.

The Beatles and the Maharishi. Cosmic confrontation. But who is the guru? Who is sent to teach whom? What?

The first rule of the God-seeker game is that all the secular game rules are reversed. In the interaction between guru and disciple it is the guru who learns the most. The Beatles were sent to the Maharishi *to teach him* and all the other Indian mystics and saddhus and Western seekers after the wisdom of the East that if you keep traveling east you'll end up back home where you started from. The planet is round.

There comes a time in the spiritual growth of the seeker when the direction points east. Walk to the sun. When you go east you are really going past. Orient means ancient. A voyage to India is a trip down the time tunnel. Take it, by all means. But don't get caught in the history tube. There comes a time to . . . drop out again.

You realize that the past teaches us how to face the future and, indeed, create the future. Thanks for the trip, Maharishi. Thanks for showing us your way. Thanks, old friend. Are you going to come along with us to the future?

So the Beatles return to the twentieth century.

Where are they going next?

The Beatles of course, produced the greatest album of all time. Every Boomer remembers where, when and with whom they were when they first heard *Sgt. Pepper*.

Well, they didn't get to Woodstock and by 1970 the four Mop Tops had all married wonderful women and were nurturant to a wonderful New Breed of kids.

So here's the very happy ending. Zak Starkey, Jason Starkey, Lee Starkey, Julian Lennon, Sean Lennon, Heather McCartney, Mary McCartney, Stella McCartney, James McCartney and Dhani Harrison.

August 6, 1994
Beverly Hills, California

ACKNOWLEDGMENTS

Editor: Matthew Carnicelli
Associate Researcher: Sesa Nichole Giuliano
Intern: Devin Giuliano

The authors would like to thank the following people for their kindness and selfless hard work in helping realize this book.

Sriman Jagannatha Dasa Adikari
Charles Artley
Dr. Mirza Beg
Deborah Lynn Black
Deni Bouchard
Fred Brown
Stefano Castino
Tony Cohen
Sara Colledge
Srimati Vrinda Rani Devi Dasi
Durkin Hayes Publishing
Chris Eborn
Michael Fragnito
Avalon and India Giuliano

Robin Scot Giuliano
Robert Noel Giuliano
Caesar Glebbeek
His Divine Grace B. H. Mangalniloy Maharajia Goswami
Tim Hailstone
Dr. Albert Hofman
Jasper Humphreys
ISKCON
Joseph and Myrna Juliana
Larry Kahn
Dr. Michael Klapper
Allan Lang
Pattie Lang
Tim Leary
Leif Leavesley
Donald Lehr
Andrew Lownie
George Lucas
Mark Studios, Clarence, New York
Gates McFaddon
David Lloyd McIntyre
His Divine Grace A. C. Bhaktivedanta Swami Prabhupada
Jeniffer Romanello
Steven Rosen
Charles F. Rosenay
Martha Schueneman
Tony Secunda
Self Realization Institute of America (SRI)
Paul Slovak
Wendell and Joan Smith
Dave Thompson
Enzo of Valentino
Edward Veltman
Robert Wallace
Doug "My Guy" Young
Dr. Ronald Zucker

CONTRIBUTING
JOURNALISTS

A. C. BHAKTIVEDANTA SWAMI PRABHUPADA and the Beatles, Ascot, Berkshire, conversation, September 11, 1969. Copyright The Bhaktivedanta Book Trust (BBT), used by permission.

GEORGE HARRISON, interview, Henley-On-Thames, 1984. Copyright The Bhaktivedanta Book Trust (BBT), used by permission.

RINGO STARR, interview, Los Angeles, 1990. Copyright 1992 Northeast Scene, Inc. Reprinted from *Cleveland Scene* magazine, June 4–10, 1992.

TIMOTHY LEARY: "Thank God for the Beatles." Afterword Copyright Timothy Leary, used by permission.

MARY "MIMI" SMITH, interview, Bournemouth, 1970. Copyright Alanna Nash, used by permission.

GEORGE MARTIN AND JOHN BURGESS, interview, Los Angeles. Copyright 1994 David Goggin, aka "Mr. Bonzai." Originally published in *Mix* magazine.

GEOFF EMERICK, interview, Los Angeles, March, 1993. Copyright 1994 David Goggin, aka "Mr. Bonzai." Originally published in *Mix* magazine.

INDEX

DUTTON **PLUME**

THAT'S SHOW BUSINESS

☐ **REBEL WITHOUT A CREW** *Or How a 23-Year-Old Filmmaker with $7,000 Became a Hollywood Player.* **by Robert Rodriguez.** The author discloses all the unique strategies and innovative techniques he used to make *El Mariachi* on the cheap—including filming before noon so he wouldn't have to buy the actors lunch. You'll see firsthand his whirlwind, "Mariachi-style" film-making, where creativity—not money—is used to solve problems. Culminating in his "Ten-Minute Film School," this book may render conventional film-school programs obsolete. (937943—$22.95)

☐ **LIVING IN OBLIVION by Tom DiCillo.** This book includes the original screen-play of *Living in Oblivion*, a movie about the making of a movie, in this case a very low-budget film being shot on a shoestring on the seedy side of Manhattan. Included as a bonus second feature is *Eating Crow: Notes from a Filmmaker's Diary*, in which the author offers a very uncensored story of rais-ing cash and assembling the people to shoot the film and reveals what really goes on and goes down at the Sundance Film Festival. (275997—$12.95)

☐ **MAKING PRISCILLA The Hilarious Story Behind** *The Adventures of Priscilla, Queen of the Desert.* **by Al Clark.** The author and director Stephan Elliott survived various natural disasters and acts of God, such as floods, earthquakes, bushfires, bomb threats, film festivals, confused critics, the outré L.A. bar scene, and power lunches, lurching from crisis to crisis to make the most hysterical film of the year. (274842—$12.95)

Prices slightly higher in Canada.